PEIRCE'S AND LEWIS'S THEORIES OF INDUCTION

PEIRCE'S AND LEWIS'S
THEORIES OF INDUCTION

by

CHUNG-YING CHENG

Associate Professor of Philosophy
University of Hawaii

MARTINUS NIJHOFF / THE HAGUE / 1969

PRINTED IN THE NETHERLANDS

PREFACE

This book is based on my doctoral dissertation written at Harvard University in the year of 1963. My interest in Peirce was inspired by Professor D. C. Williams and that in Lewis by Professor Roderick Firth. To both of them I owe a great deal, not only in my study of Peirce and Lewis, but in my general approach toward the problems of knowledge and reality. Specifically, I wish to acknowledge Professor Williams for his patient and careful criticisms of the original manuscripts of this book. I also wish to thank Professor Firth and Professor Israel Scheffler for their many suggestive comments regarding my discussions of induction. However, any error in this study of Peirce and Lewis is completely due to myself.

Chung-ying Cheng

Honolulu, Hawaii
March, 1967

TABLE OF CONTENTS

SUMMARY

In the light of difficulties of various recent attempts to justify induction, it is argued here that induction both as an inference and as a method needs a reformulation. It is further suggested that a study of Peirce's and Lewis's ideas regarding the nature of induction would lead to a general theory of induction. (Chapter I).

The discussion of Peirce's theory in this book will cover the writings of Peirce from 1867 to 1905 and will make explicit Peirce's justification of induction in two distinct modes, the probabilistic and the non-probabilistic. (Chapter II). First, Peirce's general conception of a valid inference as well as his formulation of the so-called statistical deduction is clarified. (Chapter III). Then, his formulation of induction in the form of a statistical syllogism is examined. Peirce's original argument for the validity of induction in such a form is shown to be unsatisfactory. However, it is also shown that induction can be interpreted as a probable inference from sample to population with its validity derived from a logical law of large numbers, as formally proved by the author in the framework of the calculus of classical probability. (Chapter IV).

The author also reveals that Peirce's requirement of fair sampling in his own formulation leads to difficulties. To avoid these, the author proposes a new principle of fair sampling. For Peirce's requirement of predesignation, the author shows that it is neither the necessary nor the sufficient condition for the validity of induction. But nevertheless, its relevancies for establishing a trustworthy inductive conclusion are pointed out. (Chapter V). As to Peirce's various interpretations of probability, it is shown that they lead to an inconsistency, not recognized by Pierce himself. (Chapter VI).

Regarding Peirce's non-probabilistic justification of induction, four arguments are formulated and examined. First, the argument for the self-correcting nature of induction is shown to be useless for adducing reasons for the validity of induction. The second and third arguments for the validity of induction, respectively on the basis of *a priori* impossibility of conceiving a chance world and on the basis of empirical unprovability of the non-existence of uniformities in our world, are found either untenable or inconclusive. Finally, Peirce's argument that inductive method can ascertain the true on the basis of finite sampling is shown to be imprecise. (Chapter VII). More criticisms concern the relation between the validity of induction and the notion of reality. (Chapter VIII).

The part of the book which deals with Lewis's theory of induction will concentrate on Lewis's main works, *Mind and the World-Order* and *An Analysis of Knowledge and Valuation*. The Theory of Induction by Lewis is again examined in the light of a general distinction between the non-probabilistic arguments and the probabilistic arguments. (Chapter IX).

Regarding Lewis's non-probabilistic argument for the validity of induction, it is made clear how according to Lewis *a priori* concepts and principles are relevant not only for determining our knowledge of reality, but for determining the real as we understand it. This leads to a refutation of the Humean skepticism which asserts that there is no necessary connections of matters of fact. (Chapter X). Indeed Lewis's "*a priori* analytical" principles which should guarantee the validity of induction, is based on the argument of *reductio ad impossible*. But it is pointed out that this argument is only plausible in the framework of his theory of reality and the related theory of knowledge. (Chapter XI). Criticisms are also made of Lewis's practical arguments for the validity of induction. (Chapters XII–XIII).

Lewis's probabilistic justification of induction is shown to be based on his conception of probability as a valid estimate of frequency. It is shown that it is in the credibility relation between an inductive conclusion and its premised data that the validity of induction ultimately consists. It is also shown how this should coincide with Peirce's argument for the validity of induction as a probable inference having a logical leading principle. (Chapter XIV). Unlike Peirce, Lewis has suggested criteria for determining credibility of inductive inference. The author attempts to formulate these criteria and show that they are no less than criteria for determining fair samples. (Chapter XV).

In concluding, the author compares Peirce's and Lewis's theories of induction and points out their similar features. Their contributions to the clarification of the validity of induction are evaluated. It is suggested that in formulating the problem of justifying induction, in addition to a distinction between the probabilistic and the non-probabilistic justification as exemplified by Pierce and Lewis, a distinction between a general and a specific justification need also be made. These distinctions should then form an adequate framework with reference to which a general theory of induction can be developed. (Chapter XVI).

CHAPTER I

INTRODUCTION

1. *Problem of Justifying Induction and Proposal for Its Dissolution*

The problem of justifying induction, as formulated by David Hume, is that of producing a logical reason [1] for asserting generalizations on the basis of particular instances which we find in experience. Hume's well-known conclusion with regard to this problem is that there is no logical reason whatsoever for asserting such empirical generalizations, because there is no necessary connections of matters of fact. In this sense, as is pointed out by Goodman, [2] there is no solution of the problem of justifying induction. But Goodman adds that though the problem of justifying induction could not be solved, it could nevertheless be *dissolved*. The *dissolution* of the problem of justifying induction consists not in proving why an empirical generalization must be true and why an inductive inference must be valid, but consists in exhibiting the meanings of the statement that an empirical generalization is true and the statement that an inductive inference is valid.

Goodman draws an analogy between the justification of deduction

---

[1] A logical reason, in contrast with an empirical reason which is a reason based on experience, is a reason based on logic. A logical reason for our assertion of or belief in an empirical generalization on the basis of particular observed instances will enable us to say that the inference from the particular observed instances to the empirical generalization is logically valid or logically warranted. It is well-known that Hume has divided objects of human inquiry into *relations of ideas* and *matters of fact:* every true statement about the former is logically valid independently of experience and in this sense demonstratively certain, while every true statement about the latter is not logically valid, has no other basis than experience and *custom* or habit, and hence is probable in the sense that its contrary is always possible and it inspires a belief of a degree in direct proportion with a past frequency. See *An Enquiry Concerning Human Understanding*, The Open Court Edition, 1955, 24–41, 45–49, 61–63.

[2] Nelson Goodman, *Fact, Fiction, and Forecast*, Cambridge, 1955, 63–83.

and that of induction. To justify a deduction we show that it conforms to valid rules of deductive inference. That is, if we seek any reason why we trust a deductive conclusion, we point out that the deductive conclusion is derived from its premises in accordance with valid deductive rules. Conforming to deductive rules provides a reason for our trusting deductive conclusions, and hence is its justification. But, on the other hand, a request for justifying deductive rules themselves leads Goodman to say that the justification resides in the conformity of the rule with "accepted deductive practice," i.e., "the particular inferences we actually make and sanction." Thus, he concludes that the rules of deduction and the individual deductive inferences are justified by being brought into agreement with each other and that a rule should be amended in view of acceptable particular cases of inference and an inference should be rejected because of its violating an accepted rule.

According to Goodman, a similar conclusion may be drawn in the case of justifying induction. To justify an inductive conclusion, so it is argued by him, we merely need to examine whether the inductive conclusion is derived from the premises in conformity with valid rules or principles. As valid deductive inferences must presuppose valid deductive rules or principles, valid inductive inferences must presuppose valid inductive rules or principles. The crux of the problem of justifying induction then lies in formulating correct or valid rules as well as in justifying them on the basis of our inductive practice.

To put Goodman's point in brief. Suppose an inductive rule is given. How are we to justify it as correct or valid? Goodman replies that we have to see whether it actually "codifies" accepted inductive practice. If it does actually codify or formulate a rule used in accepted inductive inferences, it is valid. If, on the contrary, it does not, it is invalid and is therefore to be rejected. There is no other problem of justifying induction beside this.

Now I see no particular objection to Goodman's thesis that the *new* problem of justifying induction could be conceived as one of formulating rules of induction and defining differences between valid and invalid inductive inferences on the basis of our common practice. But, I do not see any reason why we should stop here. For there is no reason why this view should prevent us from seeking other formulations for the basis of valid induction.

Regarding the specific thesis of Goodman, one must recognize that it is always legitimate to question whether a rule of induction is *really* valid in spite of its being a codification of accepted inductive practice, just as it is no less legitimate to question whether an inductive inference is *really* valid in spite of its being interpretable as conforming to an inductive rule. There is always a problem of justifying induction, because there is always a possibility of raising doubts against a given explanation of the validity of induction either in the light of new instances or new rules of induction, or with reference to questions pertaining to relations of induction to other philosophical problems such as our interpretations of probability and knowledge of reality. In the light of a new instance or a new rule of induction, we may always ask why this new instance must be justified by our accepted rules of induction, or why this new rule must be justified by our accepted instances of induction. With reference to philosophical problems such as our interpretations of probability and knowledge of reality, we may always ask whether and how induction is valid in relation to a given interpretation of probability or in relation to a given interpretation of knowledge of reality. This indicates the difficulty of justifying induction and gives a reason why a new examination of the problem of justifying induction can always be attempted.

2. Two Types of Recent Arguments for the Validity of Induction

It should be sufficient, for my purpose of making clear the difficulty of justifying induction, to examine briefly two main types of arguments for the validity of induction which many recent philosophers seem to have accepted as valid, before I go on to suggest the relevance and necessity of reconsidering the problem of justifying induction through a critical examination of the theories of induction proposed by Peirce and Lewis.

Arguments of the first type are in general provided by the linguist or ordinary language philosophers. They hold that individual inductions are valid because they conform to standard examples of induction or conforms to standard rules of induction, and that standard examples or standard rules of induction are valid simply because they are standard. Arguments of the second type are provided by the so-called practicists. According to them, the reason why principles of induction formulated from particular inductive inferences are valid and credible is that they are inductively justified. They argue that an inductive inference or an inductive rule is valid if it is factually effective in the past and that the inductive support for an inductive inference or an inductive rule is no less a good reason for the trustworthiness of induction. I shall first consider arguments by the linguist philosophers.

3. *Arguments from Paradigm Cases and Uses of Words*

A more exact description of the position of the linguist or ordinary language philosophers is this. The problem of justifying induction is to provide good reasons for each specific inductive conclusion which we make if their validity is challenged. These reasons should be of such a pattern that rules or standards are conformed to. If there exists such a good reason for an inductive conclusion, the inductive conclusion in question is valid, otherwise it is not. But it is improper to ask questions about the validity of rules or standards which are what we appeal to in case of doubt or in face of challenge. Hence there is no way of proving the general validity of induction, i.e., there exists no logically valid proposition which describes the general rule of induction in all particular cases of induction such that conforming to it guarantees the validity of new instances of induction other than those which are already accepted as valid and those from which this rule is abstracted.

The above position is illustrated by the view of Strawson: [3] Strawson suggests that the justification of induction consists merely in giving particular reasons for particular inductions in conformity with inductive standards. "For it is generally proper to inquire of a particular belief whether its adoption is justified," says Strawson, "and, in asking this, we are asking whether there is good, bad, or any, evidence for it. In applying or witholding the epithets 'justified,' 'well-founded,' etc., in the case of specific beliefs, we are appealing to, and applying, inductive standards. But to what standards are we appealing when we ask whether the application of inductive standards is justified or well-founded? If we cannot answer, then no sense has been given to the question." [4] He further suggests that if there is a general justification of induction, then every inductive inference which we choose to make would be valid, and this certainly is not the case. The reason for this is that an inductive conclusion is warranted by an inductive rule if this rule codifies an accepted practice of induction of a particular kind to which the inference of the given inductive conclusion belongs, whereas an abstract rule of induction which bears resemblance to accepted in-

---

[3] Cf. P. F. Strawson, *Introduction to Logical Theory*, London, 1952, 248–252, 256–263.
[4] P. F. Strawson, *Ibid.*, 257.

ductive rules only in form does not necessarily warrant any given inductive conclusions based on it.

A variant of the above view is recently suggested by S. F. Barker. According to Barker, "We do not know with certainty that people who practice induction will be more successful in reaching true conclusions than will those who practice some form of anti-induction; but what we do know with certainty is that those who practice induction will probably be more successfull – that is, that it is reasonable to believe that they will be more successful." [5] This is a justification of induction by way of dissolving the problem of justifying induction, because "just as it is inconceivable that *modus ponens* should be unreliable," suggests Barker, "so it is inconceivable that inductive inferences should not *probably* be the most successful kind in the long run."[6] But that this is so, however, is simply due to the fact that a commitment to the practice of induction is built into the normal sense of the word "probable." Thus he says, "Already built into the normal sense of the word 'rational,' a rational man is necessarily one who, among other things, reasons inductively rather rhan anti-inductively." [7] To justify induction by way of dissolving the problem of justifying induction, therefore, is to recognize that the conclusions of the general practice of induction are *probable* and *rational* by our uses of the words "probable," "inductive practice," and "rational."

One powerful objection to this line of dealing with the problem o fjustifying induction is to point out that it confines justification of induction only to that of known or accepted standard examples of induction or known or accepted standard examples of uses of inductive words ("inductive practice," "rational," and "probable") without shedding light on the problem concerning justifying inductive conclusions which are not standard or are not yet known as standard. It also presupposes that we know what constitutes a standard for us and what does not. But, in fact, a genuine solution or dissolution of the justification problem could not be made without an investigation of the criteria or standards for justification. We must inquire what constitutes a standard example or a standard rule of practice or use of words and what makes them acceptable or trustworthy to us in the first place. For example, we

---

[5] S. F. Barker, "Discussion: Is There a Problem of Induction?" in the Symposium on Inductive Evidence by W. C. Salmon, S. F. Barker and H. E. Kybury, in *American Philosophical Quarterly*, Volume 2, Number 4, October, 1965, 265–280. The reference here to Barker's articles is on page 272.

[6] S. F. Barker, *Ibid.*, 272.

[7] S. F. Barker, *Ibid.*, 273.

want to know what makes the inductive conclusion that all European and American swans are white, or the inductive conclusion that the sun will rise tomorrow, a good and standard one, if it is good and standard at all. We want to know what explications we could give to the meanings or uses of the words "probable" or "rational" in the statements "it is probable that all European and American swans are white" and "it is rational to believe that the sun will rise tomorrow." We want to know why inductive conclusions of this kind are acceptable or trustworthy to us, if their premises are true. We want to know further what the true principles and true premises of standard inductive conclusions are.

We may also raise the question whether or not a standard or a rule of induction can be challenged or evaluated. Mathematical laws and logical principles function as standards and rules for deductive inferences. As standards and rules they are indeed either accepted or violated. It is impossible to condemn them or to evaluate them in the way in which we may condemn the things which fall under them – as breaching rules or failing to conform to standards; but this is because they could be strictly formulated and proved as true propositions by logic. Now in the case where an example of inference becomes a standard or a rule because it is used by us as a criterion for judging particular inferences as valid or invalid, we should not ignore the significance of the question whether a supposed standard is *really* a standard. As we have noted before, and as has been pointed out by Urmson,[8] it is always legitimate and meaningful to ask in the spirits of philosophical inquiry or genuine doubt whether we should accept those standards which we do accept and also what should justify our acceptance of an example of induction as a standard one. Questions of this sort can be intelligibly formed in our language, because, in the first place, our language, though embodying common sense, evidently cannot be said to comprehend all the truths there is as there is demonstrably far more thruths than all our linguistic expressions can express;[9] in the second place, our language is flexible and open enough to allow expresssion of alternative thoughts and incompatible ideas as evidenced in the history of philosophy.[10]

---

[8] Cf. J. Q. Urmson, "Some Questions Concerning Validity", in *Essays in Conceptual Analysis*, selected and edited by Antony Flew, London, 1956, 120–133.

[9] The set of linguistic expressions which can be formed from any given natural language cannot be more than denumerably infinite. But, it could be argued on the basis of Cantor's Theorem in logic that there are non-denumerably infinite truths, say, about numbers, in the world.

[10] Salmon has illustrated this point by saying that the language which expresses our common sense is also the language in which Hume wrote, etc., See his "Rejoinder to Barker and Kyburg", in The Symposium on Inductive Evidence mentioned above, *op. cit.*, 278.

As we may sensibly ask if any social practice or social norm is itself right or wrong and compare it with some ideal norm or alternative, we may ask whether standards and rules of induction are trustworthy or not and compare them with paradigms of what we would like or choose to call a trustworthy inference and its rules.[11] Surely, this is not simply a matter of "contrasting the given practice with other *accepted* practices, trying to show that it does not gibe with them." [12] The choice of one standard (practice) or another may be dictated by pragmatical considerations and these are again inductively guided, being found to be congenial to our faculties. But this does not put an end to our question. In a process of empirical inquiry the question could be repeatedly raised and studied. It is certain that, in making inductive inferences, we depend upon rules just as we depend upon rules in playing a game. But this should not be taken to imply that the use of an inductive rule or standard instead of another is purely conventional. It might be quite true that we accept a standard or rule by an act of legislation or a decision. But even if this is true, we still can question the rational as well as the pragmatical grounds of the act of legislation or decision in question.

If there are good reasons for rejecting or modifying a standard as seen in a process of an open-end empirical inquiry, clearly we are justified in doing it. The very possibility of an open-end inquiry gives meaning to the problem as to the very ground of accepting a proposition as a standard rather than accepting another one. Indeed, there are always conclusions to be reached in the process of an open-end inquiry. This suggests that evaluation should be more than an appeal to existing rules or standards and that accepting a rule as a standard is more than an act of legislation. Indeed, we may hold that in a process of empirical inquiry, both inductive standards or rules and individual inductive conclusions are subject to continual modification and reformulation in the light of empirical findings or in the light of new theoretical considerations. These standards or rules shall not be absolutely fixed by our present practice, but must be checked against what we shall and could find and formulate in a process of empirical inquiry.

---

[11] W. Salmon has also suggested this point. He says, "We *can* ask whether moral practices commended by our society are worthy of commendation, and we *can* ask whether the inductive practices commended by our society are worthy of commendation". (*Ibid.*, 278.) (*American Philosophical Quarterly*, Volume 2, Number 4, October, 1965, 278.) "The fundamental question arises for cognitive evaluation just as it did for moral evaluation. Are the things we actually commend really worthy of commendation? Are the inductive methods we regard as correct really correct?" (*Ibid.*, 279.)

[12] Quoted from Barker, *op. cit.*, 273.

4. *Practical Arguments*

Now let me come to the arguments for an inductive or practical justification of induction as held by the practicist philosophers. They maintain that induction could be inductively justified instead of being
deductively justified by conforming to a rule or a standard of induction.
They suggest that the reason why we accept an inductive conclusion is
that an inductive conclusion of this kind has proved successful [13] in the
past. Consider the example that all humans are mortal. The ground for
asserting this, according to the practicist view, is that all known
humans have proved mortal in the past. That all known humans in the
past have proved mortal, the practicists urge, is a good reason why we
should trust the inductive conclusion in question. Thus, Braithwaite
says that an inductive policy could be expected to be effective in the
future if it has the characteristic of being effective-in-the-past.[14] In
this sense the inductive principle, that, whenever known members of a
class are found to possess a certain character, it is probable that all
members of the class possess that character, is a valid one, if it has
proved to be true and successful in most cases in the past.

The practicists further point out that insofar as we do not raise the
objection that there is no logical reason why we should accept this
abstract general inductive principle, it is all right for us to be content
with the fact that we do draw inductive conclusions in conformity with
the principle. Hence if we do in fact accept this principle of induction,
and if we do draw inductive conclusions in accordance with this principle, our inductive conclusions are to be considered as valid in accordance with this principle of induction. But as soon as the objection that
there is no logical reason for accepting this rule as a valid one is raised,
this principle must be justified by itself in the sense that most of its
applications in specific cases have been successful in the past. Braithwaite has proposed this way of justifying induction, which in a slightly
different way has been accepted and re-presented by Black.[15]

It is obvious that to argue that the inductive principle is valid on
the ground of its verification in the past in most cases is to beg the
question, because the very principle is presupposed. One way which

---

[13] Or as Salmon might put it: more frequently truth-preserving. Cf. *op. cit.*, 279–280.
[14] R. B. Braithwaite, *Scientific Explanation*, Cambridge, 1953, 225–292.
[15] Max Black, *Problems of Analysis*, Ithaca, Part 3, 1954. Also, cf. *Language and Philosophy*, Ithaca, 1941.

Braithwaite and Black propose to defend their position is by making a distinction between recognition of the factual effectiveness of an inductive principle and justification of that principle. We shall recognize the factual effectiveness of the principle if we recognize that it is always an effective *rule* of inference. But to justify the inductive principle, we have to formulate this principle in the form of a proposition and derive the proposition in an inductive argument according to the inductive rule. Hence, the inductive principle could be justified in the sense that it leads to true conclusions in a majority of cases. But then it is justified only on the basis of our already accepting this principle as an operative rule of inference in the first place. Thus, the difficulty of this justification is that the validity of the inductive rule remains unexplained.

The practicists even go further to assert that there is no other reason for the validity of induction than the reason that the inductive principle has proved successful in most cases in the past. In fact, the practicists, like the linguist philosophers, have pointed out that it is rational to accept an inductive conclusion in accordance with the inductive principle and that to act upon an acceptable inductive policy is what we intend by using the phrase "to act rationally." [16] Thus, the justification of induction again becomes a matter of recognizing specific inductive reasons for specific inductive conclusions. It is on this point that we find the convergence of opinions of both the practicist and the linguist philosophers. At this point, it is not unfair to conclude that the inductive justification of induction does not lead to any new solution or new dissolution of the problem of justifying induction, although the practicists' argument, like the argument of the linguist philosophers, may be useful in pinpointing the difficulties of justifying induction.

As we have emphasized, it is an open question whether we do intend by the validity of an inductive inference merely that it is acceptable by "standard" rules. It is further doubtful that the inductive principle in general and inductive rules in particular must have no other justification than that they have been effective in the past for the most part. It is always significant for us to inquire how we may justify inductive rules and the inductive principle in general in a formal manner in which deductive rules and the deductive principle in general are to be justified. If there is any formal similarity between an inductive principle and a deductive principle, there is no reason why a logical inquiry

<hr />

[16] This is the position which von Wright and Burks, among others, seem to have adopted. Cf. G. H. von Wright, *The Logical Problem of Induction*, New York, 1957, 159–175. Arthur W. Burks, "Presupposition Theory of Induction," *Philosophy of Science*, Vol. 20, 1953, 177–196.

should not be made so as to see wherein this formal similarity consists and how this will bear upon the problem of justifying the inductive principle.

5. *Induction as a Genuine Problem and*
Study of Peirce and Lewis

So far our brief examination of the linguist and the practicist arguments for the validity of induction has shown that they give no conclusive reason for regarding justifying induction as a pseudo-problem. In fact, we have shown that these arguments are inadequate and inconclusive in explaining the validity of induction, and that limitations in these arguments suggetst hat even if these arguments are valid, they need not be the only ones which affect the validity of induction. This conclusion should then justify our attempt to treat the problem of justifying induction as a genuine problem and to seek a *better* formulation of the problem and to inquire whether a *better* explanation of the validity of induction is possible.

In the history of modern and contemporary Anglo-American philosophers, Charles Sanders Peirce (1839–1914) and C. I. Lewis (1883–1964) are two original thinkers, who hold different opinions from ordinary language philosophers and practicists, in regard to the problem of justifying induction. For them, induction is a genuine problem, and deserves serious philosophical considerations. In their writings on the nature of the validity of induction, they have virtually developed their own theories of induction to the effect that the validity of induction is explainable in terms of more fundamental concepts involved in our understanding of logic and reality.

It is the purpose of this book to attempt a close examination of Peirce's and Lewis's theories of induction in order to shed light on the problem of justifying induction. I shall first confine myself to the discussion of various ways in which Peirce and Lewis formulate the problem of justifying induction and present solutions to the problem. I shall then make clear to what extent their solutions are valid and to what extent they are not. I shall conclude that, if the problem of justifying induction, in the last analysis, should be that of defining conditions and formulating criteria of making trustworthy inductive conclusions from inductive premises, those conditions or criteria, by which we define and explain the validity of induction, must be carefully examined and their relevance to logic and reality made clear.

The composition of this book is as follows. From Chapter II to Chapter VIII, I shall concentrate on explicating and examining the main theses of Peirce's theory of induction. Then from Chapter IX to Chapter XV, I shall concern myself with Lewis's theory of induction by clarifying and criticizing Lewis's arguments for the validity of induction. Finally, in Chapter XVI, I shall conclude with a general comparison between Peirce's and Lewis's theories of induction and an evaluation of their contributions in the light of their constructive efforts toward a general theory of induction.

CHAPTER II

SCOPE OF PEIRCE'S THEORY OF INDUCTION

By Peirce's "theory of induction," I refer to a system or collection of ideas which Peirce formulated about the nature and validity of inductive inference or inductive reasoning. This system or collection of ideas covers Peirce's writings from 1867 to 1905.[1] During this period, Peirce wrote his most important papers on the logic of science and probability in his long philosophical career from 1857 to 1914.[2] These papers, though only a minor portion of Peirce's philosophical works, constitute a self-explanatory unit of study, simply because they deal with one single subject: the validity of synthetic inference.

In the year of 1867, Peirce wrote his paper "On the Natural Classification of Arguments," which provides a natural introduction to his treatment of inference and its validity in syllogistic terms and to his trichotomy of inference into deduction, induction, and hypothesis. Through the year from 1877 to 1878, Peirce wrote a series of papers on "Illustrations of the Logic of Science." Beside the well-known articles "The Fixation of Belief" and "How to Make Our Ideas Clear," there are four other important but comparatively little discussed papers which are essentially concerned with the logic of science and probability. They are in the following order: "Doctrines of Chances" (with corrections 1893 and notes 1910). "The Probability of Induction" (with corrections 1893), "Deduction, Induction, and Hypothesis" (with corrections 1893), and "The Order of Nature." In these papers, Peirce laid out his rationale for the validity of ampliative or synthetic inference and indicated a justification of induction in terms of probability. He also made explicit his conception of probability in terms of empirical frequency.

---

[1] See the "Chronological Listing of Peirce's Papers Directly Bearing Upon Induction and Probability" in Appendix I.

[2] The earliest of his papers which we have is dated 1857, and his philosophical activity continued until his death in 1914.

But very often his ideas concerning the validity of synthetic inference appear disconnected and do not fit into a consistent, not to say a well-organized, whole.

It is not until 1883 that Peirce wrote a comparatively systematic treatise on his general theory concerning the validity of ampliative or synthetic inference. This is his "A Theory of Probable Inference," in which we find Peirce's statement of what a probable inference is and his argument that inductive inference is valid on account of its being a probable inference.

After the year 1883, Peirce's philosophical writings appear to bear little upon his earlier problems in logic of science and probability. But here and there, we find a variety of topics under which Peirce touched the problem of justifying kinds of inference. One significant feature among these is Peirce's recurrent distinction between kinds of induction, a distinction which he had not ever made in his earlier writings. The distinction is between a "crude induction" (or "pooh-pooh" argument), a "quantitative induction," and a "qualitative induction." This distinction is found in the following three short papers: "Three Kinds of Induction" (from "The Logic of Drawing History from Ancient Documents," 1901), "Kinds of Induction" (1903, and "The Varieties and Validity of Induction," (c. 1905).

What Peirce calls a "crude induction" is an inference which concludes a universal generalization from what has been found in common in a group of instances. It is induction by simple enumeration. A quantitative induction is an inference from our knowledge of a statistical proportion of individual things having a certain character in a given sample to a conclusion regarding that in the population, from which the sample is chosen.[3] A qualitative induction, on the other hand, is a method of ascertaining factual truths by postulating hypothesis and confirming them on the basis of relevant evidences. That all these three forms of inference are considered induction by Peirce is due to the fact that they do not usually have the form of deduction, and they usually give rise to generalizations which are not deductively warranted by their premises. They differ, nevertheless, because they have different bases for generalizations and their generalizations have different contents.[4]

[3] In later discussion, the proportion of individual things having a certain character in a given sample is called the "composition" of the sample with respect to that character; the proportion of individual things having a certain character in a population is called the "composition" of the population with respect to that character.

[4] A crude induction generalizes from a number of observed instances of a homogeneous

In the light of Peirce's distinction between these three forms of induction, we find that what Peirse calls an induction, before and in his papers of 1883, is induction chiefly in the sense of quantitative induction: it is formulated in a syllogistic form, and considered as a species of probable inference, or inference involving the notion of probability, as we shall see. After his 1883 papers, Peirce tends to focus his attention on the general features of induction as a method of inquiry, and chiefly in the sense of qualitative induction. He considers induction as a "trustworthy" method for pursuing truth, and in particular, truth of any scientific subject matter, by way of sampling.

Taking account of Peirce's considerations of induction in various senses in different periods, we may say, for the purpose of our discussion in succeeding Chapters, that Peirce's theory of induction is marked by two aspects: one aspect consists in Peirce's treatment of induction as an individual inference from sample to population, and as a valid form of probable inference; the other consists in his treatment of induction as a "trustworthy" method for pursuing scientific truth.

When Peirce treats induction as an individual inference from sample to population in a syllogistic form, he validates induction by showing that it always draws conclusions, with probability, in a manner comparable to a valid deductive probable inference. In this sense, we say that Peirce attempts a probabilistic justification of induction. On the other hand, when Peirce comes to treat induction as a "trustworthy" method for pursuing truth, he argues that induction is a self-correcting process, which does not ascribe probabilities to its conclusions, but which must lead to truth in the long run of experience. In this sense, we say that Peirce attempts a non-probabilistic justification of induction. That there exist these two modes of justification of induction in Peirce's theory of induction, is a point which we shall establish in our study of Peirce's theory of induction. But no less important than this point is my clarification, and my improvement of the formulation, of Peirce's probabilistic justification of induction. This is because the latter will point to the true difficulty of justifying induction and relating inductive inference to probability in a correct way. In his discussion, Peirce does

---

kind, and the generalization takes the form of a universal statement concerning common sense objects. A quantitative induction generalizes from a sample, given in the present or in the past, and the generalization takes the form of a statistical statement, a statement concerning a proportion in a population. A qualitative induction, finally, generalizes over a class of observed instances of various kinds, and is conducive to the establishment of a scientific law.

not make clear wherein the validity of induction as a form of probable inference lies, and he does not even make clear how a probable inference should be construed. It must be through a careful analysis and comparison of those of Peirce's papers we have mentioned, that we may expect to find answers to these questions. When we know these answers, we shall know also how Peirce's argument for the validity of induction from sample to population should contribute to a genuine explanation of the validity of induction in general.

I shall formulate Peirce's probabilistic justification of induction as an argument for the validity of probable inference from fair samples to populations: an argument which asserts that fairness of given samples is a criterion for determining probabilities and therefore for determining the validity of inductive inference in general. To clarify this argument, we have to inquire into the meanings which Peirce has given to such key terms as "probable" and "fair." The validity of induction as a form of probable inference may simply depend upon whether its conclusions can be rightly said to be probable, and in which sense of "probable." Hence, an investigation of Peirce's various conceptions of probability must play an important role in making clear the very basis of Peirce's argument for the validity of induction. I shall show that Peirce's argument for the validity of probable inference from fair samples presupposes a conception of probability which should rightly justify induction as a valid probable inference, whereas Peirce's explicit definition of probability is incompatible with this sense of probability, and therefore does not serve the purpose of justifying induction as a probable inference from fair samples.

One more thing needs to be pointed out in connection with Peirce's argument for the validity of induction as a probable inference from fair samples. It has a great inadequacy: his definition of fairness of samples in terms of equi-probabilities in an empirical sense. In this sence of fairness of samples, we should not know a fair sample, or if we know it, we should not be making an induction, but a deduction instead. When this inadequacy is overcome, we shall see that the problem of justifying induction, in Peirce's argument for the validity of probable inference from fair samples, is no more than that of formulating and establishing criteria or rules for determining fair samples of various kinds, in a proper sense of fairness. This is an important conclusion in my clarification and examination of Peirce's probabilistic justification of induction.

My study of Pierce's theory of induction will be based chiefly on

Peirce's papers mentioned above, but I shall draw upon other relevant materials which are contained in *The Collected Papers of Charles Sanders Peirce*, I–VIII. References to Peirce will accord with the standard form of referring to paragraph numbers in *The Collected Papers*.

CHAPTER III

THE NATURE AND VALIDITY OF INFERENCE *

1. A General Theory of Inference

Peirce's probabilistic justification of induction has much to do with his conceptions of an inference and its validity, for he conceives induction as an inference from sample to population, and contends that it is valid in the sense in which any valid inference is valid. The following passages, taken from "On the Natural Classification of Arguments," provides a summary description of Peirce's conceptions of an inference and its validity.

Every inference involves the judgment that, if *such* propositions as the premises are true, then a proposition related to them, as the conclusion is, must be or is likely to be, true. The principle implied in this judgment, respecting a genus of argument, is termed the *leading principle* of the argument.[1]

A valid argument is one whose leading principle is true.[2]

In order that an argument should determine the necessary or probable truth of its conclusions, both the premises and leading principle must be true.[3]

It appears that there are three things which are relevant for determining an inference and its validity: the premises, the conclusion and the leading principle. What needs explanation here is the leading principle of an inference. The leading principle of an inference is a rule which we are conscious of following when we make an inference, a rule by which the premises of the inference are related to its conclusion. A leading principle defines a class of inferences or a "genus of argument," which

---

* Both this Chapter and the next have been simplified to form a paper entitled "Peirce's Probabilistic Theory of Inductive Validity", published in *The Transactions of the Charles S. Peirce Society*, Vol. II, no. 2, Fall, 1966, 86–105.
[1] *The Collected Papers of Charles Sanders Peirce*, 2.462.
[2] *Ibid.*, 2.463.
[3] *Ibid.*, 2.464.

is its extension. Any inference which conforms to this leading principle belongs to the class of inferences defined by the leading principle. We know that an inference is valid if we know that its leading principle is true. We believe that the conclusion of an inference must be, or is likely to be true if we believe that its leading principle and premises are true. In this sense of being capable of fixing a true belief from a true belief or beliefs, a leading principle is essentially a belief-habit, or "a cerebral habit," as Peirce calls it, which we have accepted as leading in general from truth to truth.

A "cerebral habit" should be distinguished from a "physiological habit," according to Peirce. When we respond to physical stimulus by way of physiological reaction, we follow a "physiological habit." A "cerebral habit," on the other hand, is something which we follow when we relate beliefs to beliefs. It is in terms of a "cerebral habit" that the leading principle of inference and the process of inference are more clearly delineated in the following passage:

A cerebral habit of the highest kind, which will determine what we do in fancy as well as what we do in action, is called a *belief*. The representation to ourselves that we have a specified habit of this kind is called a *judgment*. A belief-habit in its development begins by being vague, special, and meager: it becomes more precise, general, and full, without limit. The process of this development, so far as it takes place in the imagination, is called *thought*. A judgment is formed; and under the influence of a belief-habit this gives rise to a new judgment, indicating an addition to belief. Such a process is called an *inference*; the antecedent judgment is called the premise; the consequent judgment, the *conclusion;* the habit of thought, which determined the passage from one to the other (when formulated as a proposition), the leading principle.[4]

According to this passage, a leading principle is both a belief and a habit by which a belief is related to or gives rise to another. The process of relating a belief to another is then called an inference. In this broad sense of habit and belief, we may meaningfully speak of a true leading principle, or of a false leading principle, as we may meaningfully speak of a true belief or of a false belief. But, then, what is a true or false leading principle? How is it determined to be true or false? Peirce's answers to these questions must be constructed from his idea of the relation of a leading principle to a valid inference.

Peirce has indicated, as we have seen, that a valid inference is one whose leading principle is true. He also says:

A habit of inference may be formulated in a proposition which shall state that every proposition C, related in a given general way to any true proposition P, is

4 *Ibid.*, 3.160.

true; such a proposition is called the *leading principle* of the class of inferences whose validity it implies.[5]

Thus, on account of the fact that a valid inference has a true leading principle, and the fact that a valid inference is one in which every proposition, related in a given general way to any true proposition, is true, we may safely suggest that a true leading principle is one which enables us to draw true conclusions from true premises, and that a leading principle is determined true in this way. On the other hand, we may infer that a leading principle is false or is determinable as false, if it does not enable us to draw true conclusions from true premises. It is also clear from this that when an inference does not give true conclusions from true premises, it is invalid because it has a false leading principle.

Now we must mention one important modification of this description of a true leading principle. It is this. When we say that a true leading principle is one which enables us to draw true conclusions from true premises, we do not mean that it must enable us to draw true conclusions from true premises *in all cases*. Sometimes there exist true leading principles which enable us to draw true conclusions from true premises in only a proportion of cases. Such an inference Peirce calls *probable inference* in distinction from the universal necessary influence under discussion. The point that, there exist true leading principles which enable us to draw true conclusions from true premises in only a proportion of cases, indicates that if a valid inference is to be defined in terms of a true leading principle, it must be defined as a process or a passage by which we *in general* derive true conclusions from true premises.

Though we have made clear how a true leading principle is related to a valid inference, it is still a question as to in which sense we may say that there exist true leading principles, and, therefore, in which sense that there exist valid inferences of the above description. In this connection, we may distinguish what Peirce calls a "logical" leading principle from a "factual" or "material" leading principle.[6] A "logical" leading principle, according to Peirce, is a formal or logical proposition which, when explicitly stated, adds nothing to the premises of the inference which it governs. In this sense, a logical leading principle is simply a logical truth, or a statement of logic, which is ascertainable as true on the ground of logic. A "factual" or "material "leading principle, on the other hand, is a non-logical leading principle. It is, in other words, a

[5] *Ibid.*, 3.164.
[6] Cf., *Ibid.*, 2.589.

material proposition, which, if it is true, must be ascertained as true on ground other than logic. Now, on this distinction between logical leading principle and material leading principle, it is clear that we may always refer to logical truths or logical principles (including rules of formal logic and probability calculus) as leading principles which we know to be true, and which we should follow for inferences. Similarly, we may always refer to the class of inferences in accordance with logical rules as inferences which we know to be valid. It will be in this sense of logical truth that we shall speak of a true leading principle or the leading principle of a valid inference, and it will be in this sense of following a logical rule we shall speak of a valid inference or an inference with a true leading principle.

2. *Necessary Inference and Probable Inference*

In order for us to see how a conception of a valid inference, in the above sense, is relevant for Peirce's justification of induction in terms of the validity of a probable inference, we have to see how Peirce distinguishes induction and the so-called "ampliative inference" in general from explicative or necessary inference on the one hand, and how he relates induction to probable inference on the other.

Peirce defines "explicative inferences" as those in which facts stated in conclusions are already implied in the premises, but are not made explicit or noticed until the inferences are made.[7] They are also called "analytical" inferences or deductions. Logical and mathematical demonstrations are examples of inferences of this sort. "Ampliative inferences," on the other hand, are such that "the facts summed up in the conclusion are not among those stated in the premises, "because they are different facts. They are also called synthetic or inductive inferences. They are further subdivided by Peirce into induction and hypothesis. Deduction, induction, and hypothesis have different features as we may see in Peirce's representations of them in syllogistic forms as follows: [8]

Deduction	Induction	Hypothesis
All M is P,	S is M,	All M is P,
S is M,	S is P,	S is P,
Therefore, S is P.	Therefore, all M is P.	Therefore, S is M.

---

[7] Cf., *Ibid.*, 2.680.
[8] Cf., *Ibid.*, 2.623, 2.508–514, 1.559.

It is obvious that induction in the above form does not exactly coincide with our ordinary or normal conception of induction as a process of generalization from many instances instead from one. A general and hence a better representation of induction is given by Peirce as follows:

S_1, S_2, S_3, etc. are instances of M,
S_1, S_2, S_3, etc. are instances of P,
Hence, all instances of M are instances of P.[9]

An example of induction in this form is:

These beans are from this bag,
These beans are white,
Hence, all the beans from this bag are white.[10]

With Peirce's distinction of induction and hypothesis from deduction, we may raise the question as to whether or how they are valid in our defined sense. As we have seen, every inference has a leading principle which enables us to draw its conclusion from its premises. The leading principle of deduction obviously is a proposition which relates the conclusion to the premises with logical necessity. It is in fact the well-known logical principle of *nota notae est nota rei ipsius*, which in modern logic can be expressed as follows: $(x) (Fx \supset Gx): Fa: \supset Ga$. As it has a logical principle as its leading principle, any deduction, obviously, is a valid inference in our defined sense. The leading principles of induction and hypothesis, on the other hand, when formulated in propositions, seem not to be logically true, because from the premises of induction and hypothesis we cannot logically prove, in an *obvious* way, that their conclusions follow. In view of this, induction and hypothesis cannot be said to be valid in the obvious sense of having logically true leading principles. Our conclusions by induction or by hypothesis from true premises may be true, but may also be false: neither is inconceivable in the cases of induction and hypothesis. But to say this does not imply in any sense that there do not exist true

[9] Cf., *Ibid.*, 2.508–2.514.
[10] Cf., *Ibid.*, 2.623. Similarly, a general form of deduction and a general form of hypothesis are, according to Peirce, respectively, as follows: Cf., 2.508–2.514.

All instances of M are instances of P,
S_1, S_2, S_3, etc. are instances of M,
Hence, S_1, S_2, S_3, etc. are instances of P.

All instances of M are instances of P,
S_1, S_2, S_3, etc. are instances of P,
Hence, S_1, S_2, S_3, etc. are instances of M.

Examples for these inferences are obviously easily constructible. Cf., 2.623.

leading principles or logical rules, by which we know that from true premises in an induction or in a hypothesis, we may draw true conclusions or a determinable number of true conclusions. In fact, when the premises of induction and hypothesis are rephrased in such a manner so as to allow us ro draw true conclusions from them (they are assumed true), according to some true or logically true principle, they must be considered valid in a sense consistent with our earlier defined conception of validity of an inference. This validity accrues to induction and hypothesis, however, when Peirce relates them to probable inference, and reformulates them in terms of probable inference.

Peirce mentions "probable inference" in connection with his distinction of a universal necessary inference or deduction from an inference or deduction which is necessary but is not universal. The latter Peirce calls "probable deduction," or more often "probable inference," the former he simply calls "necessary deduction." "Necessary deductions" are such that their true premises must invariably produce true conclusions,[11] that is, their true premises must produce true conclusions without exception for all cases mentioned in the premises. Probable inferences, on the other hand, are such that their true premises do not *invariably* produce true conclusions, but must produce true conclusions for a definite number of cases mentioned in the premises, but not for all cases.[12]

Before we go on to illustrate what Peirce means by a "probable inference," we may first mention four differences between a necessary deduction and a "probable inference," which Peirce thinks important. First, necessary deduction (in the sense of universal deduction) recognizes only the inclusion or non-inclusion of one class under another (as illustrated by the deductive syllogism on page 20), whereas probable inference takes account of the proportion of one class subsumed under another: that is to say, probable inference admits statement of the proportion of one class subsumed under another into its premises. Second, for the existence of necessary deduction, objects in the universe may not be countable, whereas for the existence of probable inference, there must be countable units in the universe in order that a proportion of one class can be meaningfully said to be contained in another. What Peirce maintains in essence here is that, in making a necessary deduction, we need not inquire into the nature of cases mentioned in the premises, in order to see whether the quantifier "all" supplies to them,

---

[11] Cf., *Ibid.*, 2.267.
[12] Cf., *Ibid.*, 2.267.

whereas, in making a probable inference, we do need to inquire, in order to see whether the term " a proportion of"applies to them. This means again that necessary deduction applies to both discrete and continuous objects, whereas probable inference applies only to discrete objects. Third, necessary deduction always leads to true conclusions from true premises, whereas probable inference leads *usually* to true conclusion from true premises. This is a repetition of our earlier description of necessary deduction and probable inference. Fourthly and finally, there is a cardinal difference between a necessary deduction and a probable inference, according to Peirce:

[A cardinal distinction between the two kinds of inference is, that] in demonstrative reasoning the conclusion follows from the existence of the objective facts laid down in the premises; while in probable reasoning these reasoning facts in themselves do not even render the conclusion probable, but account has to be taken of various subjective circumstances – of the manner in which the premises have been obtained, of their being no countervailing considerations, etc.; in short, good faith and honesty are essential to good logic in probable reasoning.[13]

When Peirce says that, in probable inference, the reasoning facts in themselves (presumably the facts of reasoning *per se*) do not even render the conclusion probable, but account has to be taken of various subjective circumstances, Peirce does not mean that the conclusion of a probable inference cannot be said to be probable in any sense, assuming there is no neglect of the "subjective circumstances." All what Peirce means is that, in order to make a valid probable inference, an observance of a true leading principle is not a sufficient, though it is a necessary, condition for the trustworthiness of its conclusion. The conclusion mustbe probable or trustworthy not only in respect of a logical principle, but in respect of the proper ways in which the premises are established and are related to other known facts, here "proper ways" referring to ways of sampling which give rise to fair samples. In this sense one has to restrict the nature of the premises in a probable inference in a certain way. There are two general conditions which Peirce requires the reasoner in a probable inference to take account of in his premises: First, if the premises mention a sample, it is required that the sample is drawn at random or fairly from its population; second, the conclusions must be drawn in advance of any other knowledge of the subject mentioned in the premises than is given by the premises. These two conditions we must recognize as two criteria for determining the legitimacy of the premises of a probable inference, in order that the conclu-

---

[13] *Ibid.*, 2.696.

sion could be held as probable or trustworthy. For clarification of these two conditions, and for criticism of their relevance in Peirce's probabilistic justification of induction, we shall wait till the next chapter.

We may come back now to illustrate what Peirce means by a probable inference. There are two kinds of probable inference, which Peirce respectively calls "simple probable deductions" and "probable deductions proper" or "statistical deductions." Simple probable deductions are in fact implicit definitions of probability in terms of proportions known to us. The following form of inference is an illustration of simple probable deduction given by Peirce:

(1)   A proportion r of instances of M are instances of P.
      S is an instance of M.
      It follows, with probability r, that S is an instance of P.[14]

This inference is an implicit definition of probability in the classical or Laplacian sense because, according to the classical definition of probability, a probabillity is a proportion of favorable alternatives to all alternatives, favorable or unfavorable. If we accept this definition of probability, it is obvious that the conclusion of (1) is true and that (1) is valid, insofar as a definition is a true leading principle.

With (1) as illustration of a kind of "probable inference," we may test whether it conforms to Peirce's definition of a probable inference as an inference which draws true conclusions from true premises for a determinable number of cases mentioned in the premises. Concerning inference (1), suppose we have $r + s$ instances of M, $a_1, a_2, \ldots, a_r$, $a_{r+1} \ldots, a_{r+s}$. $a_1, a_2, \ldots, a_r$ are also instances of N, and $a_{r+1}, \ldots,$ a_{r+s} are not instances of N. Let the ratio of r to $r + s$ be P. Then let us consider the following set of inferences and assume that each possible inference is drawn just once.

If a_1 is M, then a_1 is N.
If a_2 is M, then a_2 is N.
. . . .
If a_r is M, then a_r is N.
If a_{r+1} is M, then a_{r+1} is N.
. . . .
If a_s is M, then a_{r+s} is N.

Now given a which belongs to the set $(a_1, a_2. \ldots a_s)$, a must be either a_1 or $a_2, \ldots$ or a_s. It is clear from the above set of inferences that, the conclusion that a is N or a is an instance of N is true only when $a = a_1$, or $a = a_2$, ... or $a = a_r$; and it is false when $a = a_{r+1}$ ... or $a = a_{r+s}$. In other words, the conclusion that a is N can only be true in a proportion $r/_{r+s} = P$ of cases when the above true premises are given, and must be true only in such a proportion of cases, because the above premises show that s instances of M are not N. The probability with which the conclusion "a is N" follows from given premises in the above system of inferences is defined in terms of the proportion of cases in which it is true from true premises in the given system of inferences.

We have thus shown what Peirce calls a "simple probable deduction" does conform to his definition of a probable inference. We turn now to his characterization of a "probable deduction proper" or a "statistical deduction." A "probable deduction proper" or a "statistical deduction", according to Peirce, is a valid inference by which precisely analogous reasonings would from true premises produce true conclusions *in a majority of cases*. It is of the following form:

$S_1, S_2, \ldots, S_n$ form a numerous random sample of the instances of M,
A proportion r of instances of M are instances of P,
Hence, probably and approximately, a proportion r of instances of M in the sample $S_1, S_2, \ldots, S_n$ are instances of P.[15]

Now the validity of the statistical deduction, according to Peirce, consists in the fact that this inference follows a true leading principle. This true leading principle in question is one of the *probable* and *approximate* equality of the compositions in the sample to the composition of the population, from which the sample is taken. For Peirce says, "The principle of statistical deduction is that these two proportions – namely, that of the P's (N's) among M's, and that of the P's (N's) among the S's (i.e. the sample of $S_1, S_2 \ldots S_n$) are probably and approximately equal." [16] As Peirce does not make any explanation of the nature and the truth of this principle, in the following, we shall discuss how this principle should be understood and how its truth can be logically proved, and, finally, how the statistical deduction, in conformity with this principle, will lead to true conclusions in a majority of cases.

We may suggest that the above leading principle of the statistical deduction is no other than a law of the classical calculus of probability which, for the convenience of our discussion, we may title as the logical law of large numbers. This law of large numbers states that, given any

---

[15] *Ibid.*, 2.700; also Cf. 2.710. I have reformulated Peirce's statement of this syllogism in order to make it intelligible to our modern readers.
[16] *Ibid.*, 2.702; also Cf. 2.718.

large population, a majority of samples of a fairly large size in the population have the same or nearly the same (such as allowing a small range of approximation) value for its composition ratio as the value for the composition ratio of the population. Stated in this way, this law is an arithmetical truth about the proportion of samples or subclasses which have a certain composition in a population or a class. But in the framework of the classical calculus of probability, this law becomes a law of the maximum value for the so-called hypergeometric probability. For a precise formulation of this law, and for a rigorous mathematical proof of this law, we shall refer the readers to Appendix II of this book.[17] It suffices here for our purpose to explain how we may formulate this law as a law of probability so that we may ascribe meanings to the terms "probably" and "approximately" used in Peirce's brief sketch of the law and in his statement of the syllogism of statistical deduction.

First, we mention the classical or Laplacian principle of defining a probability. A probability, according to this principle, is defined in terms of a finite proportion of favorable alternatives among all alternatives, favorable and unfavorable, assuming that these alternatives are collectively exhaustive and mutually exclusive in a universe of discourse. With this definition of probability available, it should be clear that the probability of a sample having a certain composition is the proportion of all the samples having that composition among all samples having or not having that composition in a population.

Now as the logical law of large numbers asserts that given any population, a major number of samples in the population are samples which have the same or nearly the same composition as that of the population, there should be a proportion P of these samples in the population among all samples greater than any other proportion of samples of other compositions among all the samples in the population. Hence, there should be a probability P (in the classical sense of finite frequency or proportion) of samples in a population having the same or nearly the same composition as that of the population greater than any other probabilities of samples having other compositions. It is in those terms that the logical law of large numbers becomes a law of classical probability. When Peirce uses the term "probably equal" to describe the numerical relation between the composition ratios of the population-matching

---

[17] The precise formulation of this law and the rigorous mathematical proof of this law which I propose in Appendix II are reached by me independently of other sources. As far as I know, no standard texts in mathematical statistics or probability theory have given a proof, or sometimes, even a formulation, of this important, although seemingly obvious principle.

samples and the population, he should refer to no more than a probability P in this law of probability.

To give meaning to the term "approximately" in Peirce's statement of the logical law of large numbers, we may call attention to the fact that in our statement of the logical law of large numbers we do not require a major number of samples in the population to have *exactly* the same composition ratio, as that of the population, but merely require them to have exactly the same or *nearly the same* composition ratio as that of the population. This is because the number of samples having exactly the same composition ratio as that of the population is very small. A sample having nearly the same composition ratio as that of the population is a sample which has a value r for its composition ratio such that

$$p - e \leqslant r \leqslant p + e$$

where p is the exact value for the composition ratio of the population and e the small difference of r from p. When Peirce uses the term "approximately equal" to describe a numerical relation of composition ratios of certain samples and population, he should then mean no more than the fact that these samples in question do not have exactly the same, but only have nearly the same composition ratio as that of the population, with "nearly the same composition ratio" of the samples explained in the above manner.

At this point, we may mention several important facts about this logical law of large numbers conceived as a law of probability. First, if the value of the composition ratio of a population is known, this law can be used to calculate high probabilities of a sample assuming the same composition ratio as that of the population, within ranges of difference such as prescribed by the standard deviation of the so-called hypergeometric distribution; second, if we do not know the value for the composition ratio of a population, and if we want to estimate the value for the composition ratio of the population on the basis of known value for the composition ratio of a sample, we shall still have high probabilities, within small range of difference, according to this law. But actually to determine these probabilities and the ranges of difference, we may utilize the Central Limit Theorem of the probability theory to the effect that we shall always know the following: For a range of difference prescribed by the so-called "standard error of the mean," $\sigma_x = \sqrt{p(1 - p)/n}$ (where p is the value for the composition ratio of the sample, and n the size of the sample,) there will be at least a probability of 0.6826 that the sample composition ratio (or the mean) will coincide with that of the population. For a range of difference prescribed by 2σ, there will be at least such probability of 0.9544, and so on. For an explanation of these mathematical-statistical results, we refer the readers to Appendix III of this book.[18]

3. Validity of Probable Inference

With the above explanation of the logical law of large numbers in mind, we may go back to Peirce's statistical deduction and consider how it must be a valid probable inference which leads to true conclusions in a majority of cases, in acccordance with its leading principle – the logical law of large numbers. Our consideration will proceed in the following way. First and foremost, we must note that the first premise of the statistical deduction [19] states that a given sample is a fair or a numerous random sample from a given population. Disregarding for the present the question as to what meaning Peirce attaches to the term "fair sample" or "numerous random sample," we may point out that it is not essential for a fair sample to be objectively representative, i.e., to have a composition ratio similar to that of the population, or more precisely, to have a value for its composition ratio different from the value for the composition ratio of the population by a small number, in regard to the given property P. It is only required that a fair sample is not known to be objectively unrepresentative, i.e., not known to have a value for its composition ratio very different from the value for the composition ratio of the population. In this sense of a fair sample, we may indeed show that a statistical deduction is a valid probable inference.

Second, let us explain how a statistical deduction is a valid inference, with a probability relation determined by the logical law of large numbers. Our explanation is this. A statistical deduction is related to a class of possible inferences from premises of the form "S is a sample of size n," to conclusions of the form "S has a composition ratio similar to

---

[18] Cf., *Ibid.*, 2.287; also 2.724. In spite of the fact that Peirce does not develop any systematic statistics, he has nevertheless often referred to probability formulas such as that of the probable errors. Therefore, in connection with his discussion of probable inference, it should be to our benefit to understand Peirce's argument which uses statistical laws or laws of probability to draw conclusions of statistical deduction and induction, as we shall soon see, that a somewhat detailed presentation of the essential laws in mathematical statistics and probability theory be made in appendices.

[19] As we shall see in the next Chapter, this same premise of a statistical deduction is also the premise of an induction.

that of the population," where S ranges over all samples of size n which can be possibly drawn from the population, and it can take as its value each such sample only once. Since, by the logical law of large numbers, a high proportion of samples of same size, which can be possibly drawn from a population, have composition ratios similar to that of the population, a class of possible inferences of the above description will therefore have true conclusions in a high proportion of times. This is because a major proportion of samples in the population would verify a major proportion of conclusions of the inferences, whereas the rest would falsify the rest of conclusions of the inferences. It is in this sense that the logical law of large numbers is a leading principle of statistical deduction, and we should draw a major proportion of true conclusions from true premises according to the law.

Now, when we say that a statistical deduction is related to a class of possible inferences of the above description, we mean that it can be considered as one of the possible inferences in the given class. This is because its first premise states that a given sample is a fair one, which, in our sense, is a sample capable of being drawn once from the given population. With this understanding, we may define the probability of the statistical deduction in terms of the high proportion with which the above-mentioned class of possible inferences carries true conclusions, on the Laplacian principle that a probability is a proportion of favorable alternatives among all possible alternatives, favorable and unfavorable. It is only in this sense of probability, and in view of the probability relation between the premise that a given sample is fair and the conclusion that the given sample has a composition ratio similar to that of the population, that we may understand statistical deduction as a valid inference. This is because the probability relation between its premise and its conclusion is a logical one in virtue of the logical law of large numbers.

At this point, we should also make two criticisms of Peirce's formulation of the statistical deduction. First, since the probability of the statistical deduction is one between its premises and its conclusion, it should not be mentioned in the conclusion of the inference. When it is mentioned in the conclusion of the inference, we are misled to think that the probability is concluded from the premises of the inference. Peirce's use of the term "probably" in the conclusion of the statistical deduction in his formulation does seem to make this impression upon us, in spite of the fact that what Peirce intends to do is to suggest that the conclusion about the composition ratio in the sample *probably* follows from the premises about the composition ratio in the population and about a fair sample.[20]

Second, the statement that the given sample has a composition ratio similar to that of the population can be more precisely expressed by the statement that the value of the composition ratio in the given sample differs from that of the composition ratio in the population by a given small value. When Peirce uses the term "approximately" together with the term "probably" in the conclusion of the statistical deduction, we do not know exactly what he refers to by that term, although it should by all means refer to the fact of "differing by a given small value" mentioned in the conclusion of the statistical deduction that "the value of the composition ratio in the given sample differs from that of the composition ratio in the population by a given small value."

In view of these two criticisms of Peirce's formulation of the statistical deduction, we may give the statistical deduction a better formulation:

$S_1, S_2, \ldots, S_n$ form a numerous random sample of the instances of M,
A proportion r of instances of M are instances of P,
Hence, the proportion of instances of P to all instances of M in the given sample differs from r by a small numbers.

or

Hence, with a difference of a small number, a proportion r of instances of M in the given sample are instances of P.

We can validate this inference by saying that the probability of this inference and of its conclusion (as we may define the probability of the conclusion of an inference in terms of the probability of the inference) has a high value in virtue of the logical law of large numbers.

So far we have seen how Peirce distinguishes "probable inference" from "universal necessary or explicative inferences," and we have explained how a probable inference can be said to be valid, and to have a probability truth as its leading principle.[21] We have seen that induction and hypothesis are not valid inferences in the sense in which "universal necessary deductions" are. But it is an open question whether they can be interpreted as having a validity in the same sense in which a probable inference can, i.e., as having probability truth as their

---

[20] Peirce says at one place that "The conclusion of the statistical deduction is here regarded as being 'the proportion r of the S's are P's', and the words 'probably about' as indicating the modality with which this conclusion is drawn and held for true." (2.721nl).

[21] It is clear that, if we take logic in a broad sense, so as to include the classical calculus of probability, a probable inference with a leading principle from the calculus of probability should be considered valid in the sense of having a logical leading principle.

leading principle. Indeed, Peirce formulates and interprets induction and hypothesis in terms of probable inferences and assigns principles from the calculus of probability to them as their leading principles. In this way, he intends to justify ampliative inference in general. In the following Chapter, therefore, we shall concentrate on Peirce's attempt to formulate and interpret induction as a probable inference with the same logical law of large numbers as we have discussed above as its leading principle. In this will consist Peirce's probabilistic justification of induction.

CHAPTER IV

PROBABLE INFERENCE AND
JUSTIFYING INDUCTION

1. *Induction and Apagogical Inversion of Statistical Deduction*

In his essay "A Theory of Probable Inference," Pierce formulates induction in the following syllogistic form:

S_1, S_2, ..., S_n form a numerous random sample of the instances of M,
A proportion r of S_1, ... S_n are instances of P,
Hence, probably and approximately, a proportion r of instances of M are instances of P.[1]

To justify induction as a valid probable inference, Peirce shows that induction as formulated in the above form can be obtained from an "apagogical inversion" of a statistical deduction. I shall explain this in the following.

An "apagogical inversion" in Peirce's usage is a transposition of one inference into a corresponding inference in the following way. Given an ordinary necessary inference

> All P's are M's,
> These S's are P's,
> Hence, these S's are M's.

the operation of "apagogical inversion" on this inference will give the following corresponding necessary inference:

> These S's are not M's,
> These S's are P's,
> Hence, some P's are not M's.

In this sense, an "apagogical inversion" is simply the operation of denying an antecedent of an inference by denying its consequent. By this operation, a valid inference always yields a valid inference. Now it is

---

[1] *The Collected Papers of Charles Sanders Peirce*, 2.702; Cf. Also 2.720.

Peirce's point that we can prove the validity of induction in the form he gave above by showing that it can be obtained from the valid inference of statistical deduction by the operation of "apagogical inversion." [2] He calls this kind of proof an "apagogical proof" and refers to the statistical deduction as an "explanatory syllogism" of induction.[3]

Let us examine whether we can really understand the validity of induction from an "apagogical inversion" of a statistical deduction. The following quotation explains in Peirce's own words how we can produce a form of induction from an "apagogical inversion" of a form of statistical deduction:

> Now suppose we ask ourselves what would be the result of thus apagogically inverting a statistical deduction. Let us take, for example, Form IV:
>> The S's are a numerous random sample of the M's,
>> The proportion r of the M's are P's,
>> Hence, probably about the proportion r of the S's are P's,
> The ratio r, as we have already noticed, is not necessarily perfectly definite; it may be only known to have a certain maximum or minimum; in fact it may have any kind of indeterminacy. Of all possible values between O and I, it admits of some and excludes others. The logical negative of the ratio r is, therefore, itself a ratio, which we may name p; it admits of every value which r excludes, and excludes every value of which r admits. Transposing, then, the major premise and conclusion of our statistical deduction, and at the same time denying both, we obtain the following inverted form:
>> The S's are a numerous random sample of the M's,
>> The proportion p of the S's are P's,
>> Hence, probably about the proportion p of the M's are P's.
> But this coincides with the formula of induction.[4]

Now if we admit that statistical deduction in the above form is a valid inference, and further that induction in the above form is indeed a result of an "apagogical inversion" of the statistical deduction, we must grant that induction in the above form is also a valid inference. We have shown that we must reformulate a statistical deduction in a better form in order to see its validity. Here we want to show that, given Peirce's formulation of the statistical deduction, it is difficult to decide what should be the apagogically inverted form of the statistical deduction.

The difficulty in question is due to the ambiguity involved in the negation of the conclusion of the statistical deduction, namely, the

---

[2] He concludes as a rule for determining the validity of ampliative inference that the "syllogism of which the induction or hypothesis is the apagogical modification (in the traditional language of logic, the reduction) must be valid" (2.723; 2.718). The "apagogical modification" or "reduction" in this passage is precisely the "apagogical inversion" in question.

[3] Cf., *Ibid.*, 2.511; 2.717–723.

[4] *Ibid.*, 2.719–721.

statement "Hence, probably about the proportion r of the S's are P's." The scope of negation in this conclusion can be taken to include either the whole statement "Hence, probably about the proportion r of the S's are P's"; or the statement "About the proportion r of the S's are P's," or, (as intended by Peirce) the statement "The proportion r of the S's are P's", or finally, merely the part "The S's are P's." The results of negation for these different scopes of negation are correspondingly statements "Not probably about the proportion r of the S's are P's" "Probably, not about the proportion r of the S's are P's (meaning that probably, not with a difference of a small number, the proportion r of the S's are P's)," "Probably, about not the proportion r (therefore, the proportion p) of the S's are P's," or finally "probably about the proposition r of the S's are not P's." With these possible results from the negation of the conclusion of the statistical deduction, we may construct various apagogically inverted forms of statistical deduction. Without actually doing this, our point is clear: As there is no unique apagogically inverted form of a statistical deduction in Peirce's formulation, an apagogical inversion on a statistical deduction need not necessarily produce an induction in Peirce's formulation.

It might be suggested, however, that we consider an apagogically inverted form of a statistical deduction as *the* apagogically inverted form of statistical deduction if it preserves validity. But then the difficulty is that we have to inquire which of the possible apagogically inverted forms of statistical deduction preserves validity. In particular, we have to inquire whether induction in Peirce's formulation preserves validity as a result of the apagogical inversion on the given statistical deduction, and how it does, if it does. In fact, it is not obvious that induction in Peirce's formulation in the quoted passage does preserve validity. The explanation or the proof of the validity of induction, as intended by an "apagogical proof" or an "explanatory syllogism," is not successfully made by Peirce. Rather, because of the ambiguities involved in such an "apagogical proof," it confuses the issue regarding how we may regard induction as a probable inference from sample to population, according to some logical principle in probability theory.

2. Induction As a Valid Probable Inference

The true explanation of the validity of induction as a probable inference from sample to population follows from Peirce's own suggestion that an inductive conclusion must not merely follow from its premises, but must follow from them upon a principle of probability. This principle Peirce mentions in his suggestion as to why a statistical deduction is invertible into an induction of his formulation: "because it proceeds upon the principle of an approximate equality between the ratio of P's in the whole class and the ratio in a well-drawn sample, and because equality is a convertible relation." [5] The principle in question, as we have noticed, is the logical law of large numbers. In the following, we shall consider how induction could be shown to be a valid inference from sample to population in virtue of the logical law of large numbers, without any reference to anything like an "apagogical proof."

Like in the case of our reformulation of a statistical deduction in a better form, in order to avoid misleading interpretations, we may reformulate induction as given by Peirce in his form on page 32 as follows:

$S_1, S_2 \ldots S_n$ form a numerous random sample of the instances of M,
A proportion r of instances of M in the given sample are instances of P,
Hence, the proportion of instances of P to all instances of M in the population differs from r by a small number.

or

Hence, with a difference of a small number, a proportion r of instances of M in the population are instances of P.

Now we are to show that induction in this form is a valid inference, with a probability relation of its premises to its conclusion, as determined by the logical law of large numbers.

First, we may make clear that induction in the above form is related to a class of possible inferences of the following description in such a way that it can be considered as one of the possible inferences in the class. The class of possible inferences in question consists of inferences from premises of the form "S is a sample of size n" to conclusions of the form "The population has a composition ratio value which differs from the composition ratio x of S by a small number e," where S is a variable ranging over all samples of size n which can be possibly drawn from the population, and can take as its value each such sample only once, and where x is a variable ranging over all the fractions in the closed interval (o,1). Now as the given $S_1, S_2, \ldots, S_n$ form a fair sample of size n from the population, and as we interpret a fair sample as one which we do not know to be objectively unrepresentative, the given sample may take any value of composition ratio which any one of the samples of size n, which can be possibly drawn from the population, may take. In

[5] *Ibid.*, 2.718.

this sense, it may be considered as belonging to the set of all samples of size n, which can be possibly drawn from the population. With the sample of S_1, S_2, ..., S_n conceived this way, it is clear that induction in our formulation can be conceived as one of the possible inferences in the class of inferences described above: induction in our formulation is just an inference from premises of the form "S is a sample of size n," to the conclusion of the form "The population has a composition ratio value which differs from the composition ratio x of S by a small number e," where the variable S takes a particular sample S_1, S_2, ..., S_n as its value, and x is substituted for the known composition ratio r of S_1, S_2, ..., S_n.

Next, we are to show that the class of possible inferences described above, including induction in our formulation, assumes the same form as the class of possible inferences indicated in connection with our discussion of the validity of a statistical deduction. This latter class of possible inferences can be more precisely described as one consisting of inferences from premises of the form "S is a sample of size n" to the conclusions of the form "S has a composition ratio value which differs from the composition ratio x of the population by a small number e," where the variable S ranges over all samples, which can be possibly drawn from the population, and can take as its value each such sample only once, and where x assumes as its values fractions within the close interval (0,1). Now to show that this class of possible inferences assumes the same form as the class of possible inferences from premises of the form "S is a sample of size n" to conclusions of the form "The population has a composition ratio value which differs from the composition ratio x of S by a small number e," where S and x have domains of the same values, we need only show that the conclusion that "S has a composition ratio value which differs from the composition ratio x of the population by a small number e," and the conclusion that "The population has a composition ratio value which differs from the composition ratio x of S by a small number e," state the same thing. That they do state the same thing can be clearly seen, if we assume that the value of the composition ratio for the population is p and the value of the composition ratio for the sample is r, and then express the first conclusion by the inequality

$$p - e \leqslant r \leqslant p + e$$

and express the second conclusion by the inequality

$$r - e \leqslant p \leqslant r + e$$

These two inequalities are obviously indentical in reference. This shows that our conclusions do state the same thing. This shows that the class of possible inferences to which induction in our formulation belongs assumes the same form as the class of possible inferences to which a statistical deduction belongs.

With the above understanding, we may finally argue that as the logical law of large numbers, which states that a high proportion of samples which can be possibly drawn from the population have composition ratio values which differ from the composition ratio of the population by a small number, should determine a high proportion of true conclusions for the class of possible inferences from population to sample, to which a statistical deduction belongs, it should at the same time determine a high proportion of true conclusions for the class of possible inferences from sample to population, to which an induction belongs. This is because both classes refer to the same form of inference. Indeed, we may restate the logical law of large numbers as follows: the population has a composition ratio value which differs from the composition ratios of a high proportion of samples of a given size by a small number. In view of this law, we may readily check that the class of possible inferences which we have described above, and to which induction in our formulation belongs, should carry true conclusions in a high proportion of times. At this point, we may recall that we have defined the probability of a statistical deduction in terms of the high proportion with which the class of possible inferences from population to sample carries true conclusions, on the Laplacian principle of probability. Similarly, we may define the probability of an induction in our formulation in terms of the high proportion, with which the class of possible inferences from sample to population carries true conclusions also on the Laplacian principle of probability. We may further define the probability of the inductive conclusion in terms of the probability of the induction itself. The probability relation of the inductive premises to the inductive conclusion in an induction in our formulation is explained by the probability of the inference, and hence by reference to the logical law of large numbers. It is by reference to the logical law of large numbers that we are always able to infer with a high probability from an appropriate inductive premise to an appropriate inductive conclusion, as represented in our formulation of induction on page 35. It is in this sense that we say that induction is a valid inference, and that there is a logical relation between an appropriate inductive premise and an appropriate inductive conclusion.

In the above sense, we have shown the induction in our formulation is a probable inference with the logical law of large numbers as its leading principle. That is, on the basis of the logical law of large numbers, we have validated inductive inference from given fair sample to conclusion about population. It is therefore more appropriate to say that the validity of induction as a probable inference derives from the fact that it is an inference from fair samples to population, upon the logical law of large numbers, than to say that it derives from its being an "apagogical inverse" of a valid statistical deduction. This is not to say that there is no relation between a statistical deduction and an induction: their relation is made explicit in our above analysis of the validity of induction, but is not to be revealed in the notion of an "apagogical inversion."

Since a valid induction is such that its premises should give us information concerning a fair sample, and stand in a probability relation to its conclusion, we should consider Peirce's argument for the validity of induction always and essentially in these terms, and call this argument in this sense an argument for the validity of probable inference from fair samples. In this should consist Peirce's probabilistic justification of induction as a valid inference.

CHAPTER V

REQUIREMENTS FOR THE VALIDITY
OF INDUCTION *

1. *General Remarks*

In this Chapter I shall examine two requirements which Peirce considers to be essential for the validity of inductive inference. One, as we have seen, is that of fair sampling or obtaining fair samples for the inductive premises. Peirce says, "The first premises of a scientific inference (i.e., an ampliative inference such as induction) is that certain things (in the case of induction) or certain characters (in the case of hypothesis) constitute a fairly chosen sample of the class of things or the run of characters from which they have been drawn." [1] The other requirement is that of predesignation, which Peirce calls a condition *sine qua non* of valid inductions.[2] It requires us to ascertain with respect to which particular character we are to sample a given population and how many instances we propose to sample the population, before instances of the population are actually selected, and, therefore, before we know whether they are instances of the population or how many of them are instances of the population.

In the following I shall first examine Peirce's formulation of the principle of fair sampling as a basis for making valid probable inductive inference and point out certain difficulties involved in his notion of fair sampling. This criticism will lead to a new formulation of the principle of fair sampling and a new interpretation of fairness of samples on my part. Then I shall proceed to examine Peirce's requirement of predesignation and its supposed necessity for the validity of induction. I shall show that Peirce's notion of predesignation is not at all clear and that

---

* A simplified version of this Chapter has been presented at the Annual Meetings of the Western Division of the American Philosophical Association in Chicago, April, 1965.
[1] *The Collected Papers of Charles Sanders Peirce*, 2.726.
[2] Cf., *Ibid.*, 2.783.

it contains a weak claim and a strong claim, the former being false, whereas the latter being in need of substantiation.

2. *Peirce on Fair Sampling and Fair Samples*

Peirce formulates his principle of fair sampling in the following terms:

> The rule requires that the sample should be drawn at random and independently from the whole lot sampled. That is to say, the sample must be taken according to a precept or method which, being applied over and over again independently, would in the long run result in the drawing of any set of instances as often as any other set of the same number.[3]

Two observations can be immediately made for our proper understanding of this principle of fair sampling. First, the method in question must be one by which samples of a certain composition must be drawn in the long run of experience with a relative frequency equal to the proportion of samples of this composition in the population. The "long run" must be understood as an indefinitely long run if the sampling is to be done "over and over again indefinitely." A relative frequency in an indefinitely long run is a probability in the so-called empirical sense, as we shall see.

Second, when Peirce writes of drawing sets or samples from a population, he means drawing with replacement. The system of drawing with replacement differs from the system of drawing without replacement in the following essential respect. The former allows us to draw the same set or sample over and over again, because the same set or sample, after each time it is drawn, is returned to the population, whereas the latter does not allow us to draw the same set or sample a second time, because a set or sample, after being drawn the first time, is not to be returned to the population. Hence the content of a finite population can be exhausted by drawing without replacement, but cannot be exhausted by drawing with replacement.

With a system of drawing with replacement, the population in fact becomes one of drawings of an indefinitely large size. When Peirce requires that a method or a principle of fair sampling must draw every set or sample in the population with equal frequency in the long run, he cannot possibly mean that a system of drawing without replacement is used. For then there would not be any such "long run." Furthermore,

---

[3] *Ibid.*, 2.726.

it is theoretically impossible to draw samples or sets of the same size from a population with equal frequency, using the system of drawing without replacement. For example, after we have drawn the set (a, b) of two things a, b from the population (a, b, c) of three things a, b, c, we would not have equal chance to draw the set (a, b) of a, b or the set (b, c) of b, c because we have only c in the population.[4]

We may now say that when Peirce states that a fair sample (or a fairly chosen sample) is one drawn according to a method, by which every sample in the population would be drawn equally often in the long run, he understands a fair sample as a subset in the population, which is chosen with the same frequency in the long run as all other subsets of the same size. A fair sample can also be understood as one such that samples of its composition are drawn with a relative frequency in the long run, equal to the proportion of samples of that composition in the population.

Now there are serious objections to this way of defining what a fair sample is. First, we can never know whether any given rule or method will enable us to choose every sample, which can possibly be drawn from a population with equal frequency, in the long run, nor whether it will enable us to choose samples of a certain composition in a population with a relative frequency equal to their proportion in the population in the long run. As the long run is an indefinitely long process of sampling, the assertion that the given method or rule will or would enable us to choose every sample from a population with equal frequency in the long run will be beyond confirmation and disconfirmation, and therefore loses empirical meaningfulness. There is also no unequivocal criterion to which we may appeal for distinguishing between a method which has the characteristic of enabling us to choose every sample from a population with equal frequency in the long run and a method which does not have this characteristic. Even if we may suppose, as Peirce does not, that the long run is a finite process of sampling, how can we be sure that the method in question will draw all samples with equal frequency? Thus, given a population (a, b, c). of three things a, b, c, we may first draw a sample (a, b) of a, b, then draw a sample (b, c) of b, c and then draw a sample (a, c) of a, c. But there is

---

[4] Following the law of combination, we may calculate all the possible ways of drawing samples of size r with distinct constitutions from a population of size n. The number of such possible ways is given by

$$C_r{}^n = \frac{n!}{r!(n-r)!}$$

no telling from our drawing (a, b) that the next drawing would be that of (b, c), and the second next would be that of (a, c). In other words, from what we already know about what we have drawn, we have no idea whether or not we are going to draw the same sample over again. Even if our method *has* resulted in choosing certain samples with equal frequency, and thus we have inductive evidence for the fairness of our sampling method, there is no telling from this that all samples have been chosen or that in the long run this will continue. In short, no empirical evidence can give us a certainty that our method have brought out all samples from a population or will bring them out with equal frequency in any finite process.

For the sake of argument, we might grant that there is a sense in which we may say that we know that a given method enables us to draw every sample from a population with equal frequency in a finite process, and this sense is expressed by saying that we have chosen all samples from a population with equal frequency by using the given method and *that* we *know* that this is true. Then by the definition of this method, we must have *a fortiori* observed all samples of all constitutions in the population, and we also *a fortiori* know all the proportions of samples of different compositions in the population. This means that we know everything about the population, and there would be no need in making induction from sample to population. We know in fact, by knowing that our method has brought our samples of all constitutions with equal frequency, which sample is approximately objectively representative of the population. We should indeed know the approximate objective composition ratio of the population by knowing the approximate composition ratio of samples which have appeared most frequently. If our knowledge of a sample's being fair should presuppose that we already know the objective composition ratio of the population, then there would be no need in making induction from sample to population.

Perhaps Peirce might reply that by his formularion of the principle of fair sampling, he merely means that if the method has not in fact enabled us to choose every sample from the population with equal frequency, appropriate conditions must be stated under which we are justified in saying that our method would enable us to choose every sample from the population with equal frequency. Let us ask, however, what those appropriate conditions are. Peirce has not specified them just as he has not given any *a priori* criterion by which we may identify a method which will enable us to choose every sample from a population with equal frequency in the long run. We may perhaps suggest that these appropriate conditions are those under which we might validly induce from the fairness, so far, of a method of sampling that the method will be always fair. But certainly this does not help. For in asserting that we choose a fair sample, which is the basis for valid induction, by using a method of fair sampling warranted by valid induction, we are begging the question.

In the light of these considerations, it appears that there is neither an *a priori* reason nor an empirical reason by which we may be assured with certainty that a sampling method would enable us to choose every sample from a population with equal frequency in the long run. We may safely conclude that there is no use for Peirce's principle of sampling, that any proof we had of a fair sampling method in Peirce's sense would make induction unnecessary, and consequently that a fair sample specified in Peirce's sense is no genuine basis for probable induction.

3. *Principle of Fair Sampling: A New Formulation*

One clue to a proper understanding of fair sampling method, or of fair samples specified by reference to a fair sampling method, lies in the fact that it must not be the case that (A) we *know for certain* that a fair sampling method yields objectively representative samples, nor must it be the case that (B) we *know for certain* that the fair sampling method does not yield objectively representative samples. Because, if (A) is true, we have no need [5] to make an induction to a conclusion concerning the composition ratio of a population, while if (B) is true, we could not make a valid induction, since our inductive conclusion would be false on the basis of (B). Hence (A) and (B) must be excluded in a definition of a fair sample, as one entails deduction, and the other leads to a false inductive conclusion. Now there are two alternatives which do not entail deduction, nor lead to false inductive conclusions, but are not for this reason irrelevant for defining a fair sample; they are:

(A′) We know that the given large sample has a composition ratio r, and we do not know that the given sample is objectively representative.

(B′) We know that the given large sample has a composition ratio r, and we do not know that the given sample is not objectively representative.

---

[5] That would be good, of course; but any such requirement is (normally) impossible to fulfill.

We may combine (A') and (B') in the following statement (C):

(C) We know that the given large sample has a composition ratio r, and we do
not know whether or not the given sample is objectively representative.

Certainly, from (C) we cannot deduce with certainty the conclusion
that the population, from which the given sample is taken, has the composition ratio r, as we can from (A); nor can we deduce with certainty
from (C) the conclusion that the population, from which the given
sample is taken, does not have the composition ratio r, as we can from
(B). It is only likely or probable (in an intuitive sense) from (C) that the
population has the composition ratio r. We may suggest that under this
condition the sample is a fair one, fair in the sense that we do not know
that the sample is not objectively representative. We may define a
method of fair sampling in terms of a fair sample in our sense: a method
of sampling is fair if we can draw a fair sample in our sense by using that
method. Of course, we may first define a method of fair sampling as one
which is not known to be unfair, or in other words, as one which is not
known to enable us to draw objectively unrepresentative samples, and
then we may simply define a fair sample as one which is drawn by a
method of fair sampling in our sense.

There are two important observations on this new definition of a
fair sample. First, when we say that a sample is fair in our sense, we do
not imply that we do not know anything about the sample, i.e., we do
not imply that we are in a state of complete ignorance with regard to the
sample in question. Instead, we assume that we know that the sample in
question has a composition ratio r and that it has a statistically significant large size.[6] The probability of an empirical generalization asserted
or established on the basis of the given sample is not in this sense merely established on the basis of the doctrine of chances without empirical
basis. For the probability in question has an empirical basis, namely
our empirical knowledge of a certain composition ratio r and a certain
large size n of the sample, even though the probability is determined
in virtue of a logical law in the probability calculus. Insofar as it is
rational to accept or believe an inductive conclusion on the basis of a
fair sample in our sense, the probability of the inductive conclusion
defined by the calculus of probability can be considered as an explication of its rational credibility. This point will be further explained in

---

[6] We cannot formalize this notion here in this paper. The notion refers to the fact that in
mathematical statistics various numerical sizes of samples systematically affect their
representativeness in regard to population.

Chapter XIV in connection with our discussion of Lewis's "credibility theory of probability."

The second important observation is that in suggesting our new sense of a fair sample, we in fact suggest that the probability that a fair sample has a composition ratio similar to that of the population be defined in terms of the proportion of the samples, which can be possibly drawn from the population and which have composition ratios similar to that of the population. This I shall explain briefly: first, we regard all samples which can be possibly drawn from a population as equally probable in a certain sense: [7] (1) they are a set of collectively exhaustive and mutually exclusive alternatives, (2) they are symmetric with regard to the operation of drawing, that is to say, if there is any reason for expecting one particular sample to be drawn, there is as much reason for expecting other individual samples to be drawn; and if there is no reason for expecting one particular sample to be drawn, nor is there reason for expecting other individual samples to be drawn. Next, as a fair sample is one of which we do not know whether or not it is objectively representative, we regard it as belonging to the set of all equally probable samples in the population. Then by the fact that we know that there is a major or high proportion of samples which can be possibly drawn among all the samples and which have composition ratios similar to that of the population, we know that the probability in the classical (Laplacian) sense that the fair sample has a composition ratio similar to that of the population is the value of the proportion in question.

With this new sense of fair sample, induction can be defined as an inference from fair samples, without presupposition of the validity of induction, for the definition of a sample does not presuppose the validity of induction. The statement that S is a fair sample does not imply that we must know that S is fair on inductive ground. It only presupposes that we choose a sample as a basis for induction, if it is not known (*a priori* or inductively) to be objectively unrepresentative. Insofar as a fair sample in this new sense can be taken as evidence for asserting an inductive conclusion, we may suggest that induction can be construed as an inference in which the premise refers to a fair sample in the new sense, and the conclusion follows from the premise logically with probability in the Laplacian sense according to a principle of probability, say

---

[7] This is a formulation of the well-known principle of non-difference. What needs emphasis here for our purpose is that (1) the principle of non-difference as stated does not rule out our empirical knowledge about the composition ratio and the size of a given sample, and (2) this principle is used here to *explicate*, not to justify, our notion of probability as based on a fair sample.

the logical law of large numbers. We may thus formulate the inductive inference from a fair sample in our sense in the following statistical syllogism:

(1) The predicate P is true of a certain proportion r of a large sample S from the population M,
(2) P is not known to be untrue of about the same proportion r of the population and nothing is known to the contrary,
(3) Therefore, P is true of about the same proportion of the population M.[8]

The premises of this inference imply, by way of a definite probability, its conclusion. We may interpret the statement that it is probable that (3), as referring to no more than the fact that the premises imply with a definite probability c of the conclusion (3).

By suggesting this new sense of fair sample, we only formulate a very general criterion for ascertaining adequate premises for inductions; namely, the criterion that a fair sample in our sense is an adequate basis for making a probabilistic inductive conclusion. It is in general satisfied by any valid induction, for any valid genuine induction must be such that although its conclusion may not be known absolutely to be true, it should not be known absolutely to be false.

At this point, one may raise the question as to how samples in specific cases my be judged fair. To say that a sample is fair if it is not known to be objectively unrepresentative does not necessarily help us to decide whether in a specific case a given sample is fair in the new sense, or to justify our decision concerning the fairness of the given sample. We have to have specific grounds for saying that a specific sample is fair. For example, given a large sample of white swans, we may say that this sample is fair because we do not know that this sample is objectively unrepresentative with respect to the character "white." But then it is always legitimate to ask (1) what grounds should justify us in asserting that we do not know that swans in the sample are objectively unrepresentative, and (2) how large the size of the sample is. These questions should be appropriately answered, if we want to make specific grounds of our assertion clear. Thus, to reply to question(1), we say that we choose the sample in such and such a way so as to prevent us from producing objectively unrepresentative samples, in the light of our general knowledge of the population from previous experience or from testing.[9]

---

[8] An interesting observation is that Hempel's objection to statistical syllogism (Cf., Hempel's essay "Inductive Inconsistencies" in *Synthese* 12, 439–69, 1960) does not apply to this form of inductive inference.

[9] The so-called "sampling techniques" in modern mathematical statistics are the study of ways or methods of sampling population, utilizing known facts about kinds of populations, to

That is to say, what should justify us in making our assertion is that our general knowledge of the population from previous experience or from testing does not provide us a ground for drawing a false conclusion concerning the population, and we know nothing to the contrary that our sampling method should not enable us to produce objectively representative samples. To reply to question (2), we say that the sample at least contains such and such a number of instances.

To ascertain specific grounds for asserting fairness of samples in specific cases, we should always make reference to criteria or rules. For example, in order that we may decide whether a given sample in a specific case is sufficiently large in size if it is to be a fair sample, we should make reference to the following criteria: (1) A sample in a certain specific case should contain at least a certain number of instances; and (2) What we know in general and what we know about the relevant population in the specific case do not contradict the fact that the sample in question is not known to be objectively unrepresentative. There are criteria or rules of similar kinds for determining fair samples in various kinds of specific cases. By making reference to them we may make assertions about the fairness of samples in similar specific cases. In the light of these considerations, we may indeed reformulate the minor premise (2) on page 46 as follows:

(2') We *know* that the given sample is fair according to relevant criteria or rules.

Here we do not want to detail on how specific criteria or rules for determining fairness or unfairness of samples in specific cases are to be formulated or justified.[10] We may in general indicate that their formulation and justification should depend upon considerations of natures of specific inductive problems and the purposes which we want specific valid inductive conclusions to serve. They should be formulated and justified relative to different kinds of samples, different kinds of populations, and different kinds of sampling methods. The number of instances required in a sample for a trustworthy inductive conclusion, for example, should not be *a priori* uniformly settled, but must be settled for each specific inductive problem, as conformable to the pur-

---

design methods for producing objectively representative samples or at least to prevent producing unrepresentative samples. E.g., we may stratify a population into a set of strata and take sub-samples from each of the strata, so that the collated samples will be better representative than we do otherwise.

[10] In Chapter XIV where I formulate Lewis's criteria for determining rational credibility of empirical generalizations, we shall suggest that these criteria can be construed as criteria for determining fairness of samples in specific cases. We shall also discuss to some extent the question as to how our acceptance of these criteria should be justified.

pose which the criteria or rules concerning the sizes of samples in specific cases are intended to serve.

4. *Peirce on Predesignation*

The second requirement for making a valid induction, according to Peirce, is that of predesignation, according to which induction must be made in regard to a predesignate character and a predesignate number of instances. In an inductive process, predesignation means the following:

> If in sampling any class, say the M's, we first decide what the character P is for which we propose to sample that class, and also how many instances we propose to draw, our inference is really made before these latter are drawn, that the proportion of P's in the whole class is probably about the same as the instances that are to be drawn, and the only thing we have to do is to draw them and observe the ratio.[11]

In other words, for induction, we have to lay down a premise of the form "... M's are P's in the sample of the size n" from which the conclusion of the form "... M's are P's in the population" can be drawn, where "..." represents the proportion of instances of M which are instances of P. Induction then becomes a mere process of observing the proportion of instances of M represented by "...," which are instances of P.

Peirce's argument for the necessity of predesignation for the validity of induction is as follows. Suppose we were to draw our inference without predesignation of the character P and the number n, then, according to Peirce, we might always find a character which belongs merely to a group of instances examined, and does not belong to the whole population from which the group of instances examined is taken. It is always theoretically possible to find a common character or characters in any given group of things belonging only to that group of things. Without predesignation, our post-designate character may be just such a common character and very often it is. If it is, it would be an inadequate basis for making an inductive conclusion. Peirce gives the following example to show this.[12] Take the ages of death of the first five poets given in Wheeler's *Biographical Dictionary*. They are Argard, 48; Abeille, 76; Abulola, 84; Abunowas, 48; Accords, 45. We find that these five ages have the following characters in common:

---

[11] *Ibid.*, 2.737.
[12] Cf., *Ibid.*, 2.738.

(1) The difference of the two digits composing the number, divided by three, leaves a remainder of one;
(2) The first digit raised to the power indicated by the second, and then divided by three, leaves a remainder of one;
(3) The sum of the prime factors of each age, including one as a prime factor is divisible by three.

Presumably, these characters are all post-designate, i.e., found only after we have looked into the dictionary. On account of this, Peirce concludes that there is not the smallest reason to believe that the next poet's age would possess these characters. Peirce also draws other examples from the history of science: Playfair's assumption that the specific gravities of the allotropic forms of elements would, if we know them, be found to be equal to the different roots of their atomic weight; "Bode's law" concerning the relative distances of the planets. All these generalizations are untrustworthy, and are quickly disconfirmed by experience, because the character "being equal to the root of a certain atomic weight" in Playfair's assumption, and the character "being of a certain distance from a given planet" in "Bode's law" are not predesignate, but presumably found *post hoc*.

Two points are made in Peirce's argument. First, he calls our attention to the fact that we can always find some character shared in common by a group of things collected at hand, and since there is no way whatsoever to tell that a character does not exclusively belong to a given group of things, that group of things may therefore not be used as a sample for induction. Next, he shows how absurd an inductive conclusion one could arrive at from a group of things whose common character is observed after the group of things is given us, but not predesignated and found to be such. Presumably he would generalize this to the effect that all inductions short of predesignation are invalid and therefore that predesignation is a necessary condition of induction without which no induction will be valid.

Now I wish to point out that these two points made by Peirce represent two different claims on the necessity of predesignation for induction. The first point represents a weak claim to the effect the predesignation will prevent us from arbitrarily attributing to a population the character which we notice in an off-hand sample, but it does not follow from this that all inductions short of predesignation must be invalid for thatreason. The second point, on the other hand, represents a strong claim to the effect that predesignation is a necessary condition for the validity of induction. In the following I shall show that the strong claim of Peirce is unacceptable, because it is false, whereas the weak claim of

Peirce is acceptable, but as it stands, needs substantiation and further specification. When this is done, it will become clear that predesignation is a specific use of the principle of fair sampling, and hence is not an independent requirement for valid induction over and above the requirement of fair sampling.

5. Relevancy of Predesignation for the Validity of Induction

Consider the strong claim first. Is predesignation a necessary condition of valid induction? Can we make valid induction without predesignation at all if other conditions for making a valid induction are present? Suppose we have observed that a certain number of swans being white, and also have ascertained that the number of swans we have observed is statistically significant and we know nothing to the contrary. Then can we make the valid generalization to the effect that all swans are white? The answer is yes, because there is no reason why a specific sample considered fair may not validly lead to an inductive conclusion in the form of inductive inference as formulated by the statistical syllogism of induction. If the conclusion of the inference leads to a false conclusion, we may certainly criticize the sample as being unfair, because it is not large enough, or because it is known to be biased or not randomly collected. We will not criticize the sample as being short of predesignation with respect to its characters, or as being merely observed as such. Then in what sense a valid induction must depend upon predesignation? And in what sense, when an induction is invalid, it is the lack of predesignation of characters to blame?

The example about the poets' ages given by Peirce does not show why predesignation is necessary for the validity of induction. The reason why ages of all poets of names of a certain type do not seem to have those arithmetical characters is not that these characters are not predesignate, for even if they are all predesignate, conceivably, the conclusions would not hold for ages of all poets with names of the given type. The reasons why they do not have these characters are rather: (1) the very procedure for deciding the poets' names is arbitrary; (2) we have reasonable doubts from our *background knowledge* about any necessary relation between poets' names and those characters of their ages. In the case of Playfair's assumption and "Bode's Law," they are not credible, not because they lack predesignation of their kind, but because they were in fact disconfirmed, or because the samples on which they are based are not fair at all, according to criteria appropriate for determining the validity of generalizations of their kind. It is quite conceivable that even if the characters in question are predesignate, the samples are unfair. Thus we may conclude that predesignation is not a necessary, not to say both a sufficient and a necessary, condition for every case of valid induction.[13]

Unlike the strong claim, the weak claim of Peirce in regard to the requirement of predesignation is a true one. We may note first that, that an inductive conclusion may be false, because the character which we find in a sample may not be possessed by the whole class is a trivial truth about inductive inference. An inductive conclusion, insofar as it is inductive, could not be a necessary truth. But that it may be false is not incompatible with the induction's being valid. Insofar as a given sample is a fair one, our induction based on it is valid, and our conclusion should be probable or credible. There is no proof, however, that the character we notice in a group of things must not belong only to that group of things. Nor is there a proof that the character we notice in a group of things must be unworthy for making inductions. In order to make a valid induction, we want to guard against unfair sampling, and we may indeed regard predesignation as a necessary condition of induction in some cases in the sense that it is one of the ways of obtaining fair samples in those cases.

To elucidate predesignation as one of the ways for obtaining fair samples in some cases, we should make more specific the nature of predesignation. Peirce has himself made the following suggestion:

The Inductive Method springs directly out of dissatisfaction with existing knowledge. The great rule of predesignation, which must guide it, is as much as to say that an induction, to be valid, must be prompted by a definite doubt or at least an interrogation; and what is such an interrogation but first, a sense that we do not know something; second, a desire to know it; and third, an effort – implying a willingness to labor – for the sake of seeing how the truth may really be. If the interrogation inspires you, you will be sure to examine the instances, while if it does not, you will pass them by without attention.[14]

This means that predesignation should be understood as a rule by which we are required to devise hypotheses and proceed to test them in the course of experience for the sake of obtaining valid inductive knowledge. The hypotheses which are relevant for drawing inductive conclusions are of the form "... M's are P's in a sample of the size n," where the

---

[13] Unless, of course, we take the requirement of predesignation as stating that we should predesignate only when fair samples are guaranteed. But in this sense the requirement of predesignation is superseded by that of fair sampling.

[14] *Ibid.*, 5.584.

blank ""..." indicates the proportion of M's which are P's, which is to be determined on the basis of observation of n instances of M. A hypothesis of this form should bring out the relevant feature, say P, of a population, the instances of M, for our empirical investigation. With respect to the character P in this hypothesis, we can devise methods which would enable us to obtain fair samples from the given population M. Very often when we know what feature of the population we are looking for ,we can devise methods for collecting fair samples in the light of what we have already known.

The following well-known example perhaps will illustrate the usefulness of predesignation for gathering a fair sample. Knowing that we are to find how many American citizens in a state are pro- Republican, we may devise methods of sampling which will prevent us from collecting an unfair sample from the population of the American citizens in that state. Thus, we may collect a sample from parts of a given population stratified with respect to professions and locations. The reason why we do so is that we know that the character "pro-Republican" ranges over citizens in various locations and professions and that the stratified sampling will prevent us from choosing samples in ways in which this particular knowledge is not taken into account. Suppose we have not predesignated the character "pro-Republican" and we happen to find that in one town of the given state all the residents are American citizens and "pro-Republican." Then our conclusion thereupon that all Americans in the given state are "pro-Republicans" is as untrustworthy as the sample is considered as known to be unfair. To the extent that predesignation of a character, say, "pro-Republican," may lead us to make use of our background knowledge for the sake of collecting a fair sample, and to the extent that this is admittedly a relevant procedure for drawing a trustworthy conclusion, lack of predesignation of a character could be responsible for an invalid induction, or for drawing an untrustworthy inductive conclusion.

To conclude, there are inductions which are invalid because we have not purposefully collected samples according to well-devised criteria. But, what kind of fair samples we want, and what kind of criteria or methods we need for judging the presence of a fair sample, will be known, however, only when we decide what our inductive problem is, i.e., only when we know the character with respect to which we are to do sampling. It is in this manner that predesignation of a character is often essential for defining an inductive problem and for solving it in the light of what we have already known and in the light of findings by adequate investigation. In this sense, we must admit that, even though predesignation is not essential for determining the validity of induction as an inference from sample to population, it is relevant for establishing a trustworthy inductive conclusion on good grounds as hypothesis is relevant for establishing a trustworthy law.

CHAPTER VI

PROBABILITY AND THE VALIDITY
OF INDUCTION

1. *General Remarks*

We have seen that probability in a logical or Laplacian sense is essential to, and in fact presupposed in, Peirce's probabilistic justification of induction. In other places, when Peirce comes to discuss probability independently of his argument for the validity of induction in terms of probable inference, he no longer accepts probability in a logical sense, but instead interprets probability in an empirical sense, i.e., in the sense that probability is to be determined only in terms of empirical findings in the long run. On account of this, Peirce must virtually vitiate his own probabilistic justification of induction. This, I believe, should become clear in this chapter after my close examination of Peirce's description of probability, and of its relation to inductive validity in important passages of his writings from 1878 to 1903.

Both the logical and the empirical views of probability of Peirce are derived from Locke's notion that probability characterizes an argument which "for the most part, carries truth with it." [1] For Peirce has in general defined probability as the proportion of inferences leading from true premises to true conclusions in a class or genus of inference. That is why he says that "Probability is a kind of relative number; namely, it is the ratio of the number of arguments of a certain genus which carry truth with them to the total number of arguments of that genus." [2]

Two closely related conceptions of probability in the empirical sense can be identified in Peirce's writings on probability. First, probability is something objective, to be determined in the long run of experience,

---

[1] John Locke, *An Essay Concerning Human Understanding*, Bk. i. Chap. xv, Sect. i. Quoted by Peirce in 2.649 and 2.696. Cf. also 2.650.
[2] *The Collected Papers of Charles Sanders Peirce*, 2.657.

and hence in an indefinite future; second, probability is something inherent in a thing as a habit is inherent in a man, and is to be determined under appropriate conditions. We shall discuss these two empirical conceptions of probability in the following section. After this, we shall examine Peirce's objections to the Laplacian view of probability.

2. Peirce's Two Empirical Conceptions of Probability

By the first conception, Peirce defines probability as the relative frequency in the long run of experience. He says,

An objective probability is the ratio in the long run of experience of the number of events which present the character of which the probability is predicated to the total number of events which fulfill certain conditions often not explicitly stated, which all the events considered fulfill.[3]

Probability is a statistical ratio, and further, in order to satisfy still more special conditions, it is convenient ... to make it the statistical ratio of the number of experiential occurrences of a specific kind to the number of experiential occurrences of a generic kind in the long run.[4]

This statistical ratio in the long run of experience is the same as the limit of an endless succession of empirical relative frequencies. It can be conveniently expressed by the following mathematical notation:

$$\lim_{n \to \infty} \mathrm{fr}_n \, (\phi, \, \psi)$$

where $\mathrm{fr}_n \, (\phi, \, \psi)$ represents the relative frequency of events of a certain property ϕ occurring in a sequence of n events of a certain other property ψ, and $\lim_{n \to \infty}$ indicates the limit of the relative frequency in question when n approaches infinity.[5] This limit must be determined under special conditions which are fulfilled by events whose probability is in question. In other words, it is something real to be recognized in the long run of empirical inquiry under special conditions.

It is that when we say that a certain ratio will have a certain value in the "long run," we refer to the probability-limit of an endless succession of fractional values; that is, to the only possible value from 0 to ∞, inclusive, about which the values of the endless succession will never cease to oscillate, so that no matter what place in the succession you may choose, there will follow both values above the probability-limit and value below it; while if V be any other

---

[3] Ibid., 2.785.
[4] Ibid., 5.21.
[5] Cf., Ernest Nagel, Principles of the Theory of Probability, Chicago, 1939, 21–22.

value from o to ∞, but not the probability-limit there will be some place in the succession beyond which all the values of the succession will agree, either in all being greater than V, or else in all being less.[6]

As inferences are also events, the following description of probability also coincides with the above.

In the long run, there is a real fact which corresponds to the idea of probability, and it is that a given mode of inference sometimes proves successful and sometimes not, and in a ratio ultimately fixed. As we go on drawing inference after inference of the given kind, during the first ten or hundred cases the ratio of successes may be expected to show considerable fluctuations; but when we come into the thousands and millions, these fluctuations become less and less; and if we continue long enough, the ratio will approximate toward a fixed limit.[7]

Empirical probability in this sense differs from probability in the Laplacian sense on two counts: (1) an empirical probability refers to a unique limit of a convergent sequence of "experimental occurrences" of events, whereas the Laplacian probability refers to a finite proportion of favorable alternatives among all alternatives, favorable and unfavorable; (2) an empirical probability is to be reached in an indefinite future or in the long run of experience, whereas a Laplacian probability can be determined on a known proportion. When Peirce says that an empirical probability is to be predicated to the total number of events which fulfill certain conditions, he does not make explicit what these conditions are. It seems appropriate to point out that these conditions are those which will make the assertion of a probability in the empirical sense true. Clearly, these conditions are: (1) there exists a sequence which will converge to a unique limit; (2) this limit will be reached in the long run of experience.

Two obvious criticisms of this notion of probability can be immediately induced: (1) we cannot know an empirical probability before we reach a ratio which is supposed to be ultimately fixed in a long run. Moreover, a supposed probability can never be conclusively verified because there is an indefinite course of experience in the future relevant for verifying the probability in question. (2) As an empirical probability refers to a unique limit of a sequence, we have the problem as to how we can ascertain the uniqueness of a limit of a sequence, even if we reach a limit of the sequence. For these reasons, we can say either that we do not know such a probability or that any assertion of a probability lacks conclusive ground. One way to avoid this difficulty is to say that probability is, in an empirical sense, always indeterminate, i.e., that proba-

[6] *The Collected Papers of Charles Sanders Peirce*, 2.758.
[7] *Ibid.*, 2.650.

bility or the limit of a sequence of events cannot be determined by a definite empirical relative frequency in any finitely terminable course of experience. Peirce is aware of this way of avoiding the difficulty, for he says, "This long run can be nothing but an endlessly long run, and even if it be correct to speak of an infinite 'number'; yet ∞/∞ (infinity by infinity) has certainly, in itself, no definite value." [8] But this way of avoiding the difficulty comes to nothing other than that we cannot make any probability statement in a good sense.

Another way in which Peirce undertakes to avoid the difficulty in question is by considering a probability-statement as a statistical law, which must be verified in the long run of experience, but which can be only known by induction, if it can be known at all. Thus, to say that a normal die will show a number divisible by three with a probability of $1/3$ is to assert the truth of a statistical law that the throwing of three or six of the die will occur on $1/3$ of all its throws in the long run of experience, a statistical law which can be known and certified by induction. To say that this probability-statement is a statistical law is to say that the probability-statement *would* come out true if the die should undergo an endless succession of trials under appropriate conditions. It is in view of this consideration that Peirce concludes that probability is a habit or "would-be" inherent in a thing just as a habit is inherent in a man. Thus Peirce says,

I am, then, to define the meanings of the statement that the probability, that, if a die be thrown from a dice box it will turn up a number divisible by three, is one-third. The statement means that the die has a certain 'would-be'; and to say that a die has a 'would-be' is to say that it has a property, quite analogous to any habit that a man might have.[9]

But this "would-be" of the die does not consist in any character of each single throw or of any finite number of throws, just as the habit of a man does not consist in his single actions. Peirce continues,

and just as it would be necessary, in order to define a man's habit, to describe how it would lead him to behave and upon what sort of occasion – albeit that this statement would by no means imply that the habit *consists* in that action – so to define the die's 'would-be,' it is necessary to say how it would lead the die to behave on an occasion that would bring out the full consequence of the 'would-be'; and this statement will not of itself imply that the 'would-be' of the die *consists* in such behavior.[10]

[8] *Ibid.*, 2.662.
[9] *Ibid.*, 2.664.
[10] *Ibid.*, 2.664–665.

To describe how a probability or its "would-be" would lead the die to behave so that the probability would become actualized is to describe the general conditions under which we are justified in saying that the probability would be actualized in the long run of experience; in other words, it is to describe how we *know* that the probability would be actualized in the long run of experience.

But do we know that the probability would be actualized in the long run of experience? What are the general conditions under which we are justified in saying that the probability would be actualized in the long run of experience? Peirce makes no suggestion on this. But obviously, by taking a probability-statement as a statistical law which states that a certain proportion must obtain in cases of a certain character, we have no way of knowing a probability except by inductive sampling. When we have observed that we have thrown three or six with a proportion of 1/3 in a long process of throws, we may decide that we *know* that this die has a probability 1/3 in the stated respect or that a proportion 1/3 must obtain in cases of throws of this dice. This is a case of knowing a proportion by "inductive sampling."

But on the basis of inductive sampling, our conclusions about a probability as a statistical law may at any point be disconfirmed or falsified. In spite of this, Peirce suggests that "It is only when the series is endless that we can be sure that it will have a particular character. Even when there is an endless series of throws, there is no syllogistic certainty, no 'mathematical' certainty that the die will not turn up a six obstinately at every single throw." [11] But if we do now have *certain* knowledge of a statistical law, must we say that we have *probable* knowledge of the law? More precisely, must we consider the statement that the die would evince a probability 1/3 of throwing a three or a six should the process of throwing be indefinitely prolonged, to be *probable* under conditions which would warrant an inductive conclusion from finite sampling? Now Peirce's answer to this question is negative. A probability is not to be ascribed to a law or to any individual inference or singular statement, because in an empirical sense, or in the sense of habit,

The idea of probability essentially belongs to a kind of inference which is repeated indefinitely. An individual inference must be either true or false, and can show no effect of probability; and therefore, in reference to a single case considered in itself, probability can have no meaning.[12]

[11] *Ibid.*, 2.667.
[12] *Ibid.*, 2.652.

This is indeed true, for on the empirical theory or on the "habit" theory, a probability statement or a statement of statistical law is meaningful only with reference to a series of events which converges to a unique limit of relative frequencies. It becomes meaningless with reference to a single law or a singular statement which cannot be said to have a limit at all. Even if we know a statistical law on the ground of induction, the statistical law does not therefore become probable in the empirical sense, or for that matter, according to Peirce, probable in any other sense. But the law or statistical statement is itself a probabilistic statement. For Peirce says,

... an induction may conform to the formula of induction, but it may be conceived, and often is conceived, that induction lends a probability to its conclusion. Now that is not the way in which induction leads to the truth. It lends no probability to its conclusion. *It is nonsense to talk of the probability of a law, as if we could pick universes out of a grab-bag and find in what proportion of them the law held good.*[13]

Two observations can be made upon the above quoted passage. First, it is clear that in writing this passage, Peirce has made himself a proponent of the modern frequency theory of probability as has been developed by von Mises and Reichenbach.[14] According to the modern frequency theory of probability, a propability belongs to a "collective" or an infinite series of events which has a unique limit. The probability of the "collective" is defined in terms of this limit. As there is no sense in speaking of a limit of a single event, there is no sense in speaking of the probability of a single event in a "collective," except that we may mean by it, according to Reichenbach, something termed an "appraised posit" based on a known relative frequency of the collective of events to which the given event belongs.

Second, in writing that "It is nonsense to talk of the probability of a law, as if we could pick universes out of a grab-bag and find in what proportion of them the law held good," Peirce can be understood as an opponent against the Laplacian view of probability in much the same spirit as the modern frequentists. At this point, it should be natural for us to introduce Peirce's arguments against the Laplacian conception of probability and to examine them.

---

[13] *Ibid.*, 2.780, (italics mine); also Cf., 1.92; 5.169; 6.100.
[14] Richard von Mises, *Probability, Statistics, and Truth*, New York, 1939. Hans Reichenbach, *The Theory of Probability*, Berkeley, 1949.

3. *Peirce's Objections to the Laplacian Definition of Probability and Criticisms*

The Laplacian view of probability is one according to which we may ascribe probability to single events or singular statements or laws. Peirce terms this view "conceptualistic," in contrast to his empirical view which he terms "materialistic." Now this characterization of the Laplacian view of probability certainly prejudges the Laplacian view and proves very misleading. A "conceptualistic" view of probability suggests a subjective determination of probability in terms of an actual or thought degree of belief. But the Laplacian view of probability is an objective view, and should not suggest this. Instead, it in fact suggests (1) that a probability is construed as some finite known or logically determinable proportion; and (2) that a degree of belief *ought to be* determined on the basis of this probability. Furthermore, according to this view, the probability of a single event or singular statement is construed as the proportion of alternatives favorable to the single event or relevant for verifying the singular statement among all known alternatives.

There are two grounds on which Peirce argues against the Laplacian view of probability. First, Peirce insists that this view requires the probability of an empirical proposition to be determined in terms of possibilities or possible universes in which the proposition would be true. In other words, the proponents of the Laplacian view require us to know, in determining a probability, how many will accord, out of all possible states of things, to any assigned extent, with a singular inductive conclusion. They must then assume that any one "constitution of the universe" is as probable or possible as any other. If that is the case, a single event or a singular inductive conclusion would have a determinate probability in terms of the proportion of those possible universes in which the event would occur or in which the singular inductive conclusion would be true. But then the occurrences or non-occurrences of an event would not affect the probability of its occurrence in the future, and the relative truth frequency of a singular inductive conclusion in the past would not affect its probability at all. This is so, because the number of favorable constitutions of the universe (or possible universes) would remain always the same, irrespective of the empirical frequency of the occurrence of an event or the truth frequency of a singular proposition in any given possible universe or any constitution of the universe. Thus Pierce concludes: "In short, it would be to assume that Nature is a pure chaos, or chance combination of independent elements, in which reasoning from one fact to another would be impossible, ... It would be to suppose that if we have found the order of Nature more or less regular in the past, this has been by a pure luck which we may expect is now at an end." [15]

The second ground upon which Peirce argues against the Laplacian view of probability is a well-known one: the Laplacian view of probability is an argument from complete ignorance to knowledge. Peirce charges,

But let us suppose that we are totally ignorant what colored hair the inhabitants of Saturn have. Let us, then, take a color chart in which all possible colors are shown shading into one another by imperceptible degrees. In such a chart the relative areas occupied by different classes of colors are perfectly arbitrary. Let us inclose such areas with a closed line, and ask what is the chance on conceptualistic principles that the color of the hair of the inhabitants of Saturn falls within that area? The answer cannot be indeterminate because we must be in some state of belief; and, indeed, conceptualistic writers do not admit indeterminate probabilities. As there is no certainty in the matter, the answer lies between *zero* and unity. As no numerical value is afforded by the data, the number must be determined by the nature of the scale of probability itself, and not by calculation from the data. The answer can, therefore, only be one-half, since the judgment should neither favor nor oppose the hypothesis. What is true of this area is true of any other one; and it will equally be true of a third area which embraces the other two. But the probability for each of the smaller areas being one-half, that for the larger should be at least unity, which is absurd.[16]

The objections which Peirce intends here are, in other words, (1) that the supposition of any assignable probability in the absence of empirical evidence for or against a hypothesis is groundless, and (2) that incompatible probability determinations for the same quasitum could be derived by assigning equal probabilities to alternatives representing a merely logical division.

Previously, we have suggested that a specific fair sample is supposed to be specifiable by reference to specific criteria or rules on specific empirical grounds such as the size of the sample and the procedure by which the sample is taken. Similarly, in defining a probability in the Laplacian sense, it is not implied that a probability is ascribed to an event or to a singular inductive conclusion without any empirical basis. In fact, when we ascribe a probability in this sense to the conclusion of a statistical deduction or of an induction, it is understood that we do

---

[15] *The Collected Papers of Charles Sanders Peirce*, 2.684.
[16] *Ibid.*, 2.679.

so on the grounds of an actual fair sample before us, an actual sample which is determined as fair in a proper sense.

In fact, C. I. Lewis suggests that we may always find empirical grounds for determining a probability in a proper sense. As Lewis puts it, "Complete ignorance of all relevant empirical facts is completely fictitious in the case of any meaningful empirical question." [17] That is to say, if we really know nothing about empirical data from which we may judge the probability of the case in question, we shall not be able to judge its probability, for "There are no probability problems in the complete absence of empirical data which, directly or indirectly, are indicative of the frequency in past experience." [18] Thus, for determining the probability of the hair color of inhabitants of Saturn, we always shall find some empirical grounds for making our probability judgment, e.g., as Lewis points out, we shall know more extended analogy between supposed creatures on Saturn and living beings which we are familiar with: that is implied in their being "inhabitants" and having hair. Then we may assign probabilities to alternatives in accordance with the relative frequencies indicated by the relevant empirical data which we possess. In doing this, of course, we shall need some probability principle by which to infer the probabilities of given alternatives from the given empirical data, for otherwise there is no use in appealing to empirical data.[19] As there are empirical data, on which we can establish probabilities of conclusions concerning the hair color of people on Saturn, in accordance with some probability principle, our probalilities are not arbitrarily determined, and are not determined simply on *a priori* grounds, no matter how untrustworthy our conclusions are. The absurdity of attributing two incompatible probabilities to a single event or a singular inductive conclusion, in the absence of any relevant evidence, would be non-existent.

Now a probability which we ascribe to a single event or a singular inductive conclusion on the basis of a relative frequency as indicated by relevant empirical data agrees with the Laplacian principle of probability that, a probability is a proportion of favorable cases to all cases, favorable or unfavorable, provided nothing is known to the contrary. As we cannot know a probability as a certain relative frequency of events to be obtained in an indefinite future, i.e., as a limit of a series of relative frequencies in the long run, it should be reasonable to adopt a

[17] C. I. Lewis, *An Analysis of Knowledge and Valuation*, 308–314.
[18] *Ibid.*, 309.
[19] This we shall make clear in Chapter XIV.

probability in the Laplacian sense, which is always knowable on the basis of finite proportion. In fact, the ascertainment of probability in Lewis' sense depends precisely upon our knowledge, albeit from empirical data, that there is a proportion of cases favorable to a single event or a singular inductive conclusion and nothing is known to the contrary.

In charging the Laplacian view of probability with requiring a probability to be determined in terms of a proportion of possibilities or possible universes, Peirce fails to notice (1) that what he calls "possible universes" are no more than possible alternatives for a given inductive situation, (2) that a probability as a proportion of possibilities is to be ascribed to a proposition or a single event only on empirical ground in accordance with a probability principle such as exemplified in the statistical inference from a fair sample to a population, and finally (3) that the probability relation of the probability statement to its empirical ground is a logical relation, as exemplified also in the statistical inference from a fair sample to a population. An empirical ground such as what we know from experience of a given inductive problem may be adequate or inadequate. When it is not adequate, we may not be justified in ascribing probability in the Laplacian sense to a singular inductive conclusion. But this does not give rise to the problem concerning the validity (or legitimacy) of ascribing probability in the Laplacian sense to a singular inductive conclusion on an adequate empirical ground.

Bearing in mind Peirce's conceptions of probability, we may say that Peirce in general fails to recognize a general probabilizing relation between a hypothesis and its evidence. The hypothesis may be a singular inductive conclusion or may be a statistical law. What would make a hypothesis probable is the empirical evidence drawn in its support from what we know. Carnap calls this kind of probability *probability*$_1$ or degree of confirmation, in distinction from what he calls *probability*$_2$ or probability in an empirical sense.[20] Probability$_1$ need not be established by referring to some limit in a "collective," but has to be defined, explicated, and formulated in relation to adequate empirical ground. It may be ascribed to a hypothesis or to a singular empirical statement. On the basis of this distinction between a probability$_1$ and a probability$_2$, we may say that the Laplacian definition of probability is a definition of probability$_1$, and hence that it is ascribable to singular inductive conclusions on adequate empirical grounds. In Peirce's argument for the validity of probable inference from a fair sample to a population,

[20] Rudolf Carnap, *Logical Foundations of Probability*, Chicago, 1950, 23–36.

the probable inference leading to a probabilistic justification of induction, we see that obtaining or presenting fair samples is a good empirical ground for a probability in the Laplacian sense to be ascribed to an inductive conclusion based thereupon.

Even in his attempts to show that probability must express a real fact or a statistical fact, Peirce cannot but admit the relevance of a probability in the Laplacian sense, for determining or expressing the validity of our knowledge of the probability, in an empirical sense or in a sense of habit, in relation to empirical grounds. Suppose we draw beans singly from a bag and look at them, each one thrown back, and the whole well-mixed after each drawing. When we have drawn a thousand times, if about half have been white, then, according to Peirce, we could approximately insure ourselves in the long run by betting each time upon the white, a confidence which would be entirely wanting if, instead of sampling the beans by 1,000 drawings, we had done so by only two. From this, Peirce concludes that "to express the proper state of our belief, not *one* number but *two* are requisite, the first depending on the inferred probability, the second on the amount of knowledge on which that probability is based." [21] In other words, the probability of drawing a white bean is inferred from the known class of 1,000 drawings, half of which are of white beans, while the assurance or weight of the probability so determined depends upon our knowledge of the relevance and amount of our drawings. If we have an adequate amount of relevant drawings, i.e., if we have a fair sample of relevant drawings, we would be able to define the probability (in the logical sense) of the probability (in an empirical sense) in question. The probability (in a logical sense) should express and explicate the relation of trustworthiness of our evaluation of the empirical probability in question to the given fair sample of relevant drawings.

By explicitly denying a probability in a logical or Laplacian sense which may be ascribed to a singular inductive conclusion, Peirce should therefore virtually vitiate his probabilistic justification of induction, and naturally conclude that "There is, therefore, a manifest impossibility in so tracing out any probability for a synthetic conclusion." [22] This indicates an inconsistency in Peirce's theory of induction or an incompatibility between Peirce's two theories of induction separately entertained, this incompatibility, of course, being not recognized by Peirce himself.

[21] *The Collected Papers of Charles Sanders Peirce*, 2.678.
[22] *Ibid.*, 2.681.

CHAPTER VII

A NON-PROBABILISTIC JUSTIFICATION
OF INDUCTION *

1. *General Remarks*

If a probability, either in the Laplacian sense or in an empirical sense or in a sense of habit, ought not to be ascribed to an inductive conclusion, then on what ground should we say that induction is valid? In other words, since it is nonsense to speak of the probability of a single inductive inference and its conclusions in either sense, how should we conceive of the problem of justifying induction and explain the inductive validity? In his article entitled "Validity" in Baldwin's *Dictionary of Philosophy and Psycology*, Peirce explains the validity of an argument in the following terms:

Every argument or inference professes to conform to a general method or type of reasoning, which method, it is held, has one kind of virtue or another in producing truth. In order to be valid the argument or inference must really pursue the method it professes to pursue, and furthermore, that method must have the kind of truth-producing virtue which it is supposed to have.[1]

If it has been proved that an inductive conclusion has no probability, the problem of justifying induction ceases to be that of ascribing probability to its conclusions. But, since an argument or inference is valid in virtue of its conforming to a truth-producing method, the problem of justifying induction is then that of ascertaining whether induction conforms to some such a method other than the principle of probable deduction, or simply whether inductive method is such a method. Thus, according to Peirce, if induction is valid at all, its validity must consist in the fact that "it pursues a method, which, if duly presisted in, must,

---

* A major portion of this Chapter was presented in a paper entitled "Charles Peirce's Arguments for the Non-probabilistic Validity of Induction" of the Annual Meetings of Charles S. Peirce Society in Philadelphia, December 28, 1966.
[1] *The Collected Papers of Charles Sanders Peirce*, 2.780.

in the very nature of things, lead to a result indefinitely approximating to the truth in the long run.'' [2]

But how must induction in the long run lead to the truth? Peirce's reply is that induction is a method which will always correct its errors that may temporarily lead us into, if we presist in the employment of the method for reaching conclusions. Thus, Peirce says:

> The true guarantee of the validity of induction is that it is a method of reaching conclusions, which if it be persisted in long enough, will assuredly correct any error concerning future experience into which it may temporarily lead us.[3]

> Induction is justified as a method which must in the long run lead us to the truth, and that, by gradual modification of the actual conclusion.[4]

> Nor must we lose sight of the constant tendency of the inductive process to correct itself. This is of its essence. This is the marvel of it. The probability of its conclusion only consists in the fact that if the true value of the ratio it sought has not been reached, an extension of the inductive process will lead to a closer approximation.[5]

This idea concerning the gradual modification of inductive conclusions in a process of approximating to the truth has been hinted by Peirce, even when he contrasts the validity of probable deduction with that of induction:

> A probable deductive argument is valid, if the conclusions of precisely such arguments (from true premises) would be true in the long run, in a proportion of times equal to the probability which this argument assigns to its conclusions; for that is all that is pretended ... the validity of induction is entirely different; for it is by no means certain that the conclusion actually drawn in any given case would turn out true in the majority of cases where precisely such a method was followed; but what is certain is that, in the majority of cases, the method would lead to some conclusion that was true, and that in the individual case in hand, if there is any error in the conclusion, that error will get corrected by simply persisting in the employment of the same method.[6]

The method in question is the method of fair sampling. According to Peirce's interpretation of this method, this method will in the long run present any instance of a population as often as any other, and therefore will reveal the true and objective composition of a population. Since a majority of samples of a certain size will resemble the population with regard to their composition, according to the logical law of large numbers, if every sample is to be drawn once, there certainly would be a true conclusion concerning the composition of the popu-

[2] *Ibid.*, 2.781.
[3] *Ibid.*, 2.769.
[4] *Ibid.*, 2.777.
[5] *Ibid.*, 2.729.
[6] *Ibid.*, 2.781.

lation based on a sample in a majority of samples thus drawn. But what interests us now is another point of Peirce: the method in question is also the method by following which any error in a given conclusion will get corrected, and therefore, conclusions concerning the population composition in the process of sampling will approximate to a true one in the long run. Since induction pursues such a method, it is clear that Peirce must hold it as valid. In this sense, the validity of induction, even when induction is considered as a probable inference, consists not in its inferring, with probability, conclusions, on the ground of fair samples in a proper sense, but in pursuing a method of fair sampling, which will reveal the true and objective composition of a population in the long run. The "probability" of induction becomes then only a term which indicates that induction follows such a method.

Now there are two important problems in this justification of induction in a non-probabilistic manner, namely, in a manner other than the one in which induction is said to be a logically valid probable inference like the statistical deduction. The first problem concerns in what sense induction can be said to be self-correcting and how a self-correcting process of induction will lead to the true .The second problem concerns Peirce's conception of truth and how it affects the validity of inductive method.

2. Self-Correcting Nature of Inductive Method

As Peirce does not make clear what the self-correcting process of induction means in his writings, I venture here to clarify this notion, in order to see how a self-correcting process of induction will enable us to reach truth in the long run. Roughly speaking, induction is self-correcting if its conclusions are corrected by other conclusions in the process of sampling. More precisely, one inductive conclusion corrects another if we reject one in favor of the other, because the sample on which the first conclusion is based is larger than the sample on which the second conclusion is based. But in speaking of the self-correcting character of induction in this sense, we must require the following: for any given two conclusions A and B, if B is to correct A, A must not be known to be true, whereas B must not be known to be false. The reason for this requirement is that if A is known to be true, there would be no point in saying that it is corrected; whereas if B is known to be false, there would be no point in saying that a false conclusion will correct another conclusion. Thus we arrive at an important criterion for determining the self-correcting nature of an inductive method: in a process of sampling, any two conclusions should be related in such a way that the first conclusion will not be known to be true, while the second will not be known to be false, and that the sample on which the first conclusion is based includes the sample on which the second conclusion is based, as a proper subclass.[7]

Now we may distinguish two distinct cases in which an inductive method can be regarded as a self-correcting process of sampling in the above sense. In the first case, the sampling process is non-terminable. By being "non-terminable" we mean that no criterion is given to determine objectively when a sampling process should terminate, i.e., should reach truth at a certain point after a finite process. In the second case, the sampling process is finitely terminable. By this, we mean that we are given a criterion by which we may certify the true after a finite process.

The first case may be represented by the problem of determining the objective composition of a population by drawing samples from it with replacement, i.e., by drawing samples in such a way that our drawing procedure precludes no drawn sample to be redrawn after it has been put back in the population. In this case, as we have indicated in Chapter V, Section 2, no finitely terminable process will enable us to ascertain that we have examined all samples of the same size in the population, and hence no finitely terminable process will enable us to ascertain the true objective composition of the population. Nor will our finite drawings in a lifetime give us any assurance for saying that our conclusions will, in the long run, approximate to a true one, or for saying that some conclusion is found to be true. For, by drawing samples with replacement, our limited population of samples, whose composition we intend to find out, becomes one of drawings of samples which is virtually infinite. To say that our inductive method is self-correcting this case does not imply that we shall ever approximate to a true conclusion, nor does it imply that we shall ever reach one with certainty. The most we can claim is merely that if this population has any determinate composition, it will be discoverable by the self-correcting process of sampling in the long run. However, we cannot conclude from the self-

[7] We may note in passing that first, if a sample is not known to be false, and if it is fairly large, it is said to be fair, and the conclusion based on it is said to be valid relative to the fair sample, second, if a new sample including the given fair sample as a proper subclass is also fair in a proper sense, the given fair sample will no longer be fair.

correcting nature of this process that the objective composition of the population will be known through any finite process of sampling.

Now let us contrast the non-terminable process of sampling with the finitely terminable process of sampling. In the former process, no assertion about the population composition based on finite sampling can be true with certainty, whereas in the latter, a true conclusion about the objective population composition will be reached after a finite process. The finitely terminable process of induction may be represented by drawing samples from a finite population without replacement, i.e., by drawing samples in such a way that our drawing procedure precludes that samples which have been drawn should be redrawn. Thus, given a finite population, by finite drawings we are able to exhaust the content of the population and to ascertain, with certainty ,the objective composition of the population. Our sampling process is one by which our conclusions will approximate to a true one, if each of them is made on the collated evidences of samples so far drawn. That is to say, the self-correcting process of sampling will lead to a true conclusion after a finite process, true according to some given criterion, for example, the criterion that we have examined all the content of a population after a finite process.

From the above contrast it should be clear that the self-correcting nature of induction tells us nothing about truth – how it can be ascertained or with what criteria it can be determined. Henceforth, criteria for determining the true must be given independently of the characterization of the self-correcting nature of induction, as it is in the case of the finitely terminable process of sampling. It should be also clear that in the case of a non-terminable process of sampling, as we are given no criterion for determining the true, we must formulate trustworthy criteria in order to judge the true on given findings up to a point in the process of sampling. Unless these criteria are formulated, we cannot in practice arrive at any definite conclusion about the true in the non-terminable process. The point is that, even if the process should be valid in the sense that it must lead to the true in the long run, still we cannot tell for sure that it is the true that we have arrived at without certain criteria. Hence, Peirce's thesis that induction must lead to truth in a self-correcting process must presuppose some criteria for determining the true in practice, if induction is valid in his sense at all.

3. *Criteria for Defining Truth and Justifying Induction*

We come to the second problem in connection with Peirce's non-probabilistic justification of induction, that of defining truth. Peirce gives his general definition of truth in the following terms:

> The opinion which is fated to be ultimately agreed by all who investigate, is what we mean by the truth, and the object represented in this opinion is the real.[8]

As truth requires ultimate agreement of all scientific investigators, it is hence social and intersubjective in nature. But according to Peirce, truth should also be objective in the sense that it should coincide with what we would establish as the ultimate result of our scientific inquiry. For Peirce says:

> Truth is that concordance of an abstract statement with the ideal limit toward which endless investigation would tend to bring scientific belief ... The truth of the proposition that Caesar crossed the Rubicon consists in the fact that the further we push our archaeological and other studies, the more strongly will the conclusion force itself on our minds forever – or would do so, if study were to go on forever.[9]

The truth of the statement "Caesar crossed Rubicon" should be established only when we find more and more archaeological and related evidences in its support. These evidences must surely be objective findings of investigation. Also, their relevance for the support of the truth of the statement "Caesar crossed Rubicon" must be agreed upon by the scientists who are doing the investigation. Thus, we may say in general that truth is only describable by statements which are intended to express the ultimate scientific belief agreed upon by scientists in the long run. To say that P is true is to say (1) that P is always intersubjectively and publicly verifiable by empirical findings, although P will never be conclusively verified; and (2) that the truth of P is the ideal object of an ultimate scientific discovery.

As an ideal object of an ultimate scientific discovery, the truth of the statement P must correspond to a reality. In a sense, Peirce identifies the true and the real in a process of inquiry. For we may compare the above quotations with the following:

> The real, then, is that which, sooner or later, information and reasoning would finally result in, and which is therefore independent of the vagaries of me and

[8] *Ibid.*, 5.407.
[9] *Ibid.*, 5.565.

you. Thus, the very origin of the conception of reality shows that this conception essentially involves the notion of a COMMUNITY, without definite limits, and capable of a definite increase of knowledge.[10]

The "community" in question is a community of scientific investigators who are supposed to discover the real in their inquiry and to verify what they find as the real. That is why Peirce says that the conception involves the notion of a COMMUNITY: the real, when known, is the result of inquiry by a community of scientific investigators. We may say, to the extent that the real is the ultimate result of scientific discovery, that the real is the same as the true in representing the ultimate ideal object of scientific discovery independent of individual and subjective opinions.

With the above understanding of Peirce's conception of the real or the true, we may justify induction by saying that it leads to the true or the discovery of the real in the long run by a self-correcting process. However, it is obvious that the true or the real cannot be identified with any given inductive conclusion in a process of scientific inquiry. Then there arises the question as to whether we may ascertain the true or the real in the above sense. As we cannot ascertain the true or the real until we have carried out inquiry in a long run, we cannot ascertain the validity of inductive inquiry or of the truth of any inductive conclusion at any finite stage of inquiry. Since we do not know for certain that we must arrive at the true or the real in the long run, we do not know, in like manner, that our induction should become valid in the long run. We may indeed agree with Peirce as he comes to assert that we only draw *provisional* and *experiential* conclusions relative to given evidences: [11] *provisional* because inductive conclusions are modifiable in the light of further empirical evidences collated in the future; *experimential* because they bear upon experience and are restricted by experience. But this statement does not suggest any good ground upon which we may make valid cognitive claims, nor does it suggest any good reason why inductive conclusions are necessarily true. Thus, at this point, we may note that Peirce fails to give us an adequate reason why we should believe induction by his proposed non-probabilistic justification of induction, because, he, in making truth an ideal object, makes the validity of induction an ideal object, and the justification an ideal object as well.

In the light of the above argument, if we do know reality on the

10 *Ibid.*, 5.311.
11 Cf., *Ibid.*, 6.40.

basis of induction, it must be due to certain specific good grounds on which inductive conclusions can be taken as prescribing what is the real, other than the method itself.

An immediate suggestion, in accordance with Peirce, to meet the difficulty of determining what is the true in a finite process of inquiry, is that we should take the true to be the result of inquiry as agreed upon by a community of scientific investigators at a certain time t_1. However, there are two objections to this suggestion: first, even in science, the opinions of scientific investigators are not convergent; rather, very frequently disagreements arise among reputed scientists concerning a certain scientific theory, say, for example, the interpretation of quantum mechanics. Second, at time t_2, a community of scientific investigators may very well disagree upon what they have agreed upon at time t_1, as new opinions may be formed by further inquiry and investigation. This points to the fact that agreement of scientists at a time t_1 as a criterion for the true is too unstable to warrant an objective characterization of the true in a finite process of inquiry.

A better suggestion for defining truth in a finite process of inquiry is this: the true should be the result by a community of scientific investigators which meet the criteria of *well-confirmedness*. The so-called "criteria of *well-confirmedness*" are those which the scientific investigators should accept as essential for determining inductive conclusions in prediction and guidance of action in view of our pragmatical interests. They are also essential for explaining the reasonableness of our empirical and scientific beliefs determined in accordance with them. Without going into details, I shall merely indicate that those criteria of well-confirmedness are in general those in connection with fair sampling and other pragmatical considerations such as simplicity and comprehensiveness. Besides, the criteria of well-confirmedness should be formulated in such a way that it would be contrary to our notion of reasonableness or rational trustworthiness to say that induction is rationally untrustworthy, but that it can lead to conclusions conforming to those criteria of well-confirmedness. If the true is determinable in accordance with those criteria of well-confirmedness, under suitable empirical circumstances, and in a finitely realizable process of inductive inquiry, then induction should be rationally trustworthy in a good sense. It is in these terms that Peirce's non-probabilistic justification of induction should be formulated or interpreted.

At this point, we may perhaps consider how the method of postulation and confirmation, as having a self-correcting nature, is a well-defined inductive method; and how, in order that this method may reach truth, it must presuppose a system of criteria of well-confirmedness for determining the truth of its conclusions. The method of postulation and confirmation is called by Peirce a "qualitative induction," which consists in setting up a hypothesis concerning the nature of reality, and in deducing predictions from it, so that we may confirm or disconfirm the hypothesis by confirming or disconfirming the predictions. "The principal rule of presumption (or qualitative induction) is that its conclusion should be such that definite consequences can be plentifully deduced from it of a kind which can be checked by observation." [12]

Let us suppose from a given hypothesis H we deduce predictions of kinds C_1, C_2, C_3, ..., C_n. We then subject all these predictions to empirical tests under relevant conditions. If we find that all these predictions are true, we may conclude that the hypothesis H is true in the sense of being trustworthy, because it is well-confirmed. If predictions of the kind C_r are found to be false or disconfirmed, then either we have to reject the hypothesis H, because predictions of the kind C_r are deduced from it; or we have to stipulate that H has a scope of valid predictions excluding those of the kind C_r; in other words, H will only warrant true predictions of kinds C_1, C_2, C_3, ..., C_{r-1}, C_{r+1}, ..., C_n but excluding predictions of the kind C_r. On the other hand, if we reject H because predictions of the kind C_r are disconfirmed, we may suggest a new hypothesis H' such that all known confirmed or confirmable predictions from the hypothesis H are still deducible from the new hypothesis H', whereas all known disconfirmed or disconfirmable predictions of H are not deducible from H'. To say that a qualitative induction is self-correcting is either to say that a given hypothesis is replaceable by a new hypothesis or that the scope of the given hypothesis is modifiable or limitable in the light of known confirming or disconfirming instances of the given hypothesis. As a result, we shall have a better confirmed or more trustworthy hypothesis. In general, the self-correcting nature of a qualitative induction should consist in the process of evaluating the trustworthiness of a given hypothesis in the light of given evidence according to relevant criteria of well-confirmedness.

Finally, it is clear that in order that the given hypothesis may be es-

[12] *Ibid.*, 2.786.

tablished as indicating the true, a system of criteria must be presupposed for defining well-confirmedness and for modifying inductive conclusions in the inductive procedure. Such a system of criteria should be presupposed by Peirce, when Peirce says that we may decide, in the light of evidence, "whether the hypothesis should be regarded as proved, or as well on the way toward being proved, or as worthy of further attention, or whether it ought to receive a definite modification in the light of new experience and be inductively examined *ab ovo*, or whether finally, that while not true it probably presents some analogy to the truth, and that the results of the induction may help to suggest a better hypothesis." [13]

4. *Other Arguments for the Necessity of General Validity of Induction*

Independently of his justification for induction on the basis that induction will lead to the true in a scientific inquiry, Peirce has, however, produced three supporting arguments for the general validity of induction on non-probabilistic grounds, assuming that inductive process will lead to the discovery of the real in the long run if there is the real at all. The first two arguments consist in proving that we cannot *a priori* conceive or empirically prove the existence of a world in which no uniformity or law or order can be found or will ever be found. Peirce's point in making these arguments is that, as conceivably there is always some uniformity in our world, induction should be said to be trustworthy at least in the sense that it will lead to the true in our world, if it will lead to the true in any world. Peirce's third argument proceeds in a different way. He argues that induction itself alone will suffice to guarantee that laws or uniformities will be established or known in a certain way.

Let me begin with Peirce's first argument that we cannot *a priori* conceive a chance-world or a world in which no induction is possible or no inductive conclusion is ever true. In his paper "The Order of Nature," Peirce defines a chance-world as a world with no uniformity or lawful regularity. He suggests that it is impossible to conceive such a world and hence such a world cannot exist. This argument will be made clear by first considering Peirce's definition of a uniformity or a lawful regularity.

A lawful regularity or uniformity is defined by Peirce in a very

[13] *Ibid.*, 2.759.

general way. It consists, according to him, in the non-occurrence of a certain combination of characters in the universe. He says,

Any uniformity, or law of Nature, may be stated in the form 'Every A is B'; as, every ray of light is a non-curved line, every body is accelerated toward the earth's center, etc. This is the same as to say, 'There does not exist any A which is not B'; there is no curved ray; there is no body not accelerated toward the earth; so that the uniformity consists in the non-occurrence in Nature of a certain combination of characters, in this case, the combination of being A with being non-B.[14]

On this general self-explanatory definition of uniformity or law, it is clear that if the character of idiocy is never found in combination with that of having a well-developed brain, then one can conclude that, that every idiot has an ill-developed brain, is a uniformity or a law.

Now a chance-world, according to Peirce, is one in which there is no uniformity in the above sense. That is to say, in a chance-world no logically possible combinations of characters are excluded, Thus, in connection with the above example, the combination of an idiot with a well-developed brain is logically possible and thus an idiot with a well-developed brain should exist in a chance-world by definition. Since no logically possible combinations of characters should be excluded from a chance-world, any combination would exist in some object or would be exemplified in some instance. In fact, Peirce requires that every such combination should exist in one and only one instance, because, no two distinct objects should be considered to have the same combination. Hence Peirce defines a chance-world as one in which every logically possible combination involving either the positive or the negative of every given character would belong just to one thing. To illustrate, given five original characters A, B, C, D, E, and their negatives a, b, c, d, e, there should be one object which is A, B, C, D, and E, and one which is A, B, C, D, but e, and so on through all the combinations. Since we have five characters and five negatives of them there are exactly 2^5 or 32 different combinations for five characters each, and we should have, therefore, exactly 32 objects in the chance-world which should exemplify these 32 combinations. The different combinations in question are exhibited in the following:

ABCDE	ABcDE	AbCDE	AbcDE	aBCDE	ABcDE	abCDE	abcDE
ABCDe	ABcDE	AbcDe	AbcDe	aBCDe	aBcDe	abCDe	abcDe
ABCdE	ABcdE	AbCdE	AbcdE	aBCde	aBcdE	abCdE	abcdE
ABCde	ABcde	AbCde	Abcde	aBCde	aBcde	abCde	abcde [15]

14 *Ibid.*, 6.341.
15 The representation here slightly differs from Peirce's original representation in this: while Peirce's representation consists of 8 rows and 4 columns, mine consists of 4 rows and 8 columns. Cf., *Ibid.* 6.341.

Such a chance world, according to Peirce, should be in this sense a world of complete simple order, because everything conceivable is found in it with equal frequency. From this, Peirce proceeds to argue that the notion of a chance-world involves a contradiction.

A chance-world, as defined above, is one in which every logically possible combination of given characters has just one instance. In the above example, a chance-world of 5 original characters and their negatives, has 2^5 or 32 objects or instances. Now Peirce finds that a chance-world of these 32 objects or instances should contain 3^5 or 243 characters,[16] either simple or complex. But he also notes that there is a logical principle by which the characters of the given 32 instances or objects should be 2^{32} or 4,294,976,296 instead of 243 as required by the notion of a chance-world. This principle states that for any two or more instances, we always can find some character which is peculiar to them and which does not belong to anything else. For example, for any two things, A and B, the character which they share in common and which nothing else shares, is that expressed by what Peirce termed "un-A-B-lessness" which is the negation of the conjunction of the negatives of A and B, and hence is simply the disjunction of A and B. Thus, for the given 32 things in the chance-world, there are 2^{32} or 4,294,967,296 possible groups of these things to each of which a character must be peculiar. Peirce concludes that, "This shows that a contradiction is involved in the very idea of a chance-world, for in a world of 32 things, instead of there being only 3^5 or 243 characters, as we have seen that the notion of a chance-world requires, there would, in fact, be no less than 2^{32} or 4,294,967,296 characters, which would not be all independent, but would have all possible relations with one another." [17] The number as represented by 2^{32} is obviously incompatible with that as represented by 3^5.

Since we cannot conceive a chance-world without involving a con-

---

[16] This 3^5 is calculated on the following basis. Given 5 characters and their negatives, if we choose each 5 compatible characters each time, there are 32 logically possible combinations; if we choose 4 compatible characters each time, there are 80 logically possible combinations; if we choose 3 compatible characters each time, then there are again 80 logically possible combinations; if we choose 2 compatible characters each time, there are 40 logically possible combinations; finally, if we choose one character each time, there are obviously 10 logically possible combinations, which is the number of the given positive and negative characters. The total numbers of these logically possible combinations is 242, all of which can be identified in the given 32 objects or instances. Peirce further considers "non-existence" as a character, and adds this character to the 242 characters to make it 243, written as 3^5. This is my explanation as to how the number 243 is derived by Peirce. No other explanation has been suggested in existing literature on Peirce.

[17] *Ibid.*, 6.345.

tradiction, it follows *a fortiori* that we cannot conceive our world as a chance-world ,or a world in which every logically possible combination of characters is included. In other words, uniformities cannot be conceived as missing from our world. As a non-chance world, our world must have *some* uniformities. We recall that Peirce has argued that induction will lead to truth or discovery of the real in the long run. As uniformities are real in our world, it follows that they will be discoverable or ascertainable in a process of induction. A natural conclusion from this is that induction is trustworthy or valid in the sense that if it will lead to the discovery of uniformities in any world, it will lead to the discovery of uniformities in *our* world, because there are uniformities in our world for induction to discover. This ,as I have pointed out, is the main point of Peirce's *a priori* argument why it is impossible to conceive a chance-world, in connection with his non-probabilistic justification of induction.

From a critical point of view, we may first note that in Peirce's *a priori* argument for the impossibility of conceiving a chance-world, possibilities must be limited so that we may distinguish a uniformity from a non-uniformity in Peirce's sense. But we may raise the question as to whether or not the notion of a chance-world in which possibilities are not limited really involves a logical contradition. We may indeed summarize Peirce's argument in the following statements:

1. A chance-world is one in which every logically possible combination of given characters and their negatives is not excluded.
2. For a chance-world of 5 given characters and their negatives, we have 3^5 logically possible combinations exemplified in 32 things or instances.
3. But for the same world, we should have 2^{32} characters resulting from the combinations on the basis of the 32 instances.

The contradiction asserted by Peirce lies in the fact that our chance-world of 5 original characters and their negatives is first found to be limited to 3^5 or 243 logically possible combinations, but later also found not to be limited to this number of logically possible combinations, since more characters can be generated from instances corresponding to the logically possible combinations of the 5 original characters and their negatives. But, is this *really* a logical contradiction? Does the fact that we can generate more characters from certain given instances really involve a contradiction? To avoid the supposed contradiction in question, we may say that a chance-world of 5 original characters and their negatives is only defined by statement 2, but not defined by statement 3, in the above argument. Though the chance-world of 5 original characters and their negatives is not defined by statement 3, we may still admit that, from the instances corresponding to the logically possible combinations of the given 5 characters and their negatives, more characters can be generated. In general, we need only take a chance-world as resulting from all logically possible combinations of some pre-specified characters and their negatives, but not as resulting from all logically possible combinations of instances corresponding to some or all logically possible combinations of certain prespecified characters and their negatives. For if the latter were the case, we would have an infinite number of logically possible combinations of any two characters. In the above example, we would not only have $2^{2^5} = 2^{32}$ logically possible combinations, but $2^{2^{32}}$ logically possible combinations and so on *ad infinitum*. In short, this abstract operation of multiplying characters need not be included in the definition of a chance-world, though it as an operation does not necessarily lead us into contradiction.

Let us illustrate this argument by the simple case of two characters. Given two original characters, say green and sweet, we may have a chance-world of four things, namely, one thing being green but not sweet, the second being sweet but not green, the third being both green and sweet, and the fourth being neither green nor sweet. Using the same principle with which we construct 3^5 characters from 5 original characters and their negatives, we may construct 3^2 or 9 characters for our chance-world of 4 things. But we need not get an extension of this chance-world, consisting of characters such as, for instance, either-green-but-not-sweet-or-sweet-but-not-green. We rule out this extension as meaningless or irrelevant for our definition of a chance-world of four things.

In the light of above criticism, it is clear that Peirce has in fact failed to establish *a priori* an inconsistency for the notion of a chance-world, according to which we can say that there is no uniformity in our world, and that induction cannot lead to discovery of any uniformity. In spite of our criticism, however, it is still an open question whether our world is actually a chance-world. We may always ask whether characters in our world are actually so related that no true empirical generalization can be made about them. We may also ask whether we have any good ground to suppose that there is actually no uniformity in our world. As no *a priori* argument of the above sort can decide whether or not there is uniformity in our world, we may as well attempt to establish the hypothesis that there are uniformities in our world on other grounds.

At this point, we may turn to Peirce's argument for the empirical unprovability of the existence of a world in which no uniformity or law can be found. Peirce formulates this argument in his long paper "Grounds of Validity of the Laws of Logic: Further Consequences of Four Incapacities" (1868, with corrections 1893) as follows. If we are to make an empirical investigation, there must be something real which is an object of inductive inquiry – if there is no reality of some given description, there must be reality of some other description which we may discover in the process of inquiry. That nothing exists and induction is generally invalid is not possible on empirical grounds. Let us imagine a universe in which we must not learn from induction or that inductive conclusions must be always false. What makes this universe possible, according to Peirce, then, is that there is a general rule such that when man has made an induction, the order of things as revealed in experience would undergo a revolution. But, in order to ascertain the reality of such a rule, we have to discover this rule by induction. Insofar as this rule is a law of the universe defined in the above sense, it would cease to exist if it is also discovered by induction. In this manner, a second law concerning the invalidation of an established law would be discovered, and *ad infinitum*. Hence, if there is any general rule, it would ultimately be discovered by us. Thus, the hypothesis that we cannot learn from induction by discovering rules is absurd. The absurdity of the hypothesis simply derives from the fact that any assertion about unreality or lawlessness of our world, if true, presupposes that induction is valid at least in the sense that induction is capable of discovering or ascertaining the very unreality or the lawlessness itself.

The above argument is as paradoxical as the following one: in stating that we learn from experience that we cannot learn from experience, we exactly admit the counter argument that we do learn from experience. We have no reason to assume that our world will undergo a revolution once we have no induction, nor shall we have any reason for assuming that a demon plays an anti-inductive game against us when we make inductions, if we conceive reality in terms of what our inductive inquiry is capable of leading to, and if we modify or revise what we know in the light of future experience. In this sense, induction is an instrument for determining the real on empirical grounds. Obviously, the statement that we can determine non-existence of anything on the grounds of experience involves a contradiction.

The above argument is intended by Peirce to establish the general validity of induction as a method for discovering uniformity or law in our world. But does this argument establish such validity of induction? Evidently, it only leads to the conclusion that we cannot prove the unreality or lawlessness of our world by induction, i.e., the conclusion that we have no good empirical ground for supposing the truth of the statement that "no empirical generalization will be true." From this conclusion, we may only argue that it is conceivable that there is some uniformity in our world and that induction may lead to its discovery. It does not follow from the above conclusion that some uniformity is discovered by induction or that some uniformity will be discovered by induction at a specifiable stage of making inductions. Thus, Peirce's argument for the empirical unprovability of non-existence of any uniformity in our world does not seem to establish the validity of induction as a method for having discovered, or being necessarily capable of discovering, the real in our world.

Peirce's last argument to establish the validity of induction as a method for discovering the real is to show how the very possibility of induction should indicate the presence of uniformities in our world on the basis of limited experience. This argument is a valid one insofar as it does not attempt to establish that there is some uniformity in our world for induction to discover or to lead to, but confines itself to the hypothesis that what induction actually finds out in experience should be understood as characterizing the real or as criteria for determining the real.

In this last argument, Peirce argues that the general character of an observed limited experience is ascribable to the whole experience in the long run, and this general character is what should be determined as the real in a process of sampling. This is because the real must have some character, and this character must be conceived in terms of what is revealed in this finite series of experience, as this should be a way of conceiving what the real is.[18] In this sense, the validity of our knowledge of reality is based on the validity of the argument from sample to population, or from part to whole. At this stage, it should be quite natural for Peirce to refer back to his probabilistic justification of induction as a probable inference from fair samples to populations. But as Peirce virtually rejects his probabilistic justification of induction in his writings in connection with his empirical theory of probability and

18 Cf., *Ibid.*, 2.784; 5.170.

non-probabilistic justification of induction, he does not here see the relevance of formulating the validity of the argument from sample to population in terms of a probability connection between sample and population. Instead, he argues that the validity of this argument depends upon the necessity of our knowing the whole or the real in terms of general propositions which we generate on the basis of limited experiences. The necessity in question is not explained by him. It perhaps can be explained by the fact that we have no better or rather, no other method, to know the real.

Whether or not this argument does really establish the validity of induction as a method for discovering the real, I shall not comment upon until the next Chapter. What should be appropriate for us to note is that this argument has a salutary consequence, namely the consequence that no presupposition needs be made for the possiblity of making true inductive conclusions. In other words, if we determine the real on the basis of known experience, and speak of the real only on the basis of known experience, to justify induction, we need not assume anything "Whatever about the future being like the past, or similar results following similar conditions, or the uniformity of nature, or any such principle." [19]

Peirce's point in the last-quoted passage is that we may simply use what we discover in a finite experience as the criterion for determining the real, and need not postulate anything beyond the possible proof by induction. Thus he explains, "any fact, then, which might be supposed postulated, must either be such that it would ultimately present itself in experience, or not. If it will present itself, we need not postulate it now in our provisional inference. Since we shall ultimately be entitled to use it as a premise. But if it never would present itself in experience, our conclusion is valid for the possibility of this fact being otherwise than assumed, that is, it is valid as far as possible experience goes, and that is all that we claim." [20] In other words, no presupposition of fact is requisite for justifying induction, because either anything real will be discovered in an inductive process, or nothing will be discovered, so that the fact that we do not assume the existence of anything will not affect the validity of induction. Accordingly, the validity of induction consists merely in the fact that what induction discovers in experience is a premise or ground for us to infer the real in the long run, or equivalently that what induction discovers in finite experience is a criterion

[19] *Ibid.*, 2.102; Cf. also 2.784, 6.413.
[20] *Ibid.*, 6.41.

for determining the real. It is with this belief that Peirce rejects Mill's Principle of Uniformity of the Nature as both vague and unnecessary for the validity of induction, and concludes,

Induction needs no such dubious support, since it is mathematically certain that the general character of a limited experience will, as that experience is prolonged, approximate to the character of what will be true in the long run, if anything is true in the long run. Now all that induction infers is what would be found true in the usual course of experience, if it were indefinitely prolonged. Since the method of induction must generally approximate to the truth, that is a sufficient justification for the use of the method, although no definite probability attaches to the inductive conclusion.[21]

---

[21] *Ibid.*, 6.100.

CHAPTER VIII

CONCLUDING REMARKS ON PEIRCE'S NON-PROBABILISTIC JUSTIFICATION ON INDUCTION

Peirce's non-probabilistic justification of induction as a method for discovering the real may be summarized into three important points. First, induction is a self-correcting method. Second, there are uniformities in our world for inductive method to discover. Third, the possibility of induction guarantees that we know some uniformity in our world. The first point is made by Peirce in his general argument for the trustworthiness of the inductive method. The second point is made by him in his arguments for the *a priori* impossibility of conceiving a chance-world and for the empirical unprovability of non-existence of any uniformity in our world. Finally, the third point is made by him in his argument for knowing the real on the basis of finite experience.

I have commented on the ineffectiveness of Peirce's general argument that induction is trustworthy due to its being a self-correcting process toward truth. I have also pointed out that Peirce's argument for the *a priori* impossibility of conceiving a chance-world is not a valid one, and that his argument for the empirical unprovability of non-existence of any uniformity in our world does not entail that some uniformity in our world is known or will be known or must be known by induction. The latter criticism has the consequence that if the validity of induction depends upon the existence of some unknown or inductively knowable uniformity in our world, Peirce's arguments do not tend to establish the validity of induction. However, I did not eleaborate this consequence. Nor did I raise the question as to whether Peirce's argument for the empirical unprovability has any other significance, even though it does not produce any reason for the trustworthiness of induction. Finally, I did not examine the cogency of Peirce's argument for knowing the real on the basis of finite experience. In the following I shall proceed to treat these problems in order.

I have argued that no *a priori* reason is given by Peirce why we cannot conceive our world as a chance-world or as a world in which no uniformity or law is present. Indeed it is conceivable that every empirical generalization which we make is false and that nothing exists. If in fact nothing exists, then no matter how long we conduct our inductive process, we shall never reach any point at which we may say that we have made a true conclusion. In order to say that induction cannot be a valid or trustworthy method for discovering the real it suffices to prove that there is no reality for us to dicsover. Now, as no *a priori* argument can be given to show that our world must be a chance-world, or a world in which there is no uniformity or law, although it is conceivable that our world is a chance-world, it should also be conceivable that our world is not a chance-world, our question then is whether or not induction will be valid or trustworthy granted some uniformity in our world. That is to say, granted that Peirce's argument for the *a priori* impossibility of conceiving a chance-world is a valid one, does it provide any reason in explaining why induction must be valid or trustworthy? Sure enough, if there is some uniformity in our world, and if we know it by induction, induction should be considered as valid. But this justification we cannot have. The reason is that in an inductive process, even though we may reach a point at which our conclusion is a true one, we would not know that it is indeed a true one. In other words, granted that there is the real, we would not know at which point the real should be discovered by an inductive process. Hence the very existence of some uniformity in our world does not guarantee that we know or shall ever know any particular uniformity by induction. Because of this fact, the assumption of the existence of some uniformity in our world does not guarantee the validity of induction as a method for discovering the real. Hence, Peirce's argument for the impossibility of conceiving a chance-world, even if it is valid, will not establish the validity of induction. From this, it is clear that an essential problem involved in knowing truth or in discovering the real is to define the true or the real so that we may decide whether or not induction is trustworthy as a method for discovering the real, according to whether it is capable of discovering the real thus defined.

Concerning Peirce's argument for the empirical unprovability of non-existence of any uniformity in our world, we may say that it is essentially a valid argument for the consistency of inductive method, since it shows that we cannot invalidate induction by induction. Despite the fact that this does not constitute a reason for the trustworthiness of induction, we may still ask whether it has other significances.

For our purpose here, we single out one particular significance of this argument. It is that, no one, being skeptical toward the validity of induction, can maintain a consistent view in his rejection of induction. In fact, no skeptic can give reason for believing his view when he makes the assertion that all empirical generalizations are false or untrustworthy. On the basis of Peirce's argument for the empirical unprovability of non-existence of any uniformity in our world, we may formally prove the inconsistency of the skeptic's view.

Let us consider the following syllogism:

All empirical generalizations are false (or induction in general is untrustworthy),

That all empirical generalizations are false (or induction in general is untrustworthy) is an empirical generalization,

Ergo, that all empirical generalizations are false (or induction in general is untrustworthy) is false (or is in general untrustworthy).

This is a self-contradiction, because the conclusion asserts the invalidity of the skeptic's own assertion. The skeptic may indeed defend his assertion by saying that he does not demand that all empirical generalizations made at a certain time t_1 are false, and that his own assertion is made after time t_1, say at t_2. In this fashion, the truth of his own statement should be consistent with the falsity of all empirical generalizations made at t_1. But we would like to know whether this adds any strength to the skeptic's view. In effect, insofar as the skeptic admits that his generalization made at time t_2 is a trustworthy one, Peirce's general thesis is vindicated, namely the thesis that there is some (at least one) uniformity in our world, the very uniformity which the skeptic himself advocates. This involved argument should indicate that it is even harder to defend the validity of the skeptic's view than to defend the validity of induction on empirical grounds.

In the light of consideration of the above, it seems natural to suggest that even though we have no way to tell that inductive method must discover the real or that there is necessarily some uniformity in our world, it should be, however, more reasonable to believe the validity of induction rather than its invalidity; and that it should be especially so, if induction is said to be leading to conclusions reasonable for us to accept.

In regard to Peirce's justification of induction as a method for discovering the real, in his last argument, it is noteworthy that Peirce, in this argument, attempts to establish knowledge of reality on the basis of inductive findings. But, to avoid triviality, we should note that the problem is not to define the true simply in terms of any inductive conclusion, or simply on the basis of any finite experience which we happen to encounter. For in that case, we can always raise the question why our knowledge of reality should be trustworthy. To exhibit the reason why induction is trustworthy, we need point out that there are good grounds for accepting inductive conclusions as true. We have suggested that we have to formulate criteria of *well-confirmedness* for inductive conclusions in such a way that inductive conclusions are capable of satisfying them in a finite process. When any of the inductive conclusions satisfies these criteria, it will be considered true or trustworthy. These criteria of *well-confirmedness* are truth conditions for inductive conclusions in a process of induction, and they serve to meet our general requirements of reasonableness and pragmatical usefulness. When Peirce argues that we know the real on the basis of finite experience, he should not imply that any finite experience will give rise to a true inductive conclusion. For if that is the case, the statement that induction will reach the true will be tautologous. Hence it is proper to suggest that we can make true inductive conclusions only on the basis of finite experience which can be construed as fair samples. In suggesting this, I have Peirce's probabilistic justification of induction in mind. But, instead of saying that a fair sample from experience makes a relevant inductive conclusion probable, we say that a fair sample makes it true. In this sense, having fair samples is a criterion for *well-confirming* an inductive conclusion; it is a criterion by which we shall find whether an inductive conclusion is reasonable to accept. This relevancy of the principle of fair sampling for establishing the *well-confirmedness* of truth of an inductive conclusion or hypothesis should indicate that Peirce's non-probabilistic justification of induction does not contradict his probabilistic justification of induction. For rather, it supplements the latter as they both point to the same problem of defining the true or defining the validity of induction on the basis of what we know from finite experience.

To amplify the general validity of defining reality on the basis of fair samples, perhaps, we should pursue a little further as to how we may establish a hypothesis on the basis of fair samples in similarity to thus establishing a simple empirical generalization. We may indeed indicate how a fair sample for a hypothesis can be defined, or what should constitute a fair sample for a hypothesis, so that we may speak of the validity of a hypothesis concerning a feature of reality in relation to fair samples. Consider the hypothesis, say, "The volume of gases is directly proportional to degrees of temperature under constant pressure." It may entail various predictions such as, "The volume of a definite amount of oxygen is directly proportional to degrees of temperature under constant pressure," "The volume of a definite amount of hydrogen is directly proportional to degrees of temperature under constant pressure," and so on. Now insofar as these gases constitute a fair sample of all gases, the predictions concerning the given gases constitute a fair sample of predictions concerning all gases. If all our given predictions are verifiable, we may argue that there is a high probability that all predictions, known and unknown, are verifiable, on the basis of the given sample of known verifiable predictions. Insofar as we have a reason for saying that all predictions, known and unknown, of our hypothesis are verifiable, we have a reason for saying that the hypothesis itself is verifiable. This reason is provided by a fair sample of predictions derivable from the given hypothesis, which, we may say, represents all possible predictions derivable from the given hypothesis. Of course, given predictions of each kind may be a fair sample of predictions of that kind. In that case, a fair sample of predictions from a hypothesis may be more precisely described as a fair sample of fair samples of predictions of various kinds, derivable from the given hypothesis.

CHAPTER IX

PROBLEMS IN LEWIS' THEORY OF INDUCTION

My study of Peirce's theory of induction has shown that Peirce has made two justifications of induction, the probabilistic and non-probabilistic. By the probabilistic justification of induction, induction is shown to be a valid inference which consists in having a logical leading principle and drawing conclusions with probability. This justification of induction, as stated in Peirce's own terms, as we have seen, is inadequate. But I have suggested the way in which Peirce's argument can be mended. There are two conclusions which we may draw from this probabilistic justification of induction. First, we may say that there is always a logical and *a priori*-determinable relation between premises, which assure us of the existence of a fair sample with a given composition, and the inductive conclusion drawn from such premises. This relation we express by saying that the inductive conclusion follows with probability from its premises in accordance with a logical leading principle. It is wherein the validity of inductive inference consists. In other words, the validity of inductive inference consists in a probability relation between its conclusion and its premises.

The second conclusion from Peirce's probabilistic justification of induction is this. The premises which assure us of the existence of a fair sample with a given composition are what should warrant our acceptance of or trust in an inductive conclusion drawn therefrom. Because of this fact, the validity of induction consists not only in a probability relation of premises to the conclusion, but in its yielding a credible or rationally credible conclusion from its premises. We may say that an inductive conclusion is rationally credible, because the premises which assure us of the existence of a fair sample with a given composition are true and the inference with probability is logically warranted. Both the premises and the probability between the premises and the conclusion constitute good reasons why the conclusion is rationally credible or acceptable.

Concerning his non-probabilistic justification, Peirce has suggested that induction is a trustworthy method by which we infer from what we know to what we do not know. The inductive method is trustworthy not because any singular inductive conclusion is in any proper sense probable, but because inquiry by inductive method is self-correcting and must lead to truth in the long run. I have made clear that the truth-producing nature of inductive method is indeed a reason for the trustworthiness of induction. But I have also made clear that Peirce failed to show that inductive method is, or must be, truth-producing. I have first noted that the self-correcting character of induction does not warrant that induction must be truth-producing. Next, I have noted that Peirce's general argument, as it stands, leads to the conclusion that either we do not know that induction is trustworthy because we do not know truth, or we know truth by assuming the validity of induction in the first place. Peirce has several other arguments for the trustworthiness of induction. But none of them establishes that what induction discovers must be reality or that there must be reality for induction to discover.

Despite the inadequacies of Peirce's arguments, I have nevertheless pointed out that Peirce's non-probabilistic justification of induction, on the whole, should have its value in suggesting the following: the criteria for determining the validity of induction should be those for determining knowledge of reality, and vice versa. But then the problem is what those criteria for determining the validity of induction are, and how they are to be formulated. I have suggested that these are criteria of *well-confirmedness* and that they should be formulated in such a way that it is contrary to our notion of reasonableness to say that inductive method is not trustworthy, but it leads in a finitely realizable process to conclusions which satisfy those criteria. The justification of induction or inductive method then consists in the fact that induction or inductive method leads to conclusions which will satisfy those criteria of well-confirmedness. When inductive conclusions satisfy those criteria of well-confirmedness, they are knowledge of reality. I leave open the question as to how our notion of reasonableness should be analyzed and the question as to how criteria of well-confirmedness should be exactly formulated.

A close examination of Peirce's arguments for the validity of induction and his conception of reality also reveals for us that we cannot speak of knowing reality apart from induction, and that there should be no reality other than what we may hope to discover by induction. In other words, when we say that we know that P, where P is an empirical generalization or a hypothesis concerning a feature of reality, it is implied in an important sense that P is ascertained true by induction; and when we say that P is true, it is implied in an important sense that we have no way to ascertain the truth of P other than by inductive procedure. Indeed, according to Peirce, there are the following relationships between validity of induction, knowledge of reality, and reality:

1. Induction is trustworthy, if and only if we shall know that some inductive conclusion is true.
2. We shall know that some inductive conclusion is true, if and only if there is some true inductive conclusion in an inductive process.
3. There is some true inductive conclusion in an inductive process, if and only if something exists.

In terms of the implications between (1), (2), and (3), Peirce's non-probabilistic arguments for the validity of inductive method become that inductive method is trustworthy if something exists. When he adds that we cannot conceive that nothing exists, and intends to prove this by a logical argument, he has indeed attempted to prove the validity of inductive method on *a priori* ground.

These results of the above from my investigation of Peirce's theory of induction in respect of both its probabilistic and non-probabilistic considerations are, to a considerable extent, presented and derived under another form by C. I. Lewis in his refutations of the Humean skepticism and in his theories of reality and knowledge of reality. Indeed, there is a considerable degree of similarity between Peirce's treatment of induction and Lewis' treatment of empirical generalization, which should justify our study of Lewis' theory of induction, side by side with Peirce's theory of induction. What follows will be a clarification of this justification.

Lewis has considered that empirical generalizations constitute only probable, not certain, knowledge of reality, and as such they stand in logical or *a priori*-determinable probability relations to their premises. These points certainly are in line with Peirce's probabilistic justification of induction. But probability in a logical sense, as we have pointed out, is merely presupposed in Peirce's argument for a probabilistic justification of induction, whereas it is explicitly required by Lewis for his validation of induction. Lewis has further held that our knowledge of reality depends upon the possibility of induction, because induction cannot be dispensed with in our attempt to explain the existence of things and existence of laws. This view again is comparable to Peirce's when he argues (for his non-probabilistic justification of induction) that induction is the sole method for attaining knowledge of reality and should not be *a priori* dismissed as untrustworthy. It should be noted, however, that Lewis has done more than Peirce in making clear the necessity of induction for our knowledge of reality in his theories of reality and knowledge of reality, as well as in his analyses of the nature of empirical generalizations.

Lewis would agree with Peirce in admitting true inductive conclusions as sole criteria for determining our knowledge of reality or in equating them with our knowledge of reality. But he suggests further (1) that the validity of induction is the same as the validity of conceptual interpretation of experience in a process of pursuing our knowledge of reality, and (2) that that induction in general leads to more success of predictions than not is a reason for the trustworthiness of induction. This latter pragmatical justification of induction by Lewis is distinct from the former "*a priori* analytical" justification of induction and empirical generalization, by which Lewis argues that induction and empirical generalization are in general valid, because principles governing the possibility of our knowledge of reality are "*a priori* analytical" or necessarily true in a good sense, to be explained in our later discussions.

As in the case of Peirce's theory of induction, by Lewis' theory of induction, I shall refer to a system of ideas which Lewis develops concerning how induction as an inference should be valid, and how induction as a method, by which empirical generalizations are ascribed rational credibility, is indispensable for pursuing our knowledge of reality. This system of ideas is contained in Lewis' two well-known books *Mind and the World-Order* and *An Analysis of Knowledge and Valuation*. Lewis' thesis concerning how induction is in general valid because if it is not, we shall have no knowledge of reality, and nothing exists, is formulated in his first book and is to a great extent presupposed in his later book.[1] For the explanation of Lewis' theory of induction, it should be therefore natural for me to first concentrate upon Lewis' refutations in his first book of the skeptic's thesis that since there are no necessary connections of matters of fact, induction and empirical generalization must be in general invalid and logically incredible.

---

[1] Of course, it is a question as to whether Lewis shares the same view on the nature of knowledge in his earlier book as in his later book. It is not the question which I am concerned with in this part of the book. Even if Lewis does not have the same thought in his later book, it makes no difference to my treatment of Lewis' theory of induction, which is confined to part of Lewis' ideas in *Mind and the World-Order*, and to part of his ideas in *An Analysis of Knowledge and Valuation*.

Lewis shows that the skeptical thesis is hardly testifiable in the light of a theoretical analysis of the basis of our empirical knowledge. He also reveals that induction must be valid in the sense that it must lead to our knowledge of reality and that there should be true inductive conclusions unless nothing exists. Thus, to conduct such a theoretical analysis of the basis of our empirical knowledge in order to refute the skeptic's thesis and to explain the validity of induction, I presume, should be a problem *par excellence* in Lewis' theory of induction, a problem which receives significant considerations by Lewis in his book *Mind and the World-Order*.

We find Lewis' considerations of the problem of justifying induction in terms of general principles which guarantee the validity of induction in his earlier book, but find his considerations of the problem of justifying induction in terms of criteria for determining the logical probability relation between inductive conclusions and its premises in his later book, *An Analysis of Knowledge and Valuation*. In fact, there is a certain relation between these two kinds of considerations. Lewis has answered the question, how induction is essential for determining our knowledge of the real, by saying that there is no other way of determining our knowledge of the real, and that our knowledge of the real in this sense is expressed by probable statements, not by statements which we may hold with certainty. It must be natural for him to pursue how the rational or logical credibility of empirical knowledge in this sense is to be expressed in terms of probability, and how probability, when taken as an explication of the rational credibility of empirical knowledge, should be interpreted. Lewis presents, however, little suggestion about this in his earlier book, and only in his later book does he come to a clear statement of his view on this problem.

In his *An Analysis of Knowledge and Valuation*, Lewis maintains that the credibility of an empirical generalization is determined from the data or ground upon which the empirical generalization is asserted, in accordance with criteria by which such data or ground is judged appropriate. He points out that to say that P is probable (where "P" is an empirical generalization) in the sense that P is credible on the given data, cannot be interpreted in such a way that the probability in the statement is an empirical frequency, but must be understood in a logical sense, the sense in which we may say that there is a logical or *a priori*-determinable probability relation between the conclusion or generalization P and its data. We shall see that Lewis' point is well-taken, even though he fails to bring clarity and rigor to his own conception of the logical and *a-priori*-determinable probability relation between an inductive conclusion and its data. At this point, I shall suggest that Peirce's probabilistic justification of induction can be utilized for explicating and clarifying this important conception of Lewis, important not only in the sense that it is essential for Lewis' explanation of the validity of inductive inference, but in the sense that it is essential for any intelligible explanation of the validity of inductive inference as Lewis recognizes.

CHAPTER X

INDUCTION AND ANALYSIS OF KNOWLEDGE
OF REALITY

1. *General Remarks*

Hume and skeptics following him assert that since there are no necessary connections in statements of matters of fact, our empirical generalizations are invalid and we have no rational basis for believing them. Since our empirical knowledge of laws and of reality in general appears to be based on empirical generalizations, a Humean skeptic should therefore call into question the very validity of empirical laws and of our empirical knowledge of reality in general.

Now, there are two assumptions made by a Humean skeptic in his arguments against the validity of empirical generalizations. First, it is assumed by him that necessary connections of ideas are totally absent from our empirical knowledge of reality, and that this is a good reason for maintaining that empirical knowledge has no rational basis. Second, it is assumed by him that part of the rational basis for empirical knowledge must lie in the certainty with which we may infer empirical generalizations from given data or instances, just as we may infer with certainty the conclusion from its premises in a deductive inference.

To repudiate Hume or a Humean skeptic, Lewis undertakes a number of counter-arguments to show that the first assumption of the above is false and that the second does not prove the invalidity of empirical generalization or induction. Referring to the argument that there are no necessary connections in statements of matters of fact, Lewis observes that a Humean skeptic fails to notice "the ways in which the necessary connections of *ideas* are pertinent to the interpretation of the empirically given and hence are antecedent determinations of *reality*." [1] According to Lewis, necessary connections of ideas are

---

[1] C. I. Lewis, *Mind and the World Order*, New York, 1956, 312. (Italics Lewis's).

those relations between concepts which are determined by means of logical laws and decisions regarding the meanings of concepts.

Referring to the assertion that there is no certainty that empirical generalizations are true, Lewis points out that this does not affect the validity of empirical generalizations, because "it is the validity of empirical knowledge as probable judgment only which requires to be assured." [2] That is to say, the fact that empirical generalizations are not necessarily true is no reason for maintaining that we have no rational basis for believing the empirical generalizations.

In the following, I shall analyze how, according to Lewis, necessary connections of ideas are pertinent to the interpretation of the empirically given. In the next Chapter, I shall formulate the problem of justifying induction in the context of such analysis from Lewis' point of view. I shall discuss how Lewis attempts to justify induction in the framework of a theory of reality and a related theory of knowledge. After commenting on this, I shall proceed in the rest of the book to discuss the probabilistic character of empirical generalizations and the validity of empirical knowledge as probable judgments in Lewis' theory of probability.

2. *Empirical Knowledge and "A priori" Concepts*

According to Lewis, there are two essential features which distinguish those empirical statements which formulate our knowledge of reality from those which do not. The first feature consists in the fact that empirical statements of the former sort are verifiable, or in other words, are predictive of future experience, and therefore are always capable of being confirmed by observations in experience. The second feature consists in the fact that they have a significant opposite, namely "error", and are not necessarily true; that is to say, no matter how many times they are verified by sense experience, they are always open to disconfirmation, and are therefore revisable in the light of new experience. By the first feature of our knowledge of reality, we can say that a statement which is intended to give us knowledge of reality must be projectible, i.e. it can generate predictions which we may objectively verify or disconfirm. By the second feature of empirical knowledge, we can say that a statement which is intended to give us knowledge of reality must be retractable, i.e., it can be rejected or withheld when it

---

[2] *Ibid.*, 323.

fails of the particular prediction or a set of predictions which it generates.

With empirical knowledge thus initially understood, we may proceed to inquire how Lewis explains its structure and its validity. In the first place, Lewis analyses the structure of our empirical knowledge into two elements: the immediate sense presentation and the *a priori* form or construction or interpretation which presents the activity of thought or the mind's response.[3] Next he suggests that empirical knowledge results from application of *a priori* concepts to experience or, in other words, from interpretation of experiences in terms of *a priori* concepts. This thesis is essential for proving Lewis' point that necessary connections of ideas are pertinent to the interpretation of the empirically given and are antecedent determinations of reality. For the purpose of examining this thesis, we shall first make clear the distinction between the content of experience and the *a priori* concepts of our mind, and then determine how *a priori* concepts and their relationships are principles of classification and interpretation determined in advance of particular experience, and are therefore antecedent determinations of *reality*.

The content of experience is sense-given, which, according to Lewis, involves no interpretative or constructive elements. It is what "this" denotes when we deprive "this" (an ostension) of any descriptive or interpretive properties. It is therefore not knowledge in a proper sense, because the terms "error" and "verification" have no use with regard to it. Knowledge, on the other hand, is always an interpretation or construction of our mind ascribed to the given. It is exhibited in the form of concepts which relate the immediately presented to future possible experiences, so that a temporal process of experiences may verify or prove erroneous the assertion of such a relation as implied in the conceptual interpretation of experience. Concepts, more precisely speaking, are possibilities of sense-experience; they are, according to Lewis, what lie in our minds when we communicate by the use of *substantive* words or phrases, words or phrases which designate individual (physical) things or classes of such things.[4] They are also specifiable by the method of definition. In defining one refers one concept to another or other concepts, and set up a "pattern of relationships" between them, which we may verify by way of "identity of sensation and imagery."[5] In other words, concepts or meanings could be explained ultimately by

[3] Cf., *Ibid.*, 38.
[4] Cf., *Ibid.*, 70.
[5] *Ibid.*, 81.

pointing to relationships between certain experiences or images in our minds.[6]

In point of fact, what Lewis calls "concepts" in his *Mind and the World-Order* could be better explained from the point of view of his theory of "modes of meaning" in *An Analysis of Knowledge and Valuation*. According to that theory, every expression, term or statement, is capable of naming or applying to a thing or things, state of affairs or states of affairs, of some kind, actual or thought. All expressions have four modes of meaning which can be briefly described as follows:

1. The *denotation* of an expression is the class of all actual things or an actual state of affairs to which the expression would be correctly applicable.

2. The *comprehension* of an expression is the classification of all possible or consistently thinkable things or all possible or consistently thinkable states of affairs to which the expression would be correctly applicable.

3. The *signification* of an expression is that property in things or in states of affairs, the presence of which indicates that the expression correctly applies, and the absence of which indicates that it does not apply.

4. The *intension* or connotation of an expression is to be identified with the conjunction of all other expressions each of which must be applicable to anything to which the given expression would be correctly applicable.[7]

Obviously, a concept is not the denotation of an expression. Nor is it the comprehension or the signification of an expression: it is not the comprehension of an expression, because it is not a thing or a state of affairs, actual or thought; it is not the signification of an expression, because an expression only signifies an essence or property of a thing or of a state of affairs, not a concept. Therefore, what is most relevant for the explanation of concepts, it seems, is the intensional meaning of the expressions. This Lewis has recognized:

As suggested by the derivation of the word, the intension of a term represents our intention in the use of it; the meaning it expresses in that simplest and most frequent sense which is the original meaning of "meaning"; that sense in which

---

[6] Here, "minds" or "mind" in the earlier discussion, has, presumably only an operative meaning: a mind is that which relates experiences to experiences in certain patterns; it does not have a substantive meaning: i.e., the meaning that it is something which exists independently of its relating function.

[7] *An Analysis of Knowledge and Valuation*, 39, 55 ff.

what we have meant by "A" is what we have in mind in using "A," and what is oftentimes spoken of as *the concept of A*.[8]

To say that a concept is the intensional meaning of an expression will not help us very much until we have grasped the meaning of the "intensional meaning" of an expression. There are two ways by which the intensional meaning of an expression could be specified. The intensional meaning of an expression may be specified as *linguistic meaning* and as *sense meaning*, again in Lewis' terminology. The linguistic meaning of a term could be exhibited by the totality of other terms which must be applicable to a thing if the term in question applies, while that of a statement could be exhibited by the totality of other statements deducible from it. In general, the linguistic meanings are constituted by the patterns of definitive and other analytical relationships holding between linguistic expressions, such as we may find in definitions of terms in a dictionary. Now to say that a concept is exhibited by the totality of linguistic expressions related, say, by dictionarylike definitions, certainly has not made clear what is intended by us when we use a linguistic expression, nor explained why one linguistic expression which expresses one concept is related to other expressions which express other concepts. The clarification and explanation in demand are supplied, however, by the specification of *sense-meaning* of an expression.

Lewis explains what he calls "sense-meaning" as follows:

What we indicate by this phrase *sense-meaning* is intension as a *criterion in mind*, by reference to which one is able to apply or refuse to apply the expression in question in the case of presented, or imagined, things or situations.[9]

What is then essential for the determination of a sense-meaning of an expression is a rule or scheme-test by (following) which we can determine (or check) in our imagination whether we may correctly use an expression to a thing: for example, whether we may correctly call a given figure a "triangle." In this sense, the sense-meaning of an expression is the imagined result of application of such a rule or scheme-test or standard which determines the expression to be correctly applicable to a thing or a situation. The sense-meaning of a term is what should constitute a thing for us in terms of sense-representable characters, of which the term is a correct name. The sense meaning of a statement is "the anticipatory imagery of a perceivable result," which would cor-

---

[8] *Ibid.*, 43. (Italics Lewis's)
[9] *Ibid.*, 133.

roborate or verify the statement in question. That the sense-meaning must be conceived in terms of sense-representable characters is a condition for the determination of sense-meaning of an expression. This condition is requisite because the expression whose sense-meaning is in question must apply to sense experience, if it has application at all. In this sense, sense-meanings are derived from the so-called "experiential criteria of the application" of expressions to experience. It is also required for the determination of sense meanings that they must be fixed in mind in advance of the particular experiences, because only when they are fixed in advance of the particular experience, they could be held as criteria for judging whether or not an expression is applicable to experience in the face of given experience. It is in this sense, concepts are *a priori*.[10]

To recapitulate, we may say that concepts, when they apply to experience, are sense-meanings of expressions, which we may ascertain in advance of encounter with actual experience, and which are formulated in language and give rise to patterns of linguistic meanings of expressions. Thus when a sense-meaningful statement applies to experience, we expect eventuation of certain experiences to follow other experiences under appropriate conditions. When our expectation is confirmed, the statement is also confirmed. The presence of a sequence of experiences related in a certain way can be taken as a criterion for judging the confirmation of a statement, and therefore for judging the correct application of a concept to experience. In this sense, a concept as embodied in a statement in application to experience should be correlated with a sequence of experiences related in a certain way, or in other words, an orderly sequence of experiences. We may then say that a concept correctly applies to experience, when the empirical statement which ascribes the property as denoted by the concept to experience is verifiable by experience, e.g., the concept of "red" correctly applies to experience when the statement "This is red" is verifiable. Since an empirical statement is not to be verified with certainty, the application of a concept to experience must not be taken as absolute, but must be

---

[10] The problem of *a priori* is a problem which needs not concern us here. But in regard to saying that concepts are *a priori*, we may cite two further important senses related to the sense given above:

1. They are hypotheses regarding the nature of experience and are *prima facie* acceptable if no empirical evidence runs against them. (Here the "empirical evidence" is an ambiguous term: it means either any known experience or other empirically well-supported hypothesis or both).

2. They may be held as *correct* and *trustworthy* interpretations of experiences even in the face of unfavorable experience. In this sense they should be properly called *criteria*.

granted only on the basis of an adequate (sufficient) amount of relevant (appropriate) evidence, and be rejected when the evidence is not relevant (appropriate) or the amount of relevant (appropriate) evidence is inadequate (insufficient).

We come to the question how, according to Lewis, *a priori* concepts and their relationships are principles of classification and interpretation presupposed in our knowledge of reality, and are thus antecedent determinations of reality. Let us note, first, that, for Lewis, anything conceived as the real must be conceived as an interpretation or determination of certain experience in terms of concepts. To determine or interpret given experiences in terms of concepts should be the starting point of a process of pursuing knowledge of reality, i.e., a process of pursuing knowledge of reality must begin with some sort of conceptual interpretation of experience. This is because our knowledge of reality must be based on *reality*, and this reality cannot be "pure and simple" experience, but must be experience which we already understand as things and objective facts of some kind. Lewis formulates this idea by saying that "Reality is more orderly than experience, because reality is experience categorized;" [11] and that "All generalizations are based up on reality, not upon uncategorized experience." [12] These statements should imply that whenever we speak of reality or make statements about reality, we have already presupposed some conceptual framework in which our notion of reality and our statements about reality are given meaning.

If we do not antecedently determine or interpret a general area of experience in terms of concepts, we would hardly be said to know reality, for we would hardly be said to have begun a process of investigation for pursuing our knowledge. It is only after we have pre-determined a general area of experience that we may proceed to find out by experience whether there are laws true of the area of experience thus pre-determined and what they are if any. This point Lewis makes when he observes that "Experience must, *a priori*, conform to certain principles in order to be pertinent to any particular investigation or to the validity of any particular law of nature." [13] The principles in question are principles of classification and interpretation concerning the area of experience in which we intend to do investigation for pursuing knowledge of reality.

[11] *Mind and the World-Order*, 365.
[12] *Ibid.*, 366.
[13] *Ibid.*, 321.

Lewis emphasizes the point that in order to *make* reality out of pure experience, we must classify experiences into different categories so that one kind of experience can be distinguished from the other. According to him, it must be in terms of *a priori* concepts that we may formulate "the predetermined principles of interpretation, the criteria of our distinguishing and relating, or classification, and hence the criteria of any sort." [14] For example, it must be in terms of our *a priori* concepts of physical bodies that the principles for interpreting the properties of physical bodies may be formulated. These principles will then enable us to distinguish a physical object from a non-physical object. By the same token, it must be in terms of our *a priori* concepts of reality that we may formulate principles for distinguishing the real from the unreal. The basic categories or large classes of the real such as we may find in common sense or in physical and biological sciences are in this sense determined or formulated in terms of *a priori* concepts, and are therefore potential principles for distinguishing the real from the unreal.

According to Lewis, not simply those concepts which we should call "categories," but all concepts, general or specific, can function as principles for distinguishing the real from the unreal. They all are, in other words, potential criteria for identifying the real, or determining the real of a certain type. To see Lewis' point, we may recall that, for Lewis, every concept prescribes a uniformity of experience, and is applicable to a sequence of experiences in case there is a sequence of experiences conforming to what the concept prescribes. If some sequence is actually found to conform to what the concept prescribes, this sequence of experiences is then said to be real, insofar as the concept is antecedently accepted as a criterion for the real. On the other hand, if no actual sequence of experiences is found to conform to what a concept prescribes, the status of the concept as a criterion for predetermining the real should not be affected, if it is conceivable that some sequence of experiences should conform to it. Because, what is required of a criterion for pre-determining reality is that it is applicable to experience, not that it already applies to experience. For example, the concept of an apple is a criterion for pre-determining the reality of an apple, even if there is no actual "apple-like" pattern of experiences which conforms to what the concept of apple prescribes.

In the light of the above analysis, it is clear that all concepts, insofar

[14] *Ibid.*, 230–231.

as they are intended as criteria of reality, are laws, which may not be true of given experience, but nevertheless could be true of experience under suitable conditions. Specifically, the content of a concept, say, that of an apple, according to Lewis, can be put in the form of a general lawlike statement, "For all x, if x is an apple, then if x should give us a certain sense-experience, and if we should act in a certain way, then x would give us a certain other sense-experience." Thus, our concepts, no matter how specific they are, are criteria of reality of certain types. insofar as they can be put into lawlike statements of the above form; or, in other words, insofar as they have pre-determined sense-meanings for us. When we know the real in terms of concepts thus conceived, our knowledge of reality is a system of concepts which prescribes what experience should be. Precisely in this sense, Lewis concludes,

The whole content of our knowledge of reality is the truth of such "if-then" propositions in which the hypothesis is something we conceive could be made true by our modes of acting and the consequence presents a content of experience which, though not actual now and perhaps not to become actual, is a possible experience connected with the present. For the active being such hypothetical propositions can be meaningful and true when the hypothesis is false. The attribution of what is given in connection with such a content of further possible experience is the conceptual interpretation of the presentation and our know-ledge of the object.[15]

3. *A Fundamental Principle in Establishing Criteria of Reality*

For the purpose of pursuing knowledge of reality, we should not remain content merely with classifying experiences into large classes or categories, and thus arbitrarily formulating a set of concepts as ante-cedent criteria of reality. According to Lewis, there is one fundamental principle which we must observe in our classification of experiences into large classes or categories and in our setting up a system of concepts as criteria of reality. This fundamental principle is that "Nothing is real in all categories; and everything is real in some category." [16] In other words, it is the principle that nothing is everything, and everything is something.

---

[15] *Ibid.*, 142–143.

[16] *Ibid.*, 321–322. These two statements can be formulated in the logical symbolism as follows. Let "R" stand for "being real," "εC_i" for "in the category C_i". Suppose there are n categories, then the statement "Nothing is real in all categories" can be rendered as "$\sim(x)(Rx \supset x \varepsilon C_i)$ where $i = 1, 2, \ldots, n$". The statement "Everything is real in some category" can be rendered as "$(x)(Rx \supset x \varepsilon C_1 \vee C_2 \vee \ldots \vee C_n)$."

The significance of the above principle should be obvious. If every-thing is real in all categories or anything is everything, we cannot dis-tinguish one thing from another by characterizing them in terms of different concepts; if nothing is real in some category or nothing is any-thing, we would find no instance of what we call the real. Each of these cases would render our knowledge of reality impossible. Thus, if our knowledge of reality is possible, both these cases must be ruled out, and we must designate or devise a finite system of concepts or categories so that it is *a priori* certain there are instances of experiences which con-form to the concepts in the system, and there are also instances of ex-periences which do not conform to the concepts in the system. More-over, for a given thing, though we may not know to which category it belongs, it is *a priori* certain that it must be described in terms of some uniformity or possible experience if it is to be understood as something. In this way, we can meaningfully speak of a system of concepts, say, of physical objects, which prescribes the real in terms of concepts of physical objects. We can also meaningfully speak of a system of con-cepts, say, of non-physical objects, which prescribes the real in terms of concepts of non-physical objects. This way of devising and elaborating a finite system of concepts for describing or prescribing reality is illus-trated by the scientific practice in formulating theories for explaining a given range of experiences, and for yielding predictions concerning experiences.

In regard to the possibility of devising and elaborating a system of concepts for describing or prescribing reality, Lewis has two important points to make. First, a system of *a priori* concepts which is intended for describing or prescribing reality can be formulated in the manner of deductive science,[17] so that it may have many hypothetical results for experience to verify or disconfirm. In this sense, a system of *a priori* concepts intended for describing or prescribing the real should coincide with a deductive-hypothetical hierarchy of concepts and laws. It is by developing such a system that we are enabled to make predictions of a

---

[17] In his essay "Natural Science and Abstract Concepts" appended to *Mind and the World-Order*, Lewis says, "It may well be that the inevitable movement of the exact sciences is in this direction in which mathematics has preceded them; toward the deductive mode of de-velopment and toward concepts which are laid down less in terms of those sense-qualities by which we directly identify empirical objects and more in terms of those systematic corre-lations which figure in natural law." (*Ibid.*, 393.) Also in the same essay, Lewis says, "With exact natural science, as with mathematics, a stage is possible, if it is not already reached, in which the problem of scientific truth can be phrased equally well as the discovery of empirical laws sufficiently comprehensible to constitute a systematic whole, or as the selection of an abstract system which will be applicable to the facts." (*Ibid.*, 398.)

wide range, to correlate laws governing a wide range of phenomena, and to conceive essential properties in terms of uniformities of experiences, or uniformities of uniformities of experiences. Second, it is possible that one system of *a priori* concepts may serve our interests for prediction and explanation better than another one, because it is more simple or more comprehensive or both. In fact, each system of *a priori* concepts intended for describing or prescribing the real has a greater or smaller pragmatical value than another one. In our attempt to pursue knowledge of reality, there should be no problem of making single empirical generalizations and finding evidences for each of them. But there should be the problem of devising and elaborating systems of *a priori* concepts which will be applicable to empirical facts, and which will also prove most pragmatically valuable.

To conclude our discussion, we may say that to the extent that there are *a priori* principles or *a priori* determinable principles which prescribe what general features things have, and to the extent that we depend upon patterns of relationships of concepts as criteria of reality and can elaborate them into a deductive system, so that we may maintain them even in the face of unfavorable experiences, necessary connections of ideas in a suitable sense are relevant for our knowledge of reality, and as such are *a priori* elements in our knowledge of reality. Consequently, the assertion that there are no necessary connections of ideas in our knowledge of reality when construed as meaning that there are no *a priori*-determinable connections of concepts in knowledge of reality is ill-grounded, and is in fact false. Thus, this assertion cannot be taken as a valid objection to the validity of empirical knowledge or induction as a process of reaching such knowledge. The first argument against the Humean skepticism can be formulated then simply as this: our knowledge of reality should presuppose *a priori* criteria of reality, which are antecedent principles of classification and interpretation for defining reality.

CHAPTER XI

AN "*A PRIORI* ANALYTICAL" JUSTIFICATION OF INDUCTION

1. *General Remarks*

We have seen in the light of Lewis' arguments, that necessary connections of ideas are pertinent to the interpretation of the empirically given and that our empirical knowledge of reality resulting from our conceptual interpretation of experience is not invalid on the ground that it lacks necessary connections of ideas. However, this does not necessarily show that it is therefore valid. The problem of validating empirical knowledge of reality, as Lewis deals with it in his book *Mind and the World-Order*, is the same problem of justifying induction and empirical generalization. It is the problem of producing and formulating the trustworthiness of induction.

As empirical generalizations are never certain, but are merely probable in a certain sense to be explicated later, Lewis calls them "probabilities," and maintains that they must be *in general* valid (or true) and that this is a sufficient condition for the rational credibility or trustworthiness of them. "In other words," he says, "It is essential that the world is such that probabilities *in general* are justified by the future – that the world is 'orderly': that there are certain stabilities extending through the past and future, and that the attitude which is based on past coincidence will be in general safer for the future than a different one." [1] It appears that there are two main theses involved in this passage: (1) In order that empirical generalizations be justified, the future experience should make them true, and this presupposes that the world should be orderly, and that there should be uniformities or laws in the world. (2) In order that induction and empirical generalizations be justified, our action in accordance with probabilities must

[1] C. I. Lewis, *Mind and the World-Order*, 343–344.

be in general safer or more successful than action not in accordance with them. Both these theses pose serious problems: How do we ascertain that the world is orderly? How do we know that uniformities extend through past to the future so that empirical generalizations from past must be valid? And finally, how do we know that our action must lead to more success than not by following induction?

Before attacking these problems, Lewis claims that "for the validity of empirical generalizations as *probable knowledge* – or more accurately as knowledge of probabilities – no a priori truth other than the merely analytical is required." [2] What Lewis suggests here, I take, is that we can justify induction and empirical generalization from an *a priori* analytical point of view, and this entails the fact that we need not appeal to inductive results for the justification of induction and empirical generalization, thus saving the abuse of circularity. Hence, Lewis' problems are *how the world is orderly, how uniformities extend through past to future,* and *how induction leads to more success in practice than not, from an a priori analytical point of view.*

I suggest that what Lewis does in the final two chapters in his *Mind and the World-Order,* in which he states his thesis of an *a priori* analytical justification of induction and empirical generalization, consists in justifying induction and empirical generalization in the framework of a theory of reality and a related theory of knowledge generally advocated by him. In the following, I shall formulate Lewis' theory of reality and the related theory of knowledge, in order to see how induction and empirical generalization are justified by Lewis in their framework. I shall then point out that Lewis' arguments do not succeed in ascribing rational credibility to induction and empirical generalization, and suggest alterations in Lewis' theories for a better justification of induction and empirical generalization, in line with my suggestion regarding Peirce's non-probabilistic justification of induction. After this, I shall criticize his theory concerning the pragmatical justification of induction and empirical generalization in the final section, and suggest that induction can be only justified in terms of the satisfaction of our pragmatical interests in a weak sense, but not in a strong sense.

[2] *Ibid.,* 310.

2. *Problems of Justifying Induction in the Theories of Reality and Knowledge*

Though Lewis does not give a definition of what the real is, he does indicate that the real as the totality of things and objective facts is such that it is knowable as sequences of possible sense-experiences if they are knowable at all. He says: "Things exist for our apprehension as certain sequences of possible experiences of which given presentations are probable indices." [3] From this statement of Lewis, however, we have no reason to suppose that he should imply that the real must be merely knowable as sequences of possible experiences. Nevertheless, there is a strong reason to suppose that Lewis does suggest that what is real is *always* apprehensible things and objective facts, which will *always* make our knowledge of reality possible. For he says: "What is required in the way of order if experience is to be intelligible and knowledge possible is only that there should be apprehensible things and objective facts – and to this we can conceive no alternative whatsoever, *unless it be non-existence of every thing.*" [4] This can be construed as saying if there should be apprehensible things and objective facts, we can always have knowledge of things and objective facts, because they exist as sequences of possible experiences. But if there should be no apprehensible things and objects and objective facts, then, nothing exists. By conversion, it is clear that apprehensible things and objective facts which make our knowledge of things and objective facts possible, according to Lewis, are all there is in reality. This theory of reality – reality as apprehensible things and objective facts – is closely related to Lewis' theory of knowledge as made clear in the preceding Chapter.

In the preceding Chapter, we have made clear that Lewis held the following: to apprehend or know things and objective facts is to apply concepts to experience in the presence of given sense-experience. A concept applies to experience only when we recognize some order or uniformity in experience. The order of uniformity, according to Lewis, is a sequence of certain possible experiences, which are related to one another rather than to any other experiences. It is a pattern of sense-experiences. The concept of "apple" applies to experience, for example, only when we recognize some "applelike" pattern in experience or a sequence of possible experiences and can identify it as such if it occurs.

---

[3] *Ibid.*, 367.
[4] *Ibid.*, 367. (Italics mine).

In this sense, our knowledge of reality is nothing more than a conceptual interpretation of experience, which can be formulated in terms of statements about sequences of possible experiences. To know, therefore is to recognize sequences of possible experiences by relating given experiences to possible experiences in an orderly way. Combining this theory of knowledge and the theory of reality as described above, it is clear that reality is nothing more than what we can know by way of applying concepts to experience: they are sequences of possible experiences ordered in certain ways, which are apprehensible by us, or are apprehended by us now.

Now Lewis' procedure for justifying induction and empirical generalization consists in stating the validity of induction and empirical generalization in the framework of his theory of reality and his theory of knowledge. The validity of induction and empirical generalization, according to him, lies in the fact that it is contrary to our notion of things and objective facts that empirical generalizations do not formulate our knowledge of them. To make his point clear, Lewis betakes himself to showing (1) that empirical generalizations, as instances of empirical knowledge, may be interpreted as conceptual interpretations of experience, or in other words, as results of application of concepts to experience; and (2) that we can and we must apply concepts to experience unless nothing exists. Note that (2) must be understood in the framework of Lewis' theory of reality and the related theory of knowledge, for as we have seen, according to Lewis' theory of reality, things exists for our apprehension as sequences of possible experiences, whereas according to the related theory of knowledge, to apprehend things and objective facts is to apply concepts to experience. Hence, if we *cannot* apply concept to experience, it follows that there would be non-existence of everything. In the following I shall discuss (1) and (2) in order.

3. *Empirical Generalizations as Interpretations of Experience and Principle A*

Lewis distinguishes between two kinds of empirical generalizations: empirical generalizations of the form "all swans are white" and empirical generalizations of the form "This is an apple." Now to assert that all swans are white is to assert the truth of the statement "For all x, if x is a swan, then x is white." This statement is clearly a generalization. But it also represents an interpretation of experience in terms of two concepts or an application of two concepts to experience, for the following reason. This statement is true if the predicate or concept "white" is true of anything of which the predicate or the concept "a swan" is true. According to Lewis' theory of meaning, as we have discussed in the preceding Chapter, to say that a concept is true of something is to say that a uniformity or a sequence of possible experiences conforms to the sense-meaning of the concept, which can be expressed by the statement "If x presents some sense-experience, then if we should act in a certain manner, x would present some other sense-experience." This is precisely what Lewis means by saying that a concept applies to experience or that experience is interpreted in terms of some concept. On this explanation, it should be clear that the generalization "For all x, if x is a swan, then x is white" represents an interpretation of experience in terms of the concepts "a swan" and "white," an interpretation to the effect that, whenever x is interpreted as a swan, it is also interpreted as white, or that whenever the concept "a swan" applies to x, the concept "white" also applies to x.

By the same token, the statement "This is an apple" should also represent an interpretation of experience in terms of the concept of an apple. To assert the truth of this statement is to assert that this concept "an apple" is true of "this," or the concept "apple" applies to "this" and that "this" is interpreted as an apple. But this statement, when it is asserted as true, also prescribes that the concept "an apple" is true of a class of things to which "this" belongs. Apparently it is because of this that Lewis speaks of the statement "This is an apple" as an empirical generalization. The generalization in question should take the form "For all x, if x is an apple, then if x should present certain sense experience to us, and if we should act in a certain manner, then x would present certain other sense-experience to us." [5]

The above way of explaining an empirical generalization in terms of some conceptual interpretation of experience should make it plain that a conceptual interpretation of experience conversely can be regarded as

[5] We should note, of course, that in order to determine a concept or a sequence of possible experiences as true of an individual, we cannot require that sequences of possible experiences are exactly alike for every individual of the same class. What we may at most require is that those sequences of possible experiences should belong to some similarity classes, or classes of sequences of sense-experiences which are sufficiently similar to enable us to determine the given concept as true of every individual of the same class. The problem of similarity is a difficult one, but we do not have to discuss it here. Taking into consideration the notion of a similarity class, we may say that in making a statement of the form "This is an apple" we have implicitly made a generalization of the following form: "For all x *like* 'this,' if x should present some sense-experience to us, then if we should act in a certain manner, then x would present a certain other sense-experience to us."

an empirical generalization. This can be seen very easily. When a concept F applies to a given experience, or the experience is interpreted in terms of F, we say that we have an empirical generalization of the form "This is F." When a given experience is interpreted in terms of two concepts F and G, or when the concept F applies to a given experience to which the concept G applies, we say that we have an empirical generalization of the form "For all x, if x is F, then x is G."

We come to the second point of Lewis that we can and must always apply concepts to experience unless nothing exists. Lewis formulates this point in a general principle, which he regards as very fundamental and essential for the justification of induction and empirical generalizations. It is on the strength of this principle that Lewis thinks that induction and empirical generalizations should be justified or given reason for their trustworthiness. This principle, entitled Principle A (PA) by Lewis, is formulated as follows: "It must be false, that every identifiable entity in experience is equally associated with every other." [6] What follows will be a clarification and explanation of this principle in order to show that we can always apply concepts to experience and that there must be apprehensible things and objective facts, unless nothing exists.

First, we should note that the meanings of terms "identifiable entity in experience" and "equally associated with "in PA are ambiguous. An entity in experience is identifiable or recognizable only when we can describe it in terms of some concept. Thus, when Lewis speaks of some identifiable or recognizable entity in experience, he assumes that one should already know something about experience, and hence should already have some knowledge of the real. Thus Lewis begs the question when he uses PA as a basis for asserting the possibility of our knowledge of reality. To avoid this difficulty, I think that Lewis should make a distinction between concepts describing various sorts of sense-experiences like colors, sounds, and tastes, on the one hand, and concepts describing material (or physical) objects like chairs and tables, or describing theoretical (scientific) objects like atoms and electrons, on the other. A concept of red color applies to a patch of red color, just as a concept of chair applies to a particular chair, or a concept of electron applies to a particular electron of a hydrogen atom. On this distinction, we can understand the term "identifiable entity in experience" as referring to a sense-presentation to which some concept of sense-experi-

---

[6] *Ibid.*, 368.

ence applies. In this sense, the term will not mislead us to suppose that there must be already apprehensible things or objective facts when we have identified or recognized just some kinds of sense-presentations.

To proceed, we must also ask what it means to say that "two given identifiable entities (say, x and y) are equally associated with a third (say, z)." Apparently, it means that if the occurrence of x is followed by (or goes together with) the occurrence of z, the occurrence of y is simultaneously followed by (or goes together with) that of z. But it should be pointed out that it can also mean that if the occurrence of z is followed by (or goes together with) that of x, the occurrence of z is simultaneously followed by (or goes together with) that of y. In case there are more than two identifiable entities in experience, these identifiable entities may occur together so that they may be said to be "equally associated" with one another. They may be nevertheless said to be "equally followed" by one another if and only if given one identifiable entity, others would occur in a temporal sequence, one as frequently as another. This is the meaning we have to attribute to the PA if it is to be understood free from ambiguity.

With the clarification of the relevant terms in PA, we come to consider how PA must guarantee the existence of apprehensible things and objective facts, and hence must guarantee the validity of our knowledge of reality. This can be best seen by considering how there should be no apprehensible things and objective facts, and hence there should be non-existence of everything, according to Lewis' theory of reality, if the contrary of PA holds. Suppose every identifiable entity in experience is equally associated with every other in the above sense. Then, given an identifiable entity, say, this particular piece of "dog-like" experience, on the basis of which a prediction of the existence of a dog can be made, what should be our grounds for saying that we know that there exists a dog? As our prediction will be verified less frequently (by experiences pertinent to our concept of a dog) than disconfirmed (by experiences pertinent to other possible concepts), we should have no more reason to say that "this" is a dog than to say that "this" is not a dog; and in fact we have less, because the predicate "non-doglike" would be true of the given experience more often than the predicate "doglike." Moreover, if we consider that every experience goes with every other simultaneously, we have no reason to make the prediction of the existence of a dog in the first place. The reason is simply that prediction of existence of one thing would be as good as prediction of existence of every other. In this way, no concept should explain the given experience in terms of a specific kind of experience as distinct from other kinds, since the given experience is related to all kinds of experience, all of which occur with equal frequency. Hence, we would not say that there are specific apprehensible things or objective facts, simply because we have no way or no criteria for ascertaining the existence of one thing rather than another.

It is clearly in the above manner that the contrary of PA leads to a denial of knowing the existence of anything or any objective fact. By conversion, it follows that PA should be necessary condition for *knowing* the existence of things and objective facts, and truistically, our knowing the existence of things and objective facts is therefore a sufficient condition for the truth of PA. What needs to be pointed out, however, is that PA is not only a necessry condition for, but also a necessary *and* sufficient condition for, *knowing* the existence of things and objective facts. This is so, because, if PA is true, then, by Lewis' explanation of things and objective facts in terms of uniformities or in terms of ordered sequences of possible experiences, things and objective facts should exist as sequences of possible experiences for our apprehension. That is why Lewis refers to the truth of PA as the "sole necessity" for the existence of apprehensible things and objective facts.[7]

In this connection, it should be helpful to point out that Lewis' later doctrine of the verification of "non-terminating statements" in terms of "terminating statements" as strictly implied by them [8] also presupposes PA as a necessary condition, if the doctrine is to serve the purpose of explaining how we know true statements of physical objects by verifying statements of sense-experience derived from them. The verification of a non-terminating statement is possible by verification of terminating statements, simply because PA is true. The "non-terminating statement," according to Lewis, is a statement of fact from the "simplest assertion of received fact – 'There is a piece of white paper before me' – to the most impressive of scientific generalizations – 'The universe is expanding'." [9] A "terminating statement," on the other hand, is one concerning the relationship between sense-experiences, and is of the familiar form: "If, in the presence of a certain appearance S, a certain act should seem to be performed, a certain appearance E would result." The relation of the terminating statement to a non-terminating statement lies in the fact that the sense-meaning

[7] Cf., *Ibid.*, 367.
[8] See *An Analysis of Knowledge and Valuation*, Chapter VIII.
[9] *Ibid.*, 185.

of a non-terminating statement about fact is exhibitable in terminating statements of some sort in the above form. In this sense, a non-terminating statement is explicated in terms of a set of terminating statements. The relation between a non-terminating statement and a set of terminating statements is expressible by a set of analytical statements of the form "P (a non-terminating statement) strictly implies C (the terminating statement)."

The so-called strict implication between P and C is one to the effect that if the antecedent is true, it would not only be false but also inconsistent or inconceivable to say that the consequent is false. The range of terminating statements for a non-terminating statement is inexhaustible, for it includes every statement, the truth of which would tend to confirm the non-terminating statement, and the falsity of which would tend to disconfirm it. Now as there are many distinct non-terminating statements, there are many distinct kinds of terminating statements which are respectively implied by non-terminating statements of each kind. Each non-terminating statement is confirmable through verification of terminating statements strictly implied by its own kind, but not through verification of terminating statements strictly implied by other non-terminating statements. At this point, we may say what PA requires is that the preceding statement is true. Or in other words, it requires that a non-terminating statement implies a set of terminating statements of a certain kind, while excluding in its implication sets of terminating statements of certain other kinds. This is so, because to say that every recognizable appearance is equally followed by every other, as the denial of PA should entail, is to say that sets of terminating statements of all kinds occur with equal frequency as verifying instances of any given non-terminating statement. In this way, there would be no distinction between the confirmation and disconfirmation of any non-terminating statement, and hence there would be no recognition of the existence of an object nor the presence of a law in experience as predicted by a non-terminating statement.

The applicability of concepts to experience, the confirmability of empirical (non-terminating) statements, and the existence of apprehensible things and objective facts all depend upon PA. Hence we may indeed conclude that PA is essential for explaining how we know that there should be apprehensible things and objective facts in the framework of Lewis' theory of reality and his related theory of knowledge.

4. Analyticity of Principle A

Now, there arises the question whether Principle A itself is necessarily or analytically true. In the presentation of this principle, Lewis not only suggests (1) that if some apprehensible things exist, the "sole necessity" is that every recognizable entity in experience should not be equally associated with every other, but suggests (2) that it *must* not be the case that every identifiable entity in experience is equally associated with every other. On his first suggestion, PA should be both sufficient and necessary conditions for the existence of apprehensible things and objective facts. In other words, the following logical equivalence should hold:

$$\text{Apprehensible things exist} \equiv \text{PA}$$

It should be clear from this equivalence that PA is a necessary or analytical truth if the statement that apprehensible things exist is a necessary or analytical truth. But is the statement "Apprehensible things exist" a necessary or analytical truth? According to Lewis' theory of reality which prescribes the equivalence between reality and apprehensible things and objective facts, to conceive the non-existence of apprehensible things and objective facts is to conceive nothing being real. But this is not conceivable because this will defy conceiving. To conceive this is to conceive a self-contradiction. If indeed an analytical or necessary truth is such that its denial leads to self-contradiction, the statement that apprehensible things exist is a necessary or analytical statement and hence PA is a necessary or analytical statement in virtue of the logical equivalence between the statement "Apprehensive things exist" and PA.

In fact, on Lewis's second suggestion that it *must* not be the case that every identifiable entity in experience is equally associated with every other, PA should be an "explicitly" necessary or analytically true statement.[10] That is, it should be analytically true by meanings of the words involved in the statement of PA and its analytical truth is explicitly affirmed by the statement of PA. However, if PA is considered as an assertion about an "identifiable entity in experience," and be put in the form "If x is identifiable or recognizable, then x is not equally

---

[10] Cf., *An Analysis of Knowledge and Valuation*. Lewis's definition of an explicitly analytic statement is this. "*An explicitly analytic* statement is an analytic statement (hence true) which asserts the logical necessity of something." (Italics Lewis's), 89.

associated with every other entity in experience," then, in the sense of "indentifiable entity in experience" given earlier, it is always conceivable that every identifiable entity in experience can be followed by every other with equal frequency. Thus, it would be difficult to consider PA as a necessary truth on Lewis's second suggestion, if we have accepted our earlier interpretation of the term "identifiable entity in experience." Of course, we may reinterpret "an identifiable entity in experience" as something to which a certain concept of physical object applies or as something to which a certain non-terminating statement refers. In so doing, PA can be simply considered as an assertion about a physical object or an objective fact. But then, it is still difficult to explain why we could not conceive of a case contrary to PA.

In the light of the difficulties about explaining the analytical truth of PA, perhaps, we may suggest that PA is necessary or is analytically true only when it is considered as a definition of our recognition or our identification of an entity in experience. That is to say, PA can be expanded in the following form: *x, as a sense-experience, is recognizable or identifiable in terms of some concept of physical object or some non- terminating statement, if x is not equally associated with every other sense-appearance.* It is by this explanation of recognition that we may make any confirmable prediction and non-terminating statement. If we have granted "recognition" or "identification" the above explanation, it follows that to conceive the contrary of PA would be a self-contradiction in meaning.[11]

Understanding PA in the above sense, we may proceed to show how PA, serving as both sufficient and necessary conditions for our apprehension of things and objective facts in terms of conceptual interpretation, is essential for justifying induction and empirical generalization. We recall that, according to Lewis, empirical generalizations are conceptual interpretations of experience while induction consists in applying concepts to experience. We have further noted that conceptual interpretations of experiences or applications of concepts to experiences can be regarded as empirical generalizations. Now PA guarantees that we should never fail to use induction and empirical generalization if we

---

[11] In this sense, this principle should not, as Lewis supposes that it should, compare to Keynes' Principle of Limitation of Independent Variety. The latter, as Keynes affirms, is a hypothesis supported only by inductive evidences about kinds of things in nature. For Keynes' principle, see John M. Keynes, *Treatise on Probability*, 253 ff., esp. 257, where it is stated that "the amount of variety in the universe is limited in such a way that there is no one object so complex that its qualities fall into an infinite number of independent groups." What Keynes calls independent groups are groups consisting of combinations of qualities, elements of one being irreducible to those of another.

want to know the real. The reason is simply this. According to Lewis' theory of reality, unless nothings exists, there should always be apprehensible things and objective facts, and hence there should be induction and empirical generalization. For this reason, induction and empirical generalization are indispensable for, as well as presupposed in, our conception of reality as well as our notion of knowledge of reality. The validity of induction and empirical generalization is then no more than the necessity of induction and empirical generalization for our knowledge of reality and for the definition of reality. To justify induction is to recognize this necessity and to recognize the fact that, without induction and empirical generalization, we should not only have no knowledge of reality, but have no reality at all. This kind of justification is clearly indicated by Lewis in the following passage:

The only alternative to the conception that our knowledge in general is valid, is the conception that there are no things; that nothing exists to be known and no mind exists to know it – The nearest approximation we can make to such a conception, is perhaps, that there might be an experience which is mere flitting of meaningless presentations.[12]

The statement in this passage, that "The only alternative to the conception that our knowledge in general is valid, is the conception that there are no things," is characteristic of Lewis' theory of reality. To him, the real is no more than a set of apprehensible things and objective facts or a set of sequences of possible experiences. Hence the denial of the possibility of our knowledge as valid is the denial of reality. This denial is equivalent to affirming that experience is meaningless to us. In the presence of an experience, instead of having meaningful interpretations, we would have a state of pure "aesthesis," which, in Lewis' use of the term,[13] is neither knowledge nor reality. On the basis of this state of pure "aesthesis," we can hardly say that some apprehensible things exist or that something is apprehended, because no concept applies and no empirical statement is true. Hence, for Lewis, the very indispensability of empirical generalizations for the existence of some apprehensible things or objective facts in the presence of given experience is a justification of induction and empirical generalization. That induction and empirical generalization cannot be doubted is a reason why we should not doubt the validity of induction and empirical generalization.

For a criticism of this view, we may remark that if what a Humean

---

[12] *Mind and the World-Order*, 378. (Italics mine).
[13] *Ibid.*, 53 f, 75, 275 f. Appendix B, 407.

skeptic asks for a justification of induction and empirical generalization is merely that they be shown to be presupposed in and indispensable for our knowledge of reality as well as for the existence of things and objective facts in Lewis' sense, Lewis' procedure indeed should satisfy him. But the Humean skeptic may accept the fact that induction and empirical generalization are indispensable for our knowledge of reality, as well as for the existence of things and objective facts in Lewis' sense, but may still request that some reason be given for the trustworthiness of credibility of induction and empirical generalization. The tautologous truth that induction and empirical generalization are indispensable for and are presupposed in our knowledge of reality is no reason for us to believe them, any more than they are reasons for us to believe our knowledge of reality as trustworthy, or to accept the definition of reality as adequate. The question as to how our knowledge of reality is trustworthy and how our definition of reality is adequate can be always raised. Unless there are independent grounds on which we may ascribe credibility to our knowledge of reality, that induction and empirical generalization are indispensable for and presupposed in our knowledge of reality should not itself lend any credibility to the procedure of induction and empirical generalization or to the general procedure of applying concepts to experience.

There is a second type of criticism of this procedure of justification. Lewis apparently regards the validity of induction and empirical generalization as consisting ultimately in the impossibility of our conceiving the non-existence of things and objective facts. Hence, according to Lewis, if we reject induction and empirical generalization, we not only reject our knowledge of reality, but also reject reality. But this is not a correct view. Because the fact is that when we reject induction and empirical generalization, we reject only the part of knowledge of reality which depends upon application of concepts to experience through induction and empirical generalization. We do not therefore reject the fundamental principles of classification and interpretation determined in advance of our experience and presupposed in our conception of reality. In this sense, we do not therefore reject reality.

Next, according to Lewis' theory of reality, the real is "apprehensible things and objective facts." Thus, if a thing cannot be apprehended or known, it must not be said to be real. Similarly, if nothing can be apprehended in terms of concepts, there would be no reality. It also should follow from this that there should be no meaningful statement about reality. This is because if there is no reality just because there is no valid induction and empirical generalization, any statement about the real would be meaningless. But is this position a tenable one? The fact again is that we can make perfectly meaningful statement about reality without knowing that this statement is a true one. Hence, even if we reject induction and empirical generalization, what we reject is merely the means or method by which we may find out whether a meaningful statement is true. We do not by any means reject the meaningfulness of the statement and reality itself. For example, it is perfectly meaningful to say that "A cat has five legs" or that "All galaxies other than ours in the sky recede from ours." But it does not follow from this that we *know* that a cat has five legs or that we know that it is the case that all galaxies other than ours in the sky recede from ours. Nor does it follow from this that it is the case that a cat has five legs or that it is the case that all galaxies other than ours in the sky recede from ours. Hence, the fact that we do not know that a cat has five legs or that we do not know that all galaxies other than ours in the sky recede from ours does not entail that these statements are meaningless. Since meaningful statements about reality and reality itself cannot be rejected on rejecting induction and empirical generalization, Lewis' justification of induction and empirical generalization by equating possibility of them with possibility of reality itself is no proper justification at all. It is at most a proposal as to what we should mean by reality and what we should mean by induction and empirical generalization.

Although Lewis' "*a priori* analytical" justification of induction and empirical generalization does not warrant credibility of induction and empirical generalization, it must be admitted that it does in a sense show the fundamental necessity of our conceptual interpretation and the process of induction and empirical generalization for recognizing experience as real. It points out that induction is a method of verifying meaningful statement about reality. If anyone accepts our knowledge of reality as valid without knowing that induction and empirical generalization are presupposed in it, he cannot raise doubts about the validity of induction and empirical generalization without self-contradiction. This is like one who accepts the law of contradiction as valid and who, at the same time, raises doubts about the validity of that law. This is a kind of pragmatical inconsistency. But there would be logical contradiction if the validity of his denial of the validity of empirical generalization should depend upon induction.[14]

---

[14] Cf., Chapter VIII.

A better way of justifying induction and empirical generalization may be suggested by revising parts of Lewis' conception of reality and his conception of knowledge of reality. According to Lewis' theory of reality, the real depends upon our apprehension of things and objective facts in terms of sequences of possible experiences. We have argued previously that we can make meaningful statements about the real without actually knowing whether they are true by induction, even though the meaningful statements about the real may always be analyzed into a set of statements about possible experiences, and thus about apprehensible things and objective facts. In this sense, we say that the real exists independently of our apprehension, i.e., things and objective facts need not be apprehended or even be apprehensible for their existence. To revise Lewis' conception of the real, we may take the real as things and objective facts about which we may make meaningful statements. In this sense, a meaningful statement about the real need not be true or known to be true.

With the above conception of the real, we may define our knowledge of reality in such a way that not every or any empirical generalization can be taken as knowledge of reality. Instead, a new conception of knowledge of reality should prescribe that knowledge of reality is a *well-confirmed* conceptual interpretation of experience. We have discussed the notion of *well-confirmedness* in connection with our criticism of Peirce's non-probabilistic justification of induction in Chapter V. According to this notion, induction and empirical generalization are valid and trustworthy if they are well-confirmed. That is to say, if they meet the criteria of well-confirmedness, or if they lead in a finitely realizable process to well-confirmed statements about reality. In this sense, showing that an induction or an empirical generalization is well-confirmed or that it will in a finitely realizable process lead to well-confirmed statements about reality is to show a reason for its trustworthiness. A well-confirmed empirical generalization should belong to a body of knowledge of reality, since it is equivalent to a well-confirmed conceptual interpretation of experience. This is a justification for induction and empirical generalization which Lewis might have intended in his arguments. In the light of this justification, to reject induction and empirical generalization is not to reject reality or to reject any meaningful statement about reality. Rejecting induction and empirical generalization is nothing other than rejecting a method for discovering reality, a method by which a meaningful statement of reality may be verified or disconfirmed.

CHAPTER XII

IMPLICATIONS OF LEWIS' "*A PRIORI* ANALYTICAL" JUSTIFICATION OF INDUCTION

1. *From Principle A to Justification of Argument from Past to Future*

Referring to his Principle A, Lewis says, "What I wish to point out is, first, that this single requirement satisfies everything which is necessary, in the way of order in experience or reality, for the validity of empirical generalizations, based on past experience and applicable to the future; and second, that although this has the appearance of a limitation of the possibility of experience it has in the end no alternative." [1] Before dealing with Lewis' first point in this passage, I shall attempt first to justify his second point on the basis of PA which states that we can apply concepts to any given experience unless nothing exists. That this is a consequence of PA should be obvious from the following analysis.

We have seen that PA, for Lewis, is an infallible principle. Part of the reason why PA cannot be false is that we can always apply concepts to experience. It is in this sense, according to Lewis,, that we may *know* that things exist; and because we know that things exist, we may say that things *exist*. It is precisely in this sense that the possibility of experience must be restricted according to what the concepts prescribe in terms of sense meanings. Furthermore, if the possibility of experience is not thus restricted, nothing would exist. When Lewis says that there is no alternative to the fact that we do restrict the possibility of experience, he precisely means this. From the statement that nothing exists it naturally follows that we know nothing.

For the purpose of emphasizing his point that we must *know* something in any situation where experience is given, and that we must

[1] C. I. Lewis, *Mind and the World-Order*, 368.

therefore restrict the possibility of experience, Lewis puts down the following principle (which he calls Principle B): "In any situation (if sufficiently extended) in which there are identifiable entities which fail to satisfy Principle A – i.e., whose association is random – there will be other entities, systematically connected with the former or specifiable in terms of them, which do satisfy Principle A." [2] What Lewis suggests in this principle is that PA must apply to experience in any situation if we want to avoid conceiving of non-existence of everything. The problem raised with respect to this principle is how to understand that a sequence of sense experiences, which does not satisfy PA, is systematically specifiable and can be connected with another sequence of sense-experiences which does satisfy PA. A preliminary explanation of this is that, if the given experiences are such that they cannot be described or interpreted in terms of a set of familiar concepts, we may always find a "suitable" set of concepts to describe or interpret them, "suitable" in the sense that the set of concepts will enable us to make confirmable predictions on the basis of the experiences given. Thus, in a random phenomenon we may always look for some order or pattern of experiences other than prescribed by familiar or pre-specified concepts. Note that a random phenomenon, for Lewis, is not one to which no concept whatsoever applies, it is only one to which no pre-specified concept applies. Directing toward this point, Lewis remarks: "In the process of our learning the nature of the real, what we do is to look for some order or certain general type and, if we do not find that, to look for some other." [3]

Principle B in fact maintains that we can always understand experience, because ways of understanding or interpreting experiences always exist, no matter how random the given experience is. That ways of understanding or interpreting experiences always exist is due to the fact that we can always make distinctions and classifications of given experiences, conformable to our practical considerations such as simplicity and comprehensiveness. The problem is how we may "intelligibilize" random experiences, to which familiar or pre-specified conceptual apparatus has no proper application. Lewis has suggested the following methods of apprehending experience in order that we may always say that we know something. The first method is that we may proceed from simple elements derived from analyses of the entities in experience to the discovery of conceptual relationships which would

[2] *Ibid.*, 383.
[3] *Ibid.*, 352.

qualify as criteria of reality and, in terms of which less simple elements are subject to formulation. For example, the macroscopic laws in classical physics result from analysis of this kind. We may also in other cases take a larger whole into which the entities in question may be organized and subject it to formulation in terms of some conceptual relationships. The microscopic laws in statistical mechanics are well-known examples of these. A third method which Lewis suggests is that we may always confine attention to abstracted elements, and disregard the remainder of the given as irrelevant. That is to say, if the given is not subject to any existing system of conceptual interpretation, we may simply take the existing categories as irrelevant for determining what the given is and relegate instead the given to the category which does not overlap with any existing category. This would certainly constitute a way of understanding experience, however inadequate it may be. This procedure is not rare in scientific practice. The discovery of new elements in chemistry and the discovery of new species in biology are good examples in point.

As a last ground for saying that some concepts could always be applied to experience, Lewis correctly notes the important fact that we can always impose arithmetical order upon random experience where none is directly observable. In the light of these considerations, Lewis concludes,

Our concepts are devised with the purpose to catch the significant, the subject of meaningful generalization, at whatever level and in whatever way we may. When particular concepts fail, we merely abandon them – through analysis or organization or abstraction and so on – in favor of corrected ones, which take cognizance of, and include the ground of, our previous failure. That conception *in general* should be invalid, is quite impossible. That attempt to envisage an experience or state of affairs such that *every* attempt to discover stabilities must fail, is an attempt to conceive the inconceivable – to conceive what would not be things or objective facts nor subject to any generalization which makes what is denoted conformable to concepts. The experience or reality which should be incompatible with conception, *ipso facto* cannot be conceived.[4]

That is, our given particular concepts may fail to give rise to true predictions, but this does not prevent us from making predictions on other conceptual basis in the presence of given experience and what we know from the past. Indeed, we may always revise our empirical generalizations in the light of their verifications and failures so that we may make empirical generalizations always conform to what we know from

---

[4] *Ibid.*, 385.

experience. In this sense, the self-correcting nature of induction, as we have explained in connection with Peirce's non-probabilistic justification of induction, is not only essential for determining a process of inquiry for the real, but essential for determining a valid ground for making empirical generalizations. This ground consists in all the data given to us and the fact that empirical generalizations made thereupon are open to correction in the light of further empirical findings. To make prediction is to limit the possibility of experience in some way. Since we cannot fail to make some prediction in a self-correcting process of induction, it is impossible that we should fail to limit the possibility of experience in some way or other for the purpose of understanding experience in terms of concepts. The only alternative to this is that no concept applies to given experience, and hence that we shall make no cognitive claims. This alternative, in fact, we cannot take. Thus, Lewis' assertion that there is no alternative (meaning no alternative for knowing the real) to the limitation of experience is justified in the above analysis.

In the quotations from Lewis in the beginning paragraph of this section, we see that Lewis also holds PA to be essential for justifying induction from past to future. What Lewis requires for the validation of argument from past to future, like what he requires for the validation of empirical knowledge in general, is not that any particular prediction based on past experience must be true, but that predictions from past are generally true; or, in other words, that some prediction from past must be such that by it we may determine what the real is, unless nothing exists. Lewis formulates this justification of the argument from past to future in the following principle which he calls Principle C: "The statistical prediction of the future from the past cannot be generally invalid, because whatever is future to any given past, is in turn past to some future." [5]

A statistical prediction of the future from the past is based on a statistical generalization, which takes the form "A proportion r of things which are M's are P's," and which is generalized on the basis of our knowledge of the fact that a proportion r of things which are M's are observed to be P's. This is obviously a more general way of making a generalization. A *universal* empirical generalization would correspond therefore to a statistical generalization of the form "The proportion of things M's which are P's is one." To say that a statistical prediction of

[5] *Ibid.*, 386.

the future from the past cannot be generally invalid is to say that some or at least one such statistical prediction must be valid. But then the question is how the validity of at least one such statistical prediction is to be understood. It certainly cannot mean that we know with certainty at least one statistical prediction to be true. For we simply cannot know this, I suggest, however, that the validity in question should consist in the fact that at least one statistical prediction must be definitive of our knowledge of the real and should render our knowledge of the real possible. Since it is assumed that whatever is future to any given past is in turn past to some future, if we claim that all arguments or predictions from the past are invalid, and thus fail to afford a basis by which we may know something about the real, then we shall find that we have not made, and will never be able to make, any valid prediction throughout the whole temporal process which consists of the past and the future, and hence that we do not know anything about the real. But since this, according to Lewis, is a situation which we can hardly conceive, and since it is a fundamental principle that some concept does apply to experience such that we may know something about the real, the problem of justifying the argument from past to future is reduced to one of justifying induction and empirical generalization in general. That is, the justification should show that without using the argument from past to future we would have no knowledge of the real.

The justification of the argument from past to future thus amounts to (1) an explanation of the necessity of statistical prediction from the past for our knowledge of reality and (2) a definition of the validity of this argument in terms of the fundamental principle that we must and can always apprehend something in the presence of some sense-experience. Such a justification can be cast in the following lines of reasoning:

1. Given any sense-experience, we must know some uniformity or existence of something.
2. But our prediction of uniformity or of existence of something always takes the form of a statistical prediction from past experience.
3. Hence, given any situation of sense-experience, some prediction of statistical laws from the past must be relevant for determining our knowledge of the real.

What requires explanation in the above reasoning is the second premise that a prediction of uniformity takes the form of a statistical prediction from past experience. A prediction of uniformity is always made on the basis of given experience, but a given experience is not the sole ground on which a prediction of uniformity is made. Past experience, we may recall, is also a ground on which a prediction of uniformity is made. In fact, what is in general taken as a given experience for a prediction is always understood as one which we can certify as real by perception or memory. In this case, the ground of prediction should always refer to something in the past, and should not refer merely to some "specious present" or "immediately presented data." Insofar as we grant that a prediction of uniformity always takes the form of a prediction from past experience,[6] the reasoning in the above is logically valid, and the argument from past to future is justified if PA is justified.

As we have pointed out, to justify induction and empirical generalization on the basis of PA is to recognize the indispensability of inductive procedure for pursuing knowledge of reality, and to point out the fact that if we reject induction and empirical generalization in general we shall reject any application of concepts to experience, and hence we shall also reject reality which, by Lewis' notion of reality, is understood to be apprehensible things and objective facts. Similarly, to justify the argument from past to future, according to Lewis, is to recognize the indispensability of this argument for pursuing knowledge of reality, and to point out the fact that if we reject this argument, we shall reject any application of concepts to experience, and hence we shall also reject reality. In other words, the justification of this argument lies in the fact that to deny this argument is to deny the truth of any prediction of uniformity or to deny the existence of everything. Henceforth, this argument will necessarily yield knowledge of re lity.

Without repeating my criticisms of Lewis' justification of induc ion and empirical generalization in general, which should also apply o Lewis' justification of the argument from past to future, it suffices to say that Lewis' justification of the latter argument does not really adduce reason why the argument from past to future is trustworthy. I make this statement simply because (1) induction as necessarily presupposed in our knowledge of reality does not give any such reason, and (2) to reject this argument is not necessarily to reject reality; it is merely to reject a method for knowing the real. To justify this argument and induction in general, we may indeed appeal to some independent ground for the trustworthiness of this argument and induction in general, apart

---

[6] Since past experience is a ground of our prediction of uniformity, it is assumed that we do know what past experience is and hence that memory is in generall valid. Indeed, the validity of argument from the past presupposes the validity of memory. But the validity of argument from past to future as an inference from what is certified by memory to be true to what we may take as a determination of what we accept as the real has nothing to do with memory.

from the fact that this argument is presupposed in our knowledge of reality. But whether or not, according to Lewis, induction and empirical generalization, including the argument from past to future, has such an independent ground, we shall see in the following section.

2. *Lewis on the Practical Successfulness of Induction*

We come to the question of how action or prediction in accordance with probabilities or empirical generalizations must be more successful than action or prediction not in accordance with them. This question was raised in the first section of last Chapter where we quoted from Lewis. As Lewis does not seem to separate the question as to how things in general exist or how the world is orderly in general from the question as to how induction leads to success, he seems to regard the answer to the first question as a natural answer to the second. He seems to think that if there is some uniformity in experience in a situation, we shall always make more successful predictions than if there were none.

Immediately following his statement of the general validity of the argument from the past to future, Lewis says: "That is, whoever continually revises his judgment of the probability of a statistical generalization by its successfully observed verifications and failures cannot fail to make more successful predictions than if he should disregard the past in his anticipations of the future." [7] But this is false: the self-correcting nature of induction does not guarantee that action or prediction in accordance with empirical generalizations based on what we have already known will be more successful than action or prediction not in accordance with them. Indeed, if Lewis' statement is taken as indicating the pragmatical usefulness of induction and empirical generalization, then what I shall point out in this section is that induction and empirical generalization do not have this pragmatical usefulness in the above sense, and hence that we should not trust induction and empirical generalization if such a pragmatical usefulness is required of them for their validity.

In order to prove that it is more pragmatically advantageous in the above sense to revise our empirical judgments than not to do so, Lewis invites us to conceive the worst possible experience in regard to which we are required to make predictions. This worst possible experience is one which keeps refuting and contradicting our predictions made on

[7] *Ibid.*, 387.

the basis of inductive evidences. The so-called inductive evidences are patterns of correlations which we find among recognizable items of experiences. That we may always find such patterns of correlations, according to Lewis, is due to our intelligibilizing ability which exhibits itself in our use of methods of abstracting, distinguishing, classifying, analyzing and numerical ordering. Now a demon may always produce recognizable items in experience as varied as possible, so that there is a minimum likelihood that the next sequence will resemble the given one. But insofar as these items are recognizable, they could be described always in terms of concepts which are meaningful for us. Thus our predictions based on these recognizable items in experience are always confirmable before they are disconfirmed or known to be false on further experience.

Even when experience is totally random in the sense that no specific order or correlation could be found in it, we may always describe it in very general terms such as "This experience is hardly repeatable" and so on. This shows that we are always in a position to predict, insofar as some experience is given to us, and are in a position to make some empirical generalization insofar as our empirical generalization consists in the adoption of a certain conceptual pattern based on the given experience. But the question is: could we conclude from this possibility of prediction and empirical generalization the certainty of the success of our prediction and the truth of our empirical generalization? It is not inconceivable that while our predictions are always possible, no verification of them will ever take place and no absolute ascertainment of the truth of our predictions is possible. It is also not inconceivable that for any empirical generalization, revision in the light of what we have already known does not lead us to making more successful predictions than we would otherwise.

We may indeed suppose that there are two groups of people: one group revise their inductive conclusions in the light of what they have known according to inductive rules, while the other group do not revise their generalizations in the same way. It is then imaginable that the first group may fail as often as, or more often than, the second group. When a demon antagonist always produces sequences of experiences which differ from both the predictions of the first group and the predictions of the second group, the first group may fail as often as the second group. When the demon antagonist, or bad luck indeed, always produces sequences of sense experiences which differ from the predictions of the first group, but do not differ from those of the second group, the first group would fail more often than the second group. Thus, in playing card games with such a demon antagonist, every time when we are required to bet on the next card in his hand, we may always lose and would not win if we revise our predictions in the light of open cards, and hence may lose more money than if we predict otherwise. Therefore it should not be the case, as Lewis thinks that it should, that "by nothing which he could do could he so devise it that we should not lose less of our money if we intelligently observed past dealings and continually revise our betting on the basis of accumulated experience." [8] What is said here could only be true when it is construed as saying that if we revise our betting on the basis of accumulated experiences, we should not lose less of our money than what our prediction based on revised accumulated experiences would cause us to lose. But in this way the statement in question becomes truistic.

The above example should suffice to indicate that the possibility of prediction on the basis of what we know from experience does not guarantee the necessity of the success of prediction. It may be said that if the possibility of prediction does not entail the necessity of the success of prediction, it at least entails the probability of the success of prediction. The probability in question certainly does not depend upon the necessity of the success of prediction for its explanation. We may say that it only indicates that it is *rationally believable* that prediction made on the basis of what we know is more success-producing than prediction not made thereupon. We may also say that revision of empirical generalizations in the light of empirical findings is required for the validity of empirical generalizations, not because this will lead to the necessity of the success of the predictions based on them, but because this is a way of establishing adequate grounds for rationally credible generalizations and predictions from them. In this sense of probability, the statement that it is probable that we shall not fail to make more successful predictions when we do accord, than when we do not accord, with past experience, is compatible with the falsity of the statement that we may not fail to make more successful predictions in accordance with past experience than not in accordance with them. When a prediction which is rationally credible fails, the failure is a genuine one, the explanation of which is always compatible with the rational credibility of the given prediction.

We may now conclude that pragmatical usefulness in the sense that induction must lead to practical success in both prediction and action,

[8] *Ibid.*, 389.

although being a good ground for the trustworthiness of induction and empirical generalization, is non-existent. When induction is pragmatically significant in the sense that induction must give rise to successful prediction or action, we say that induction is pragmatically significant in a *strong* sense. Although induction cannot be pragmatically significant in a *strong* sense, it nevertheless can be pragmatically significant in a *weak* sense. The pragmatical significance of induction in a *weak* sense lies in this: induction and prediction represent a practical attitude of ours and they are purposeful activities which will indeed satisfy our needs to understand the world and to adapt ourselves to it. But whether or not our induction and prediction would enable us to adapt to the world successfully is quite a different matter. In this *weak* sense, the pragmatical significance of knowledge and prediction is not that they must meet our pragmatical interests but that they are always possible and capable of being formulated in such a way that there is a rational basis for us to believe that they *probably* will meet our pragmatical interests. The justification of induction and probable knowledge then has to turn upon providing and formulating that rational basis of prediction and generalization as *probabilities*.

CHAPTER XIII

CONCLUDING REMARKS ON LEWIS'
"*A PRIORI* ANALYTICAL"
JUSTIFICATION OF INDUCTION

Lewis' argument for an "*a priori* analytical" justification of induction can be summarized in the following syllogism:

1. If something exists, then we can make some true empirical generalization,
2. Something exists,
3. *Ergo*, we can make some true empirical generalization.

This argument is "*a priori* analytical", because Lewis considers that the premises of the argument are "*a priori* analytical" or necessary truth. The first premise is necessarily true, because it is part of Lewis' definition of existence of things or reality in his theory of reality, according to which, reality consists of apprehensible things and objective facts or simply ordered sequences of possible experiences predictable by empirical generalizations. The second premise is also necessarily true for Lewis because it is necessarily true in the following sense of necessity: it is necessary that something exists if we cannot conceive that nothing exists. According to Lewis, to say that noting exists is to say that we cannot apply concepts to experience. Hence, to say that we cannot conceive that nothing exists is to say that it is inconceivable that we cannot apply concepts to experience. If we can always apply concepts to experience, and when we do apply concepts to experience, we shall say that something, of which these concepts are true, exists.

Because things and objective facts are experiences understood in terms of concepts, Lewis' argument for the "*a priori* analytical" justification of induction thus becomes the following:

1. If some concept can apply to experience, then we can make some true empirical generalization,
2. Some concept can always applyto experience,
3. *Ergo*, we can make some true empirical generalization.

In our discussion of Lewis' "*a priori* analytical" justification of induction in Chapter XI, we have made two criticisms of Lewis' argument. Now we may review these criticisms in connection with Lewis' argument as set in the form of either of the above two syllogisms.

Our first criticism of Lewis's "*a priori* analytical" justification of induction and empirical generalization is this. In showing that induction and empirical generalization are indispensable for and are presupposed in our knowledge of reality, Lewis fails to realize that this is itself no proper ground for the trustworthiness of induction. In other words, Lewis fails to distinguish the following two theses involved in his argument:

1. Induction and empirical generalization are necessary for, and are conducive to, our knowledge of reality defined as conceptual interpretation of experience (including empirical generalization).
2. They are necessary for, and conductive to, our knowledge of reality as it is trustworthy on other independent ground than induction.

On the basis of the first thesis, one may simply suggest that true empirical generalizations mean knowledge of reality. But this is no justification of induction and empirical generalization, since it is tautologous to say that true empirical generalizations are knowledge of reality. The open-question argument can be always invoked: Are induction and empirical generalization conducive to true knowledge of reality? Or simply, are they *really* true?

On the second thesis, we may certainly justify induction and empirical generalization if induction is really conducive to knowledge of reality, which is trustworthy on independent ground other than induction. But does Lewis produce such an independent ground? We have seen that Lewis has argued that induction is practically valuable, beause it will lead to more success of prediction than otherwise. That induction will lead to more success of prediction than otherwise is certainly a ground for the trustworthiness of induction, independent of the fact that induction is presupposed in our knowledge of reality. But Lewis fails to show that such a ground exists for induction. It seems therefore that if induction is practically valuable at all, it must not be practically valuable in the sense of rendering us more success than otherwise.

For our second criticism of Lewis' argument, we may indeed grant that Lewis' argument in the form of either of the above syllogisms should establish the validity of induction, but still question whether we have any reason for believing its underlying theory of reality, i.e., whether we have any reason for believing that things exist for our apprehension as sequences of possible experiences as predicted by induction. We have proposed one strong objection to this theory of reality. We have argued that it is good sense to say that something exists, without knowing whether our statement is true. Hence, it is not necessary that if something exists, some empirical generalization in terms of application of concepts to experience must be true or can be true; or equivalently, if no valid induction is made, nothing would exist. We may perhaps add that it is not even inconceivable that nothing exists or no concept is true of experience. Because, as we have pointed out, it is conceivable that our world may be merely a chance-world, in which everything follows every other with equal frequency, and hence that Lewis's Principle A is false. Even Lewis has suggested that there might be an experience which is "a mere flitting of meaningless presentations." [1] If we all have such an experience, no induction will be true, because our concepts will denote a null class of things.

At this point, we may compare Lewis's "*a priori* analytical" argument for the validity of induction and empirical generalization with Peirce's argument for the *a priori* impossibility of conceiving of a chance-world. We may note first that, for Peirce, the notion of a chance-world is self-contradictory in a logical sense, but for Lewis, the notion of a chance-world is a notion of a world in which we should not successfully predict existence of anything in experience. Second, Peirce's argument entails the fact that our world must possess some uniformity, and hence the fact that in our world some inductive conclusion could be true. In the case of Lewis's argument, the reason why we cannot conceive of our world as a chance-world is also the reason why we can conceive of our world as one of uniformities, where uniformities are understood as ordered sequences of possible experiences. Lewis explains the procedure how the uniformities of our world result from our application of concepts to experience, whereas Peirce does not. This difference should explain the following difference between Peirce's and Lewis's justifications of induction on *a priori* grounds: Peirce maintains that induction is valid, because there is some uniformity in our world which can be discovered by induction; whereas Lewis maintains that induction is valid, because we can always apply concepts to experience and ascertain the uniformities of our world by knowing the results of application of concepts to experience. Both, however, fail to give good reason for the trustworthiness of induction and empirical generalization, because both fail to establish their intended theses that induction must discover

---

[1] *Mind and the World-Order*, 378.

uniformities in our world and that what induction discovers must be uniformities in our world.

Now a third criticism of Lewis's *"a priori* analytical" argument can be added. Even if we grant that this argument for the general validity of induction and empirical generalization is valid, it is still too general to be satisfactory, The reason is that it does not serve to show how we can give reason for the trustworthiness of any particular empirical generalization.

From the principle that there should be apprehensible things in the presence of any given sense-experience, it does not follow that any particular empirical generalization should be true. In other words, granted that we must have some knowledge of reality, it is still conceivable at the same time that any given particular empirical generalization is false, and that we do not know on what ground we may credibilize a particular empirical generalization. Thus, for example, granted we do have some knowledge of the external world, it is conceivable at the same time that the empirical generalization that all swans are white is false, and that we do not know the ground of its credibility or truth even if it is true or credible. By the same token, granted that some conceptual system must be fit for describing a given collection of sense-experiencies, it is still conceivable at the same time that a given conceptual system is not fit for such a description, and that we may not know (in a good sense of knowing) which particular conceptual system is fit for such a description.

In making the last criticism, we in fact point out two things: first, to say that induction and empirical generalization are generally relevant for determining our knowledge of reality does not provide any specific ground for our credibilizing a given empirical generalization, or for our accepting a given conceptualization of reality. Hence a general justification of induction and empirical generalization does not explain the validity of a given empirical generalization or a given conceptual system. Second, in saying that a particular empirical generalization is credible or that a particular conceptual system is acceptable, we must assume some good ground for our assertion other than the fact that we can always apprehend things and objective facts in the presence of given sense-experiences. But what this good ground is, is not presently clear. This shows that we need some principle or principles which will formulate the general content of this good ground, and hence by which we may explain why a given empirical generalization should be true or rationally credible, or why a conceptual system should be acceptable and rationally credible for describing the real. Part of our criticism of Lewis' "*a priori* analytical" justification of induction and empirical generalization is that no such principle or principles are afforded by his theory. His justification is in this sense too general to be satisfactory.

At this point, we may recall that I have suggested that we have to formulate criteria by which we may determine which inductive conclusions are true and which are false. With these criteria, we can not only ascertain whether or not a given particular inductive conclusion has a good ground, but justify the general trustworthiness of inductive method by saying that the inductive method leads to conclusions which meet these criteria. As these criteria are so formulated that it is contrary to our notion of reasonableness to say that an inductive conclusion satisfies these criteria but is not rationally untrustworthy, to raise the question why induction should be rationally trustworthy would be most improper. As these criteria are not presupposed or entailed by any induction, to justify an inductive conclusion by appeal to these criteria is no trivial justification.

In our concluding remarks for Peirce's non-probabilistic justification of induction, I have suggested that the fair sampling principle, in a proper sense of fairness, should be a good criterion of well-confirmedness, because it should be reasonable or rational to trust an inductive conclusion on the basis of a fair sample in a proper sense of fairness. We may therefore suggest that the fair sampling principle will provide a good ground for the trustworthiness or credibility of a particular empirical generalization or a particular conceptual system: an empirical generalization or a conceptual system is trustworthy or credible (and hence valid) if it is established on the basis of a fair sample (or a set of fair samples) in a proper sense of fairness. In general, the principle for fair sampling can be brought to bear upon any particular empirical generalization, and has a genuine application for determining the validity of a given particular generalization on specific ground. The validity of all particular empirical generalizations could then be conceived as consisting in the truth of the following premises: "This sample A is fair," "This sample B is fair," "This sample C is fair," etc.. Similarly, in order to ascertain the validity of application of a particular concept, or of a particular conceptual system, to experience, we can find fair samples of various kinds as bases for justifying hypothesis, or hypotheses, which the application of a particular conceptual system to experience may entail. How fair samples are to be specified for hypotheses I have indicated also in Chapter VIII, Section 4.

To conclude, we must note that, in spite of our criticisms of Lewis' "*a priori* analytical" justification of induction and empirical generalization, this justification makes one important contribution, when it is viewed in the light of the theoretical analysis which Lewis makes of the nature of our knowledge of reality. We have seen that in arguing against Hume's objection to the validity of induction, Lewis has effectively shown that unless we *a priori* prescribe certain classifications to experience, we would hardly know of which kind of things we are speaking ,when we raise the question as to whether a law is true of experience. The very significance of raising a question or formulating an empirical generalization or a law depends upon the conceptual framework in which the question is raised and in which the empirical generalization is formulated. In this sense, the very possibility of empirical generalization and induction presupposes some given conceptual framework or some given system of classificatory principles. Now what needs to be pointed out is that this fact should provide a reason for the validity of induction and empirical generalization if it is rational to suppose that we will not understand reality without those classificatory principles. The validity of induction and empirical generalization should derive from the fact that they presuppose those principles and are themselves ways to understand experience. The reason why one empirical generalziation should be true, and another should not, should be then that one conforms to a given system of classificatory principles, whereas the other does not.

CHAPTER XIV

NATURE OF PROBABILITY AND RATIONAL CREDIBILITY

1. *General Remarks*

As we have seen, in retort to the other argument of the Humean skeptic, that we have to know for certain that empirical statements must be true in order to validate them, Lewis holds that it is the validity of empirical knowledge as probable judgemnts only which requires to be assured. Since an empirical generalization is subject to tests and revision in the light of further empirical findings, we should hold it not with certainty but with mere probability. Now the question is whether this probability warrants our belief in empirical generalizations or laws. By rejecting our empirical knowledge as invalid because they are not necessarily true, the skeptic may be suggesting, as many other philosophers usually do, that some principle like the principle of the uniformity of nature is requisite for the purpose of validating empirical knowledge. Lewis's answer to this is that no such principle is requisite for that purpose. He argues that no rational proof can establish that empirical knowledge must correspond to objective facts or that predictions must be infallible.

In fact, he suggests that it is unreasonable to require such a proof; it is sufficient for the validity of empirical generalizations that they be probable on grounds which genuinely establish them.

The position which Lewis adopts in *Mind and the World-Order*, regarding probability, though quite imprecise, is sufficiently clear to indicate that probability is a matter of credibility or trustworthiness to be determined and defined relative to empirical grounds. He says:

Now a common supposition seems to be that our knowledge of the law of gravitation is invalid if there are facts of nature which do not conform to the law. But if this is probable knowledge, it is a very simple and obvious fact that its validity does not require such conformity. The judgment "A is B is probable" does not require for its truth that A is B; it requires only that this should be genuinely probable.[1]

Hence Lewis affirms that our judgment "A is B is probable" may be absolutely true, when the judgment "A is B" would be absolutely false. This indicates that when we judge that "A is B" is probable, even though in fact A is not B, our knowledge that A is B is valid. The skeptic, who takes the validity of the judgment "A is B is probable" to consist in the accord between what is probably true and the objective fact, denies this. He therefore requires the truth of the empirical generalization as the ground of our assertion of this empirical generalization. This, according to Lewis, is a mistake resulting from the lack of recognition of the true ground of our empirical cognition. Our empirical generalizations as probable judgments are valid not absolutely, but in relation to given data. He thus concludes that a probable judgment is valid if there is no logical error between the probable judgment and its premises, and hence that

There is no difference in the case of probability inference between validity and truth. Whatever the judgment "A is probably B" asserts is not that A is B or that any other objective state of affairs (except what the premises assert) holds good. It asserts that "A is B" has a certain probability on the basis of certain data. If the data are actual, the probability is "actual"; if the data are merely hypothetical, the assigned probability shares this hypothetical character. But unless there has been logical error, the probable judgment is not only valid but absolutely true. There is no alternative to this account except that probability has no kind of truth, no validity, and no meaning of any sort.[2]

In other words, a probability judgment, according to Lewis, makes explicit the relation of the empirical generalization to the ground of our assertion of it, and does not refer to any objective fact. Though the empirical generalization itself does refer to something which has a temporal spread, the ground of its validity is not what it refers to, but that which makes us assert the empirical generalization as true. In this sense, the probability is indicative of our accepting on appropriate ground an empirical generalization as having an objective reference. Hence a probability judgment is to be recognized and formulated independently of empirical verification. That is to say that a probability judgment is not an empirical statement. At this point, one may raise the question in what sense, or how, empirical generalizations are genuinely probable and we have a reason for their trustworthiness or

[1] C. I. Lewis, *Mind and the World-Order*, 325.
[2] *Ibid.*, 331-332.

credibility relative to their grounds or given data. The answer will be revealed in our discussion of Lewis's "credibility theory of probability" formulated in his book *An Analysis of Knowledge and Valuation*.

In the above-mentioned work, Lewis defines probability in two senses: (1) probability should be understood as rational credibility of an empirical generalization based on appropriate ground, which make the empirical generalization in question rationally credible, and (2) probability should also be understood as a valid estimate of frequency (rational expectation), that is, an estimate of frequency which is made on adequate ground. Lewis arrives at this view as a consequence of his critical examination of the so-called empirical and *a priori* theories of probability. It combines the merits of both, but avoids their difficulties. Thus, it should be helpful to begin our discussion of Lewis's "credibility theory of probability" with an examination of the empirical and *a priori* interpretations of probability.

2. *Empirical Interpretation of Probability*

According to the empirical interpretation of probability, the statement "That p is q is probable to a degree a/b" means that instances of q occur in the class of p with a frequency measured by a/b in the long run of experience. Thus stated, this theory of probability is essentially the same as the empirical view of probability of Peirce's as examined by us in Chapter VI, Section 2. This interpretation of probability finds its use, according to Lewis, when a relative frequency established as holding in past experience may, with a certain degree of assurance, be extended to the future. On this interpretation, to make a probability statement is equivalent to making a statistical generalization under circumstances which should make the statistical generalization acceptable. For the statement "That p is q is probable to the degree of a/b" is equivalent in its meaning to the empirical statement "There are a/b members in the class of p which have the character q." But Lewis points out that the possibility of making a probability statement in this sense depends upon the following inductive principle: "The incidence of any property in a well-defined class, will be approximately indicative of the incidence of that property amongst instances of that class in general." [3] In the light of this fact, it is obvious that the empirical interpretation of probability will not explain the validity of an induction in terms of a

---

[3] *An analysis of Knowledge and Valuation*, 273.

probability statement, but has to presuppose *it* for *its* justification. In asserting the validity of an induction or a statistical generalization of the inductive rule, we presuppose induction to be valid, and this is a circular argument.

This circular argument is even found in an apparent *a priori* justification of induction, where the empirical frequency theory of probability is introduced in a very subtle way. The *a priori* justification of induction in question is one which takes the logical law of large numbers as an explanation of why our experiences accumulated by sampling a class in a certain respect should approximate to the objective character of the class. "If in fact a class has a certain property in a certain proportion of cases, and we sample the class and collate our findings as to presence and absence of this property, then our cumulative experience 'ought' progressively to approximate to the objective character of the class in the respect examined. *Because there are more samples to be selected which are closely representative of the class as a whole than there are samples which will be less closely representative.*" [4] The statement italicized by me is a formulation of the logical law of large numbers. This law is taken as a reason why we ought gradually approximate the objective composition of a population by continuous sampling. In order to make an inductive inference to a valid conclusion concerning the composition of the population, we have to state a condition or criterion by which we may use the logical law of large numbers as a reason why the given inference must be valid. The condition or criterion suggested by the frequentists for this purpose is this: the probability that an unobserved instance of p will be an instance q is m/n, if and only if the cumulative collation of the findings will show progressively smaller and smaller values of the maximum divergence, i.e., from the mean frequency m/n after later and later points in the series of cumulative frequency ratio are found. [5] This states the requirement for the convergence of the sequences of frequencies. By requiring that the cumulative collation of empirical findings will show progressively smaller and smaller values of the maximum divergence from the mean frequency in later parts of the frequency ratios series, this criterion already presupposes the notion that the series of empirical frequency ratios will approach the given mean frequency m/n as a limit. Thus, this again presupposes an empirical interpretation of probability, for it is the empirical interpretation of probability which requires a defined value

[4] *Ibid.*, 274. (Italics mine).
[5] Cf., *Ibid.*, 275, 276.

of a limit to be approximated in experience by a series of values of frequencies.

If the frequentists reply that to determine the probability of a series, no induction needs to be made, but inquiry must be conducted to find what the limit of the series is, then the most serious objection to this way of determining a limit of a series is that a series of successive empirical frequencies does not necessarily approach a limit, since a limit may not exist. Moreover, no finite process of inquiry will necessarily find the limit even if the limit exists. A series of successive empirical frequencies is not generated by a mathematical rule, but is determined by collated empirical findings. Though we may agree that an empirically determinable series of frequencies may be said to converge to a limit, m/n, provided, indeed, that for later and later points in the series there are smaller and smaller values of the maximum divergence e from the probability m/n determined in past experience, and provided that for every number e, however small, there is one point in the series beyond which the divergence (positive or negative) from m/n of every later number is less than e,[6] we would not, however, predict with certainty from observation up to a point that for later and later points in the series there are smaller and smaller values of the maximum divergence from the mean frequency so far known, nor could we know with certainty that for every number e, however small, there is some point in the actual series beyond which the divergence from the mean frequency is less than e. Therefore, we may not even know about the existence of a limit in an empirical sequence. We may indeed say that our predictions are made on the ground that the observed series *seems* to tend to a limit, which we may evaluate in terms of the mean frequency so far known, but not on the ground that we know the limit or the objective frequency of the series in the long run. In short, our predictions are made on the ground of known frequency which is *probably* true of the whole series, and hence is not certain, but merely probable with respect to the given data of the observed sequence. Then, we have the problem of defining the new term "probable" in the statement.

In sum, on the empirical interpretation of probability, as we have seen, a probability statement becomes a statistical generalization whose validity depends upon the very validity of induction. We cannot justify a statistical generalization by finding it true in the long run. Furthermore, for any given series S of empirical frequencies it is conceivable

[6] Cf., *Ibid.*, 276–277.

that S will not converge toward a limit, or that if S will converge toward a limit, it will not converge toward *the* limit which the statistical generalization predicts. Hence, the statistical generalization could be asserted with probability at the most. If we again interpret this probability according to the empirical theory, then, by saying that a given statistical generalization is probable, we make another new statistical generalization, that is, we generalize from the known truth frequency of the given statistical generalization in the long run of experience. And so on *ad infinitum.* "Thus," concludes Lewis justifiably, "when confronted with the general problem of how we are to elicit or express the cognitive status of beliefs which have some justification but less then completely certain, we find that the empirical interpretation of their probability would not provide a solution but only the beginning of a perpetual stutter." [7]

3. *Logical Interpretation of Probability*

To avoid the difficulties which the empirical interpretation of probability entails, we must interpret probability in a different sense when it is used as a rational basis for the validity or rational credibility of empirical generalizations. This different sense of probability, according to Lewis, has been suggested by the logical or *a priori* interpretation of probability.

In the *a priori* interpretation, probability is conceived as a logical and *a priori*-determinable relation between an inductive conclusion and its premises or data. Thus, the logical theorists understand the probability statement "That p is q is probable to a degree a/b" to mean that certain given premises or data "D" warrant our assertion of the proposition "p is q "with a probability a/b which is determinable according to valid or correct rules of propability. Presumably, the valid or correct rules of probability are those from the classical calculus of probability. One of them, according to Lewis, is that of equi-probability. This rule which is the most relevant for defining what a probability is states: "If two alternatives P and Q are symmetrically related to the whole body of the given data, then P and Q are, on these data, equiprobable." [8] This rule says in effect, that if we have no reason for thinking that one given alternative is more acceptable than another, or if we have no more reason for thinking that one given alternative is accepta-

[7] *Ibid.,* 289.
[8] *Ibid.,* 266.

ble than we do for other alternatives, then these alternatives are equally acceptable.[9]

Traditional probability writers such as Laplace, Quetelet and Boole [10] have taken the above rule of equi-probability as a rule which justifies a cognitive claim such as "There is a probability of one-half that the tide will rise tomorrow," on the ground of ignorance or indifference as expressed by the statement "There is no reason whatsoever either to suppose that the tide will not rise tomorrow or to suppose that it will." In agreement with the empirical frequencists, Lewis does not think that this rule of equi-probability enables us to decide a probability from mere ignorance. He correctly observes that this rule has no actual application in such a way. That is, in no case of attributing a probability to a statement do we proceed from the principle of ignorance or indifference. Thus, we should never in practice make a statement that there is a probability one-half that the tide will rise tomorrow, simply, on the ground that we know nothing about the tide. If we do not know anything about the tide, we can conclude no probability at all. But since we do know something about the tide, and we have stronger reason to suppose that it will rise tomorrow than to suppose that it will not, we can make a probability judgment concerning the rise of the tide tomorrow in accordance with our knowledge about it.

Lewis further points out that it is a mistake to assume that, because we could not determine equi-probability on the ground of ignorance or indifference, we could not establish equi-probability at all. In fact, if past experience has indicated that there were equal frequencies of a set of events, then we can always determine equi-probabilities of this set of events on the basis of the past experience. In connection with Peirce's criticism of this rule in Chapter VI, Section 3, I have shown that Lewis makes the following point: Peirce's criticism slayed only a straw man, for he was mistaken in assuming that we may make any probability judgment concerning an event without having some knowledge, direct or indirect, about the event. In practice, we cannot determine probability or equi-probability on the ground of "pure and simple" ignorance. We always know something about our experience, and our

[9] Here I have adopted a liberal interpretation of this well-known principle of indifference, and interpret equal probability in terms of equal acceptability of alternatives which indicates that if we are required to bet on equal alternatives, we shall be willing to bet on one alternative as well as on another.

[10] For a brief statement of the classical view of probability, see Ernest Nagel, *Principles of the Theory of Probability*, Vol. I, No. 6, of *International Encyclopedia of Unified Science*, 1957, 44–48.

past experience always affords us clues as to how events are to be classi-fied, as well as how their probabilities are to be evaluated according to known acceptable criteria on the basis of empirical frequencies.

Besides taking the rule of equi-probability (interpreted as a rule of ignorance or indifference) as a valid rule for determining a probability, the classical *a priori* theory of probability, according to Lewis, holds the following thesis: Probability is a kind of logical and *a priori*-deter-minable relation between what is judged probable and the data or premises on which the judgment is made. For example, if the statement that the sun will rise tomorrow is judged probable, then we must by holding or asserting this statement refer to some given data (e.g. those concerning the fact that the sun has risen in the past), on the basis of which, the statement in question can be judged probable according to valid or correct rules of probable inference.[11] In this manner, a proba-bility statement is always a statement which formulates an inductive conclusion in relation to certain given data, the validity or credibility of this relation being warranted by a probability rule. Thus, according to the *a priori* theory, to prove the validity of induction is to prove that the inference of a probable conclusion from certain given data accords with a valid rule of probability, a rule which warrants our assertion that there is a logical and *a priori*-determinable relation between the con-clusion and the data of the inference.

Just how the classical probability writers formulate and justify their rules of probability is an open question. It is a further open question as to how Lewis would formulate and justify these rules himself, as he has not given any indication on this matter. But insofar as we accept the logical interpretation of probability given in the above form, we may conclude that to say that induction is a probable inference or to state an inductive conclusion in relation to its given data need not presup-pose the validity of the induction itself. We may say that the validity of the induction consists only in the probability of its conclusion, which is expressed by the logical and *a priori* -determinable relation between the conclusion and the given data or premises, according to valid rules of probability.

---

[11] In this case, we have the famous Laplacian rule of succession, which states that given an event which has taken place m times in n observations, the probability that in next observation the event will take place is m + 1/n + 2.

4. *Rational Credibility, Fair Sampling and Logical Probability*

Lewis agrees with the logical theories of probability in considering a probability statement as capable of expressing a logical and *a priori*-determinable relation between an inductive conclusion and the ground or data on which it is asserted. But, as we have seen, he objects to the assumption of the logical theorists that ignorance or indifference is a valid ground for determining the probability of an event. To the extent that Lewis takes past frequency as a valid induction of a probability, Lewis also agrees with the empirical frequentists, who assess probability on the basis of induction. The position which Lewis adopts for his own thus combines the ideas of both the empirical and logical theories. It is this: probability is to be determined on the basis of known frequency from past experience, but only on appropriate ground in relation to which the known frequency may be said to stand in a logical and *a priori*-determinable relation according to valid rules of probability. In other words, the assertion of the frequency a/b of a character p with respect to another character q holds if and only if the given ground or data make rationally credible the claim that the frequency is indeed a/b. The rational credibility of such a claim indicates that there is an appropriate ground to which the given frequency stands in a logical or *a priori*-determinable relation. Every probability expressed as a frequency must refer to some such ground which makes it rationally credible that the frequency represents an objective composition ratio of the population.

It is by way of the above that Lewis comes to define probability as a valid estimate of frequency from the given data. He says, "That a given instance of ψ will be an instance of φ, is to be determined as probable in the degree a/b when and only when the frequency of instances of φ amongst instances of ψ is validly estimated as a/b from the given data." [12] To say that the frequency is validly estimated from the given data is to say that it is established with rational credibility from the given data. The validity of the estimate of frequency is a rational credibility which is determinable relatively to the ground or data of the given frequency.

It is clear then that only when an empirical frequency is an estimate or evaluation of some unknown objective frequency based on some ground adequate for making the estimate or evaluation a rationally

---

[12] *An Analysis of Knowledge and Valuation*, 291.

credible one, is the frequency definable as the probability of a singular statement of the form "A given instance of ψ will be an instance of ϕ." Thus, if a statistical generalization of the form "m/n ψ's are ϕ's" is asserted on some appropriate ground D, we may define m/n as the probability of the singular statement that a given instance of ψ will be an instance of ϕ, relative to the given appropriate ground D. The following quotations from Lewis will justify and illustrate what we have said about Lewis's notion of the logical relation between an estimate of a frequency and the ground which makes the estimate rationally credible and valid in this sense:

When we judge the probability that an instance of ψ will be an instance of ϕ to be measured by the fraction a/b, we justifiably do so only on some ground which indicates that the frequency of instances of ϕ amongst instances of ψ is also measured by a/b ... what it (this) suggests is that the probability in question holds if and only if the *given ground of judgment makes it probable – credible, rational to believe* – that the frequency of instance of ϕ amongst instances of ψ is a/b.[13]

The only possible kind of account which can apply to the cognitive status of less than certain empirical beliefs which nevertheless have a warrant or justification, is one which will identify such probability with some fact which is knowable *a priori* when the data on which it is to be judged are given. Rational credibility of belief can, in the nature of the case, depend on nothing more than the supporting premises of what is believed and some relationship of it to these premises which is of the general type of logical relations.[14]

If we are to say that the probability that an instance of ψ will be an instance of ϕ is a/b when and only when the frequency of ψ instances of ϕ amongst instances of ψ is validly estimated as a/b from the given data, then we must observe that this estimate of the frequency is itself no more than rationally credible, and that the degree of its credibility (the probability that the actual frequency coincides with the estimate) is *not* the probability, a/b, that an instance of ψ will be an instance of ϕ. This degree of reasonable assurance that the frequency is as estimated from the data given, is one aspect of what we may call the reliability of the probability determination.[15]

In brief, to say that an estimate of frequency is valid is to say that it is concluded from proper data or premises, and hence is rationally credible or reliable or trustworthy. A full statement of a valid estimate of frequency then takes the following form: "The frequency of instances of ϕ amongst instances of the property ψ is validly estimated from the data D, as a/b." [16] By calling an estimate of frequency an "expectation" or "rational expectation" and by explaining its validity in terms

---

[13] *Ibid.*, 289.
[14] *Ibid.*, 290.
[15] *Ibid.*, 292.
[16] *Ibid.*, 296.

of credibility, Lewis comes to reformulate a probability statement in the following form: "That c, having property ψ, will also have the property ϕ, is credible on data D, with expectation a/b, and reliability (or credibility) R." [17] Since the "expectation" is obviously a statistical generalization from a known empirical frequency, we may also formulate the above statement in the following form: "The statistical generalization that the instances of ϕ have a frequency a/b among instances of ψ, is credible or reliable to the degree R on the data D." In this way, it is obvious that the validity of induction can be seen in general to consist in a credibility relation between a statistical generalization and the data upon which it is asserted as credible.

Put in the above form, the credibility statement closely resembles a probability statement in the logical theory: "That a p is q is probable on data D." Probability in the logical theory of probability, as we have seen, is to be determined according to valid rules. But we have seen also that it remains an open question as to what these valid rules are. This is also an open question with regard to determining a credibility relation between a statistical generalization and its appropriate ground in Lewis's credibility interpretation of probability. We may ask what argument we can summon for showing that the relation between a valid or credivble estimate of frequency and its appropriate ground is a logical and a *priori*-determinable one. Lewis's discussion of the conception of probability in terms of rational credibility gives no hint on this matter. At this point, I suggest again that Peirce's argument for the validity of probable inference from fair samples is of help. This will be shown in the following.

We may take a known empirical frequency in a finite sequence S as the composition with respect to a property of a chosen sample and take the objective frequency in a sequence of which S is a proper part as the composition of a population with respect to the given property. Then a statistical generalization or an estimate of frequency on the basis of a known empirical frequency may be considered to be an inference from a sample, and a valid statistical generalization or a valid estimate of frequency may be considered to be an inference from a fair sample. Insofar as the data upon which a valid estimate or statistical generalization is asserted constitute a fair sample in the proper sense, the relation between the valid estimate of frequency and the data must be a logical and *a priori*-determinable one, in the sense that the assertion of

17 *Ibid.*, 305; Cf. also 296.

the estimate upon the given data is based on a logical inference of a conclusion about the composition of population from a fair sample, in accordance with the logical law of large numbers. Thus, to prove or show that there is indeed a logical and *a priori*-determinable relation between a valid statistical generalization and its data, we may construe Lewis's meaning of "credibility" according to what we have shown in connection with Peirce's probabilistic argument for the validity of induction in Chapter IV.

The correspondence between logical probability and credibility can then be seen as follows:

(1) An estimate of frequency is credible on appropriate grounds.

(2) An estimate of frequency is logically probable on the basis of a fair sample.

(1) expresses the validity of an induction in terms of rational credibility based on some appropriate ground without giving us any idea as to how an inductive conclusion is related to its premises or data. (2), on the other hand, indicates that, insofar as a "logical probability" is understood in the Laplacian sense, and insofar as a fair sample is understood in the proper sense, the estimate of frequency as an inductive conclusion is logically related to its appropriate ground which is construed as a fair sample. In this sense, we may say that "credibility" in (1) is an explicandum explicated by the explicans "logical probability" in (2).

However, to say that "credibility" in (1) is an explicandum explicated by the explicans "logical probability" in (2) does not imply that all the meanings or senses of the term "credibility" are explained by the term "logical probability." It only implies that some important meaning of "credibility" is explained by the term "logical probability." This important meaning is this: to say that an estimate of a frequency is valid or credible is to say that the estimate is logically probable on the given ground which constitutes a fair sample. The important problem of validating an estimate of frequency becomes one of showing whether its ground or data constitute a fair sample. The criteria for determining fairness of samples therefore *a fortiori* constitute those for determining the credibilities of the estimates of frequencies for various inductive problems, which require estimates of frequencies to be made upon given or discoverable experience. Thus, insofar as a sample is fair, an estimate of frequency is logically probable; insofar as a fair sample constitutes an appropriate ground for making an estimate of frequency, it follows, the estimate of frequency is rationally credible. The whole problem of justifying induction could be said to be thus reducible to that of formulating adequate criteria for determining fair samples, and for determining the credibilities of the estimates of frequencies of various kinds.

CHAPTER XV

CRITERIA FOR DETERMINING RATIONAL CREDIBILITY

I. *Questions Regarding Criteria for Determining Rational Credibility*

Even when any credible empirical generalization can be construed as established on the basis of a fair sample, and the credibility of this generalization is, in this sense, explicated by the logical probability of the inference from a fair sample, it still remains a question as to how credibility for specific empirical generalizations is to be determined. This question can be put in a different manner: we want to know what constitute the specific criteria for determining the credibility of a given or supposed empirical generalization.

This question can be similarly raised in the determination of the fairness of the samples on which a logical probability can be asserted. As can be seen in Chapter V, Section 3, we require a fair sample to be one which we do not know to be objectively unrepresentative. But, again, this only constitutes a general principle by which the validity of induction as a probable inference can be explained; it does not tell us how we may determine the fairness of samples in practice. To determine the fairness of samples in actual cases, we need specific criteria. Whether a given or a supposed sample is not known to be objectively unrepresentative is a decision which we have to make by virtue of the criteria relevant for determining the fairness of that given or supposed sample. Similarly, whether a given or supposed empirical generalization is acceptable or rationally credible is a decision which we have to make by virtue of the criteria relevant for determining the rational credibility of that given or supposed empirical generalization.

It should be noted that the question of what those specific criteria are cannot be answered by explaining the meaning of rational credibility, just as the question of what the criteria for determining fair samples are cannot be answered by explaining the meaning of a fair sample. For it is those criteria, not the explanation of the meaning in question, that we may use for determining the credibility of a given or supposed empirical generalization. It is also those criteria that we may adopt as regulative principles in an inquiry for credible empirical generalizations on the basis of fair samples.

2. *Degrees of Rational Credibility and Criteria for Determining Them*

Lewis asserts that there are degrees of credibility in terms of "more or less," and suggests three important specific criteria for determining them. In asserting that there are comparative degrees of credibility, Lewis says, "Although reliability (or credibility) cannot commonly be gauged in a manner making it approximately representable by a fraction, still it is plainly a matter of more or less, and hence of degree; and for convenience we may speak of reliability as the reliability coefficient." [1] In this sense, degrees of credibility are comparative, not quantitative, i.e., the credibility of an empirical generalization can be compared with that of another, or with that of the same empirical generalization on a different basis, but cannot be determined precisely in numerical terms.[2]

One justification for the recognition of various comparative degrees of credibility in common usage is this: "Different data for judging probability of the same quasitum – giving different assessments for the same problem – could be ranked in some order of their relative satisfactoriness as a basis of judgment, if one is practically to depend on the probability judgment made." [3] In other words, the credibility of an empirical generalization can be evaluated and determined in relation to different data, or data which differ in various respects essential to the specification of the credibility of an empirical generalization, and which can be ranked in some order of their relative satisfactoriness as a basis of judging the credibility of the given empirical generalization. How we are to establish the relative satisfactoriness or trustworthiness of

---

[1] C. I. Lewis, *An Analysis of Knowledge and Valuation*, 296.

[2] Evidently, what Lewis calls degrees of credibility are also what we call degrees of probability, which empirical generalizations may have upon confirmation or disconfirmation. See *An Analysis of Knowledges and Valuation*, 237 ff. He claims that, in the case for determining degrees of probability, no probability formulas allow numerically precise statement of probability, nor common use requires them. This is not quite true, at least when we recall that the logical probability which we lay down for a probabilistic justification of induction as a probable inference is numerically precise, although it is very often associated with a margin of error, the so-called standard deviation.

[3] *Ibid.*, 293.

different data depends again upon how we formulate the specific criteria for determining the credibility of the given empirical generalization on the basis of those data.

Now Lewis suggests three important specific criteria for determining comparative degrees of credibility. They arise from considerations of "the adequacy or inadequacy," "the proximateness or remoteness," and "the uniformity or disuniformity," of the data. By the "adequacy" of the data, Lewis means the extensiveness of past experience collated with respect to the frequency to be estimated; by the "inadequacy" of the data, the meagerness of our past experience collated with respect to the frequency to be estimated. If a set of given data is adequate in this sense, the estimate of frequency based on it will be in that respect credible; if, on the other hand, a set of given data is inadequate in the above sense, then the estimate of frequency based on it will be in that respect incredible. If one set of data is more extensive than another set, then the assessment of relative frequency in the first set is more credible than that in the second. Thus, we may say that Lewis has recognized one valid rule or criterion for determining the comparative degrees of credibility of an estimate of frequency or an empirical generalization. It is this: *Additional data which are pertinent to determining the estimate of frequency in question will always increase a given degree of credibility of the estimate of frequency or empirical generalization.* In other words, this rule or criterion says, *If the given data are adequate, an estimate upon the given data is credible, and is credible to a degree in proportion to the degree the given data are said to be adequate.*

By the "approximateness" of the data, Lewis means the degree of resemblance or closeness of the analogy between the data and a case relevant to the inductive problem in question. More generally speaking, it means the pertinence in respect of known specific properties whose presence or absence may affect the occurrence of instances of a quasi-tum property in a given class. Considerations of this sort are relevant for defining degrees of credibility, because to make an estimate of frequency in any given problem, we have to choose a reference class to which a given case belongs. The reference class may be similar to the case under consideration with respect to known specific properties in various degrees, more or less. If the reference class is distantly similar to the case under consideration, the estimate of frequency in the chosen reference class would generally be less credible than if the reference class were closely similsar to the case. As a particular case may have various reference classes, all these reference classes can be ranked in some order according to the relative similarity between each reference class and the given case with respect to some specific known properties.

It is usually admittedly very difficult to choose a reference class of a specific case as *the* reference class of it, in order that the estimate of frequency made with respect to this reference class may be credibly applied to define the expectation of the given case. Because, as Lewis recognizes, "Any assessment of the expectation coefficient for any problem in hand must encounter the hazard of estimating a frequency in the reference class as a whole from the given data, and the further hazard of applying this estimated frequency to an instance or instances which may differ from those of the reference class in general in ways which affect occurrence of the quasitum property." [4] From this statement, it is clear that the problem of measuring the approximateness or similarity involves two separate questions. First, how close is the similarity between the observed instances, which constitute our given data, and the members of a chosen reference class as a whole? Second, how closely similar are members of a chosen references class to the instance or instances of a prediction in general? For illustration, in assessing the frequency of throwing heads by a given penny, throws of the given penny will be closely proximate to a specified throw of the given penny in the future; throws of a different penny made in the same year as the given one will be less proximate, because that penny may lack some particular character or property which the given penny has; similarly, throws of pennies in general will be further less proximate, and throws of coins of the same size still further; while throws by coins in general will be comparatively the least proximate to a specified throw of the given penny in the future, since the former may include throws of a dime, a quarter, and so on, which may have properties quite different from those of the given penny, properties which may affect the outcome of the throws. It is thus that Lewis thinks that there are degrees of proximateness for different reference classes of a given case whose expectation we have to determine on the basis of an estimate of the frequency in a reference class.

What Lewis calls the "remoteness" of the data denotes the lack of "proximateness" of the data and could be explained in a manner similar to the above. Implicit in this meaning of proximateness or remoteness is another rule or criterion for determining the comparative degrees of credibility of an estimate of frequency. This rule or criterion

---

[4] *Ibid.*, 298.

can be briefly stated as follows: *The more similar the given data are to the case under consideration, the more credible the estimate of frequency based on the data is.*

That aspect of the data which Lewis calls "uniformity" or "disuniformity" concerns the sameness of the frequency of the quasitum property in all properly chosen subsets of the instances of the reference class. But what is a properly chosen subset? According to Lewis, it is one which is "taken in any manner not antecedently likely to affect the frequency found." [5] Precisely speaking, it should be one which is taken in a way antecedently *not known* likely to affect the frequency found. It is, in this sense, a fair sample.

According to Lewis, there are comparative degrees of uniformity, which are to be determined in the following manner. "If the frequency of the quasitum property, amongst examined instances of the reference property, be m/n, then the data are more uniform according to the frequency found, for subsets of instances, shows a divergence, e, from m/n, which is more closely the same, and according as the mean value of e is smaller." [6] The question is then: How do the degrees of uniformity affect the credibility of an estimate of frequency? The answer is that if the reference class is uniform, then we should be assured of the validity in arguing from the frequency of one subset of the reference class to that of another; if the reference class is discuniform, then we should not be thus assured. If a given refernce class is more uniform than another, then we should be more assured of the validity in an estimate based on the frequency of the first reference class than in an estimate based on the frequency of the other. In this way, Lewis may be said to arrive at a third rule or criterion for determining comparative degrees of credibility of an estimate of frequency: *the more uniform the given data with respect to a frequency in it is, the more credible the estimate of the frequency based on the given data is.*

We have thus shown that Lewis has arrived at three rules or criteria for determining comparative degrees of credibility of an estimate of frequency. These three rules or criteria are those for determining comparative degrees of the fairness of samples, insofar as degrees of credibility correspond to degrees of the fairness of samples on which they are asserted. But how these rules or criteria should combine to determine a comparative degree of credibility of a given estimate of frequency in reference to some given data is a problem which we do not intend

[5] *Ibid.*, 300.
[6] *Ibid.*, 300.

to discuss here. Indeed, Lewis himself does not indicate how one should weigh the relative importance of these rules or criteria for determining a comparative degree of credibility.[7] All that he points out is that these three rules are relevant to the determining of a comparative degree of credibility. This should give us a reason for regarding them as rules or criteria which are merely necessary but not sufficient for determining comparative degrees of credibility. In fact, as we may simply note here, more specific criteria or rules for determining comparative degrees of credibility or credibility in general must be formulated relative to considerations of the individual nature of the problem in question, the particular knowledge we have concerning it, and the purpose we want to serve when we establish an empirical generalization as rationally credible. We may formulate our rules or criteria on the basis of empirical findings by inquiry. As a matter of fact, with respect to each inductive problem on hand, experience and our background knowledge will show, or have shown how, and to what extent, these three rules or criteria, as given by Lewis, will affect our determination of comparative degrees of credibility.

3. *Justifying Acceptance of Criteria for Determining Rational Credibility*

In suggesting the above criteria for determining comparative degrees of credibility, Lewis also exposes the principle which we try to conform to when actually making an inductive conclusion. For, in making an inductive conclusion, we normally prefer a large sample, and normally prefer a reference population as pertinent as possible to our inductive problem. We also require our sample to be chosen in a way which is not known to affect the known frequency. When we have taken a sample from a reference population in this way, our conclusion based on this sample will receive a higher degree of credibility than that based on a sample which is not chosen in this way. In brief, we

---

[7] I may perhaps indicate here how we *in practice* weigh the relative importance of these rules or criteria for determining a credible empirical generalization. We first make certain that our samples are sufficiently pertinent to a well-defined population. Next, we make certain that our samples are sufficiently uniform by utilizing sampling techniques warranted by our background knowledge. Finally, we make certain that our samples are sufficiently large in number or adequate. When samples are thus collated, they should be considered *fair*. By this procedure for fair sampling, it is clear that the criteria of adequacy, pertinence, and uniformity are equally important, and we may further guess that lack of conformity to any one of these criteria should leave our empirical generalizations based on collated samples unwarranted.

normally want our sample to be as fair as possible, fair in the sense of being large, being most pertinent to the inductive problem in question, and being chosen in a proper way. At this point, one may raise the question as to how our acceptance of the criteria or principles is itself justified. That is, we certainly depend upon these criteria for determining degrees of credibility, but we want to know on what ground, and for what reason they can be held as criteria or principles for determining degrees of credibility.

It is certainly useless to suggest that our acceptance of the criteria in question are inductively justified, i.e., they are accepted as criteria for determining degrees of credibility, because they have been so accepted in the past. This justification not only presupposes the validity of induction, but also leaves open the question as to how, if they have been accepted in the past, they should be held as valid for determining degrees of credibility.

One may nevertheless suggest that those criteria are formulations of practical policies or methods, which, when followed in inductive reasoning, will lead to truth or success in a given case. This way of justifying our acceptance of them will be valid only if we know either with certainty or with probability that, as such, they do lead us to truth or success in a given case. For example, if we do know either with certainty or with probability that the criterion of collecting large samples will lead us to discovering the objective frequency in a given case, then we have reason for saying that this criterion is an acceptable one. But we may recall that this way of justifying our acceptance of a criterion is similar to the way in which Peirce seeks to justify induction by characterizing it as self-correcting and truth-producing. If so, we cannot escape our criticism of Peirce's proposal and Lewis' own criticism of the empirical theory of probability. We have no certain knowledge that any one of those criteria will not in the next step lead to some error and ultimate failure in the long run. If we say that we have such knowledge without certainty but with probability, and if the term "probability" is not used in an empirical sense but in a logical sense, that is, not as a known empirical frequency from induction, but as a logical probability relation of our knowledge to the given data, we shall come back to the original position of Lewis: the validity of induction and empirical generalization is to be explained in terms of probability or credibility in a logical sense. This still leaves open the question as to how our acceptance of criteria for determining degrees of probability or credibility is justified.

In full awareness of the difficulty of justifying our acceptance of those criteria either from an inductive or from a practical point of view, it may be well to suggest that to justify our acceptance of those criteria is to recognize that they are essential for explaining the reasonableness of our belief in the inductive conclusions which satisfy them, and that they are essential for explaining why we attach pragmatical value to the prediction and guidance of action afforded by inductive conclusions which satisfy them. *For it is a fact that we do find it reasonable to accept an empirical belief which is credible according to those criteria. It is also a fact that we find it more reasonable to accept an empirical belief which has a greater degree of credibility according to those criteria than to accept one which has a lower degree of credibility according to the same criteria. Furthermore, we do in fact find pragmatical value in the prediction and guidance of action afforded by inductive conclusions which are credible according to those criteria. Moreover, it is a fact that we find more pragmatical value in the prediction and guidance of action afforded by inductive conclusions which have higher degrees of credibility according to those criteria than in the prediction and guidance of action afforded by inductive conclusions which have lower degrees of credibility according to the same criteria.*

In brief, the justification of our acceptance of those criteria for determining degrees of credibility lies in the following two principles: (1) it should be reasonable to accept them, and (2) they should be definitive of our notion of the validity or rational credibility or trustworthiness of inductive conclusions. In other words, what we should emphasize is that those specific criteria or rules are definitive and regulative in character. They are definitive in the sense that they define what are good evidences and what are not for various kinds of inductive conclusions. In this sense, they prescribe adequate bases for drawing trustworthy inductive conclusions. They are in this sense necessary for stating the rational basis of our inductions and relevant for explaining the rational credibility of induction. They are regulative in the sense that they are standards with which we should choose our samples for making various inductive conclusions in accordance. In other words, they are ideal principles which guide our inquiry for adequate evidences for making inductive conclusions of various kinds. They do not guarantee that inductions according to them must succeed, just as our general criterion for determining a fair sample does not guarantee that a fair sample must represent the population. They are simply needed as both analytical and practical principles for the purposes of making clear what constitutes a trustworthy inductive conclusion and how we may decide one. If one queries *why we are reasonable* in the sense of accepting those criteria, we can only answer that it is a basic feature of human nature that we are reasonable in that sense. If one queries *why we should be reasonable,* we can only answer that this is like asking why we should be what we should be: and we do not know what kind of an answer we are expected to make.

In making the above justification of our acceptance of those criteria for determining degrees of credibility, we do not imply that those criteria are not formulated in the light of past experience or empirical findings. In fact, they are formulated in the light of past experience and empirical findings. But the problem of the validity of those criteria is a distinct one from the problem of the origin of their formulation, just as the problem of the validity of the Euclidean geometry is distinct from the problem of its origin in the practice of land-measuring.

CHAPTER XVI

CONCLUSION

I shall conclude by way of bringing out important points of similarity between Peirce's and Lewis's theories of induction, discussing briefly the significances of Peirce's and Lewis's arguments in their theories of induction, suggesting the framework for a comprehensive theory of justifying induction, and finally, exhibiting the relevant bearings of this theory upon the contemporary efforts to justify induction as indicated in the Introduction.

1. Similarity Between Peirce's and Lewis's Theories of Induction

In our examination of both Peirce's and Lewis's theories of induction, we have seen that induction and empirical generalization, if properly understood as probable inferences, are valid in the sense that they follow or conform to some logical leading principle, and that there is a probability connection between their premises and their conclusions. This is a probabilistic justification of induction. Furthermore, we have seen that induction and empirical generalization are valid in another sense: they are essential for our understanding experience and having knowledge of reality, and there would be self-contradiction in maintaining that no inductive conclusion or empirical generalization is true when the assertion itself can only be justified as an inductive conclusion or an empirical generalization. This is a non-probabilistic justification of induction. That both Peirce's and Lewis' theories of induction can be formulated in terms of these two types of justification of induction will be briefly reviewed.

In the case of Peirce, his argument for the validity of probable inference from fair samples is an attempt to make induction a valid logical inference, an inference which is conducted according to a logical leading principle. The validity of his argument depends upon his interpretation of a fair sample. A fair sample, according to him, is one which is chosen according to a method which would lead us to obtain samples of the population with equal frequency in the long run. But, I have argued that either no such method can be known with certainty, or the existence of such a method must be ascertained on the basis of induction. To justify induction by appealing to such a method, we would assume the validity of induction in the first place, and hence our justification would be circular. In view of this, I have suggested a reformulation of the principle of fair sampling in Chapter V. With this, I conclude that any fair sample would give rise to a well-defined valid probable inference according to a logical principle. Since any conclusion of induction may be said to be rationally credible on the basis of a fair sample which we have accepted as the referent of the inductive premise, I have suggested that a probability connection in the Laplacian sense of probability should be regarded as an explication of our conception for the relation of rational credibility between the inductive conclusion and a given fair sample. I have also suggested that the fair sample should provide a logical reason for our asserting or accepting an inductive conclusion on the strength of the probability of the inference.

In the case of Lewis, considerations of fair sample as a basis for inferring an inductive conclusion or a statistical generalization arise from his criticisms of the empirical theory of probability. Empirical probability is not a criterion for deciding the validity of induction: to say that "P" is probable where "P" is an inductive conclusion or a statistical generalization does not show why "P" is acceptable or why induction by which "P" is concluded is valid, because the statement of probability involved is a statement of fact, our acceptance of which needs justification in the first place. To make probability a criterion for the validity of induction, Lewis suggests that to say that "P" is probable is to say that "P" is rationally credible on the basis of data from which it is concluded. The assertion of a rational credibility or reliability signifies that we have good basis or ground for accepting or believing the conclusion which is said to be rationally credible. Though Lewis does not make it clear enough by what general principle we may distinguish a good ground from a bad one for accepting an inductive conclusion, he nevertheless suggests conditions relevant for determining goodness of the ground for inductive conclusions and hence for determining the rational credibility of them. I have interpreted these conditions as specific criteria for determining comparative degrees of credibility of empirical generalizations or estimates of frequency. The criteria of adequacy, pertinence and uniformity, for example, help us to realize what objective features of sets of data or samples are relevant for determining comparative degrees of credibility of empirical generalizations in specific cases and relative to specific purposes. This approach to the problem of the validity of induction and empirical generalizations should be consistent with, and also supplementary to, the general thesis that a fair sample in a proper sense is a good reason for asserting an empirical generalization or inductive conclusion as probable or credible.[1]

For the justification of our acceptance of criteria for determining credibility of empirical generalizations, it suffices to say first that they can be considered as standards which ought to be conformed to because, first, conclusions based on fair samples in conformity with them should satisfy us in regard to their use in prediction and guidance of action, and second, they can be considered as rational principles in terms of which our conception of rationality of an empirical belief upon a given or supposed set of data or sample should be defined or explained.

Now insofar as an inductive conclusion is credible upon the basis of a fair sample according to specific criteria, the credibility relation of the conclusion to its premises – the given fair sample – is also a logical relation of probability between the conclusion and the premises, according to Peirce's probabilistic justification of induction. Insofar as Lewis asserts that there is a logical and *a priori*-determinable relation between an inductive conclusion and its data, and insofar as he fails to make clear what this relation is, Peirce's probabilistic justification of induction supplies a theoretical (basis for) explanation of Lewis' assertion, and should in this sense complement Lewis' theory of probabilistic justification of induction.

Lewis's and Peirce's non-probabilistic justifications of induction are also closely related to each other, even more closely related than their probabilistic justifications of induction. As we have seen, Peirce has suggested four arguments for the validity of induction in a non-probabilistic fashion. His first argument consists in showing that induction as a method must lead to truth in the long run in a self-correcting process. His second and third arguments point out that our world must

---

[1] In a sense, those specific criteria, suggested by Lewis, are also general in character, because more specific criteria could be always formulated upon considerations of the nature of each specific inductive problem and the nature of the purpose which we want to serve in solving a specific inductive problem.

be real and hence must possess uniformities so that the method of induction can be used to discover them. His final argument consists in demonstrating that induction is always possible, given some experience. I have clarified and criticized these arguments, and have shown them to contain essentially the point that we can know the real by an inductive process and it is inconceivable that we cannot know the real by induction.

In discussing Lewis's so-called "*a priori*" analytical justification of induction, I have shown that Lewis argued as follows. First, criteria for determining the validity of empirical generalization and induction should coincide with those for determining the real, i.e., the real should be only known by a valid empirical generalization. But this argument again has only shown how the real should be related to valid induction without indicating whether or not induction does *actually* lead to genuine knowledge of the real. Then, Lewis shows that the principles upon which the possibility of our empirical knowledge relies are those which also guarantee or govern the possibility of induction and empirical generalization. Thus, Lewis asserts that we can know reality, because to deny this is to affirm that nothing exists. Finally, Lewis argues that it is impossible that we could conceive that nothing exists. By these arguments, he intends to establish that we can always learn the real because we can always apply concepts to given experience. Insofar as this is true, induction cannot be a failure in general, i.e., some true empirical generalization should be made in any conceivable situation in which some experience is given. In this, Lewis asserts, consists the general and ultimate validity of induction and empirical generalization.

In the light of the above, similarity between Peirce's and Lewis's non-probabilistic justifications of induction should be conspicuous. It suffices to emphasize some major points. Both philosophers have accepted induction as a self-correcting process, by which we may always formulate what appears to be the case in terms of some empirical generalization in the light of empirical findings. In considering the self-correcting nature of induction, Peirce indicates that induction will lead to the truth in the long run, whereas Lewis indicates that induction will give us more success than not. Again, both Peirce and Lewis argue that in proving the validity of induction, no material presupposition such as that of the uniformity of nature need be assumed or made. A material presupposition need not be made for proving the validity of induction, for doing this we beg the question. It is true that both Peirce and Lewis indicate the theoretical indispensability of some uniformity in any real world in their non-probabilistic justifications on induction. But this should not be taken to imply, as I have pointed out, that a uniformity of some pre-specified description is indispensable. The general indispensability of some uniformity for our knowledge of reality, in other words, does not lead to the necessity of postulating a uniformity of some pre-specified description, as a basis for the validity of induction.

The differences between Peirce's and Lewis's theories of induction are secondary, as we should already note in our discussion of their similar points. But one significant difference perhaps deserves our mention here. Peirce has often emphasized the importance of the future in our attempt to ascertain either a probability or a reality. He has therefore emphasized the importance of the inquiry for reality or truth *in the long run.* This has the happy effect of encouraging us to look for certainty of truth in the future, but it has the unhappy effect of suggesting to us that any given inductive conclusion, which is not known to be true with certainty, is irrational, and could not be accepted on the ground of known experience. In a sense, we may also say that Peirce has often confounded the justification of an empirical truth with the confirmation of it. Lewis, on the other hand, points out that justification and verification are distinct and different procedures for validating empirical truth.[2] To inquire in the future for truth or certainty is what counts as a procedure of confirmation, but what we have accepted or believed cannot be merely ascertained by finding whether it is true or not, with certainty, this being often impossible to do, but by finding out whether it is rationally supported or not. This means that what we have accepted or believed as true are indeed trustworthy if they are well-supported and therefore are in this sense rationally justified. This is a procedure of justification. In emphasizing the importance of warranted credibility as a basis for the validity of induction and empirical generalization, Lewis has shown himself in this respect closer to John Dewey regarding the latter's theory of "warranted assertibility" than Peirce.[3] It is due to this consideration that Lewis adopts a radically different interpretation of probability than what Peirce in his later days would profess to accept.

---

[2] Lewis says, "The validation of empirical belief has two dimensions or directions of its import, its verification and its justification; the determination of it as true and the determination of it as rationally credible. Cognitive evaluation of our assertion, or an assertive state of mind looks to the truth of what is asserted, but also it looks to the warrant or ground of the belief." *An Analysis of Knowledge and Valuation,* 254.

[3] Cf. John Dewey, *Logic, The Theory of Inquiry,* New York, 1938, 154, 172, 195, 262, 329.

2. *Significances of Peirce's and Lewis's Arguments*

One implication of Peirce's and Lewis's arguments for the validity of induction is quite clear: It effectively forestalls the epistemological skepticism inspired by Hume. The Humean skeptic points out that since induction as an inference is not logically warranted, empirical knowledge by induction cannot be rationally credible. He further contends that it is conceivable that all our empirical generalizations are false and characterize no reality. In the face of these Humean challenges, Peirce's and Lewis's arguments for the validity of induction stand out as well-coordinated answers. For we can see that their probabilistic arguments demonstrate the logicality of the inductive inference and their non-probabilistic arguments repudiates the myth that we can conceive that all our empirical generalizations are false and characterize no reality.

The mutual complementariness of the probabilistic and nonprobabilistic arguments in forestalling the skeptical position perhaps need a little elaboration. If we have only the probabilistic argument, the skeptic might grant that induction is a logically valid form of inference if properly understood, but nevertheless points out that there is no guarantee that this form of inference must lead to true conclusions about our world or about any real world, i.e., it does not have application in our world or in any real world. At this point, we have to introduce the non-probabilistic arguments which assure us that it is rationally incredible to believe that no induction leads to truth in a real world and that a real world admits no truth-producing induction. On the other hand, if we have only the non-probabilistic arguments, the skeptic may very well withdraw his doubts concerning how induction leads to conclusions which it is rational for us to accept as knowledge of reality, but insist that it is not clear why induction should be regarded as a logically valid form of inference, instead as a psychological habit not to be explained by reason or logic. This objection however can be answered by the probabilistic arguments which exhibits the logical relationship between the premises and the conclusion in an inductive inference.

In summary, the probabilistic and the non-probabilistic arguments of Peirce and Lewis exhibits the fact that induction is a valid form of inference governed by probability rules and is trustworthy as a method for pursuing knowledge as knowledge ought to be. They provide respectively the logical and metalogical grounds for induction, which should at the same time constitute general good reasons for our applying inductive inference and accepting their conclusions.

3. Toward a Comprehensive Theory of Justifying Induction

Lest we are led to think under the above favorable considerations that Peirce's and Lewis's arguments for the validity of induction cover every aspect of the problem of justifying induction, we must recognize their limitations. Among other things, Peirce and Lewis failed to draw a clear distinction between the levels of justification of induction. I shall presently explain what such a distinction is and how it is important for developing a comprehensive theory of justifying induction.

Granted the framework of Peirce's and Lewis's probabilistic and non-probabilistic arguments, we have shown that we can repudiate the skeptical position. But the answers to the skeptical questions are *general* answers as the skeptical questions are *general* questions.[4] Nothing prevents the skeptic from raising questions about the specific rational grounds for specific inductive conclusions, and demand specific reasons for accepting specific inductive conclusions for characterizing the real.[5] Answers to these questions should pertain to a justification of induction on a level of specificity. Evidently neither Peirce nor Lewis has concentrated on these questions, the importance of which can scarcely be understated. In the following I shall say a few things about these questions, and then show how a comprehensive theory of justifying induction can be developed on the basis of a distinction between the probabilistic and non-probabilistic arguments on the one hand, and a distinction between the general and specific levels of justification on the other.

Questions concerning grounds of specific inductive conclusions require us to determine specific criteria for ascribing rational credibility

---

[4] The generality of the skeptical questions can be recaptured in the following formulation: If any valid induction is made, what makes it in general valid or rationally credible? Why is any empirical generalization true? Whereas the generality of the answers to these questions can be expressed in the statement that induction is a form of inference capable of logical validation and it is contrary to our notions of rational credibility and reality that empirical generalizations are in general rationally untrustworthy for characterizing the real.

[5] We may consider a specific problem of justifying induction not only as that of ascertaining the rational credibility of specific inductive conclusions in a certain field of inquiry, but as one of ascertaining the rational credibility of a system of specific concepts which is proposed as a systematic interpretation of experiences in a certain area. In this latter case, it is obvious that the specific problem of justifying induction involves not only ascertaining the rational credibility of such a system of specific concepts in relation to experience in the given area, but explaining how this system is superior to other alternative systems under considerations of simplicity and comprehensiveness.

to specific inductive conclusions. Only when these criteria are properly determined, these questions can be adequately answered. To the question concerning a specific reason for accepting a specific inductive conclusion, the answer cannot be the generality that induction must lead to some knowledge of reality. For the generality does not entail that a given specific inductive conclusion must be rationally credible and characterize the real. Rather, the validity or rational credibility of induction in specific cases lies in the fact that it leads to rationally credible characterizations of the real in specific cases on specific grounds. Thus, a specific physical law is rationally credible, not because things in general exist and empirical generalizations are in general rationally credible, but because this very law itself characterizes reality of a specific kind on a specific adequate ground. To ask why we should take this law as rationally credible is to ask why what we should regard as the real on a specific ground should be regarded as the real. Question as such becomes either trivial or serves only the purpose of calling our attention to the fact that things of specific descriptions do exist.

Thus a very important aspect of treating the problem of justifying induction is to clarify and explicate the validity of specific inductive conclusions with reference to specific criteria that will determine specific adequate grounds for specific contents of these conclusions. It is precisely of this aspect that Peirce's and Lewis's theories of induction give little or no discussion. Of course, this cannot be done without a thorough examination of different kinds of specific inductive problems and different kinds of specific purposes which we want to serve by formulating or solving different kinds of specific inductive problems. What we wish to stress here is the importance of the problem for developing a comprehensive theory of induction.

For developing a comprehensive theory of justifying induction, one must take into considerations both the general and the specific problems of justifying induction which may be respectively examined in regard to the agreements of either the probabilistic or the non-probabilistic modes. Justifications on the general and the specific levels do not overlap, because they answer related questions on different levels. Insofar as this is true, they are necessarily complementary to each other in regard to rebuking a thorough-going skeptic.

The very relation of justification levels to the modes of justifying induction, could, perhaps, be exhibited in the following diagram:

level of justification	mode of justification	
	probabilistic	non-probabilistic
general	GP	GN
specific	SP	SN

where the terms "GP," "GN," "SP," and "SN" stand for the statements which indicate how justification of induction is intended or required under the cross headings of "general," "specific," "probabilistic," and "non-probabilistic." In the following I shall explain this and formulate the justification schemata of GP, GN, SP, and SN in the logical symbolism.

The probabilistic justification of induction on the general level (GP) consists in regarding induction as a general probable inference from fair samples to populations. Accordingly, in an inductive inference, if p is an inductive premise about a fair sample of a certain kind, then p is related to the inductive conclusion c in the relation that p highly probabilizes c. For the convenience of formalizing this form of inference, we may assume that existence of a sample always presupposes existence of a population from which the sample is drawn, and therefore that an inductive premise about a sample always entails an inductive conclusion about a population by way of high probabilization. We may further assume the validity of quantification over propositions. These assumptions granted, let p be the proposition having the characteristic ϕ of referring to fair sample S of a certain kind, c the proposition having the characteristic ψ of referring to the population from which S is drawn. Clearly c is in certain manner determined by p. Let further "hiprob (p, c)" stand for the relation that c is highly probalized by p. Then the probabilistic justification on the general level will have the logical form:

$$(p) \ (\phi p \supset . \ (\exists c) \ (\psi c \subset \text{hiprob} \ (p, c)) \ ^6 \qquad\qquad (1)$$

where "hiprob (p, c)" can be defined contextually as follows:
"hiprob (p, c)"   "there is a high probability that c can be inferred from p according to a logical principle"

Similarly, the non-probabilistic justification on the general level (GN) consists in regarding induction as a general indispensable method

---

⁶ Avoiding propositions, this logical schemata can be interpreted as meaning that if ϕ is true of some statement p, then another statement c can be always formulated such that ψ is true of c and hiprob is true of both p and c. Similar interpretations can be made for the logical schemata (2), (3), and (4).

for understanding experience, and hence is related to empirical generalizations as generally characterizing the real. Accordingly, if p is an
inductive premise about experience of some form, p is then related to
the inductive conclusion c in the relation that p is conceptually
characterized by c. Again for the sake of conveniently formalizing this
form of inductive relation, we may assume that experience of some
form can be referred to in connection with an epistemological situation
of perception. We may further assume the validity of quantification
over propositions. Then let p be the proposition having the characteristic ϕ' of referring to experience x of some form stated in epistemic
terms. Since x is always conceptualizable according to Peirce's and
Lewis's non-probabilistic arguments, given p, there will be a proposition c having the characteristic ψ' of predicating about x in non-epistemic terms. Clearly c conceptually characterizes p in the sense the c non-
epistemically predicates about x epistemically reported in p. Let
"conchar (p, c)" stand for such a relation. Then the non-probabilistic
justification on the general level will have the logical form:

$$(p) \ (\phi'p \supset. \ (\exists c) \ (\psi'c \ . \ \text{conchar} \ (p, c)) \tag{2}$$

where "conchar (p, c)" can be defined contextually:

"conchar (p, c)"   "c predicates something true in non-epistemic
terms about something to which p refers in
epistemic terms."

Since the probabilistic justification of induction on the specific level
(SP) is related to induction as a specific probable inference to a rationally credible inductive conclusion if it is a fair sample, fair according to
specific criteria, obviously it should assume the logical form:

$$\phi p_i \supset. \ \psi c_i \ . \ \text{hiprob} \ (p_i, c) \tag{3}$$

where p_i is a specific given inductive premise referring to a fair sample
of a certain kind, and c_i a specific inductive conclusion related to p_i in
the relation of high probabilization. Since the non-probabilistic justification of induction on the specific level (SN) is related to induction as a
specific empirical generalization necessary for characterizing reality of
a specific kind upon specific ground, similarly it can be represented as
having the logical form:

$$\phi'p_i \supset. \ \psi'c_i \ . \ \text{conchar} \ (p_i, c_i) \tag{4}$$

with corresponding interpretations of p_i and c_i. It should be noted that
in a specific justification the inductive conclusion ψc_i or $\psi'c_i$ are de-
tachable from the justification schemata (3) and (4).

In the framework of the theory of justifying induction outlined above, it is clear that the problem of justifying induction can be analyzed and attacked with respect to its modes and its levels. It is further clear that the notion of justification of induction can be stated in a contextual definition in terms of (1), (2), (3), and (4). Thus an argument A is a justification of induction if and only if A is equivalent to (1) (2) or (3) or (4). Finally, we may note that the relation between the general and specific justifications of induction is one of logical implication either by way of universal and existential generalizations or by way of universal and existential instantiations, under proper restrictions.[7] The philosophical significance of this relation is that in rendering a justification of induction on the specific level nothing prevents us from raising a significant question concerning justification of induction on the general level and vice versa.

4. *Bearings upon Practicist and Linguist Arguments*

In the light of the possibility of justifying induction on both its general and specific levels, we may conclude that the problem of justifying induction is a genuine problem on both general and specific levels. To the extent that induction is justifiable in the context of considerations both of its validity as a probable inference and of its validity as a reasonable method for establishing our knowledge of reality, the problem of justifying induction should be a solvable one.

Peirce's and Lewis's theories of induction have affirmed the justifiability of induction on a general level and suggested ways by which induction could be in general justified. In this sense, they have taken the problem of justifying induction as a genuine and a solvable one, and repudiated the suggestions of modern linguist philosophers that there is no general problem of justifying induction, and that the problem of justifying induction is merely a matter of finding whether an induction conforms to a standard or not. The linguist philosophers, as we have pointed out, are mistaken in assuming first that we should not raise the question concerning the trustworthiness of an inductive standard, and, second, that a standard to which induction seeks to conform has no connection with logical cogency. Our examination of Peirce's and Lewis's theories of induction has shown, on the other hand, that even inductive standards are subject to doubt, and that induction is capable of logical-

---

[7] See W. V. O. Quine, *Method of Logic*, 160—161.

ly cogent formulation in terms of probability. In this sense, the validity of induction *qua* inference is homologous with that of deduction *qua* inference, though it differs from deduction in many other essential aspects.

As to the practicists's suggestion that induction should be regarded as a practical policy which has been successful in the past in most cases, we observe that this does not adequately characterize the validity of induction. For Peirce and Lewis make us aware that induction is valid primarily on the ground that it is a valid form of inference and an indispensable method for formulating our knowledge of reality. The practicists simply fail to recognize two different questions regarding justification of induction: What is the reason for our trusting an inductive policy or principle P? Why is an effective-in-the-past inductive policy or principle P rationally trustworthy? When he asserts that the reason for our trusting P is its effectiveness-in-the-past, he has only answered the former question, but not the latter, even though he may *feel* that he has answered *all* the questions regarding the justification of induction. The answer to the latter question is given by Peirce and Lewis: An inductive policy or method, which has been successful in the past, is essential for determining our knowledge of reality in general in any conceivable situation as our knowledge of reality ought to be.

It is true that specific criteria for deciding what the real is are often adopted on the ground that they have proved successful in the past in most cases, but as regards their rational credibility, however, they cannot be thereby explained. We must instead consider them as rational principles in terms of which the notion of rationality or rational belief should be defined. At this point, we concede that there is some form of circularity in this explanation of the general validity of induction. But we insist nevertheless that the definition and explanation of the validity of our inferences about reality in terms of logic and reality should be prior to mere practical considerations. The general principles of such a definition and explanation are largely ignored by both the analysts and the practicists.

A CHRONOLOGICAL LISTING OF PEIRCE'S PAPERS DIRECTLY BEARING UPON INDUCTION AND PROBABILITY

"John Venn, The Logic of Chance" (review) 8.1–6, 1867.

"The Frequency Theory of Probability", 3.14–19, 1867.

"On the Natural Classification of Arguments," 2.461–516, 1867 (corrections 1893).

"The Social Theory of Logic," from "Grounds of Validity of the Laws of Logic," 5.318–357, 1868 (corrections 1893).

"The Fixation of Belief," 5.358–387, 1877.

"How to Make Our Ideas Clear," 5.388–412, 1878.

"The Doctrine of Chances " 2.645–668, 1878 (corrections 1893, notes 1910).

"Deduction, Induction, and Hypothesis," 2.619–644, 1878 (corrections 1893).

"The Probability of Induction," 2.669–693, 1878 (corrections 1893).

"The Order of Nature," 6.395–427, 1878.

"A Theory of Probable Inference," 2.694–754, 1883.

"Necessity Considered as a Postulate," from "The Doctrine of Necessity Examined," 6.35–65, 1892.

"Kinds of Reasoning," 1.65–74, from "Lessons from the History of Science," c. 1896.

"Reasoning from Samples," 1.92–7, from "Lessons from the History of Science," c. 1896.

"Methods for Attaining Truth," 5.574–604, 1898.

"Definition of Truth," 5.565–573, 1901.

"Abduction, Induction and Deduction," 7.202–6, from "The Logic of Drawing History from Ancient Documents," 1901.

"Three Kinds of Induction," 7.208–217, from "The Logic of Drawing History from Ancient Documents," 1901.

"The Nature of Hypothesis," 6.522–525, from "Hume on Miracles," c. 1901.

"The Testing of Hypothesis," 6.526–536, from "Hume on Miracles," c. 1901.

"What is Science," 1.232–7, 1902.

"Abduction and Deduction and Induction," from "Minute Logic," 2.100–104, 1902.

"Notes on Ampliative Reasoning," 2.773–791, 1902.

"Uniformity," 6.98–101, 1902.

"Syllogism," 2.552–580, 1902.

"Kinds of Reasoning," 7.97–109, from "Scientific Method," part undated, 1903.

"Kinds of Induction," 7.110–130, from "Scientific Method," part undated, 1903.

"Lectures on Pragmatism," 5.14–212, 1903.

"The Varieties and Validity of Induction," 2.755–772, c. 1905.

"Truth and Satisfaction," 5.555, c. 1906

"The Three Stages of Inquiry," from "A Neglected Argument for the Reality of God," 6.468–477, 1908.

"The Validity of the Three Stages," from "A Neglected Argument for the Reality of God," 6.468–477, 1908.

PROOF OF THE LOGICAL LAW OF LARGE NUMBERS (THE MAXIMUM VALUE LAW OF HYPERGEOMETRIC PROBABILITY)

We state *the logical law of large numbers* in the following three parts:

1. The probability that a sample has a certain composition ratio is greatest when that composition ratio equals the composition ratio of the population.
2. The probability that a sample has the same composition ratio as that of the population, given a certain range of difference, is greater than the probability that the sample has any other composition ratio, given the same range of difference.
3. We can make the probability that a given sample assumes the same composition ratio as that of the population as high as we want by allowing a proper range of difference, and this probability is greater than the probability that the sample has any other composition ratio, given the same range of difference.

To prove the logical law of large numbers, we need here only to prove 1. in detail, and indicate how 2. is related to 1. and can be proved in the similar way. As to 3., its first part can be easily shown to follow from the fact that the probability that a sample has a certain composition ratio greater than, equal to, or smaller than, the composition ratio of the population is a definite proper fraction, however small it may be, whereas its second part obviously follows from 2.

We may formulate 1. as the following mathematical theorem in the probability theory: Let N = size of a population T, k = number of elements having a property t in T, n = size of a sample S to be taken from T, x = number of elements having the property t in S. Then the probability that S has exact x elements having the property t, namely the hypergeometric probability

$$P(N, k, n, x) = \frac{\binom{k}{x} \cdot \binom{N-k}{n-x}}{\binom{N}{n}}$$

where $N \geqslant k$, $N \geqslant n$, $x \leqslant$ maximum (n, k), has its maximum value when $x/n = k/N$ or $x = nk/N$.

Proof: Consider the following ratios

$$A = \frac{\dfrac{\dbinom{k}{x}\dbinom{N-k}{n-x}}{\dbinom{N}{n}}}{\dfrac{\dbinom{k}{x+j}\dbinom{N-k}{n-x-j}}{\dbinom{N}{n}}} = \frac{\dbinom{k}{x}\dbinom{N-k}{n-x}}{\dbinom{k}{x+j}\dbinom{N-k}{n-x-j}}$$

$$B = \frac{\dfrac{\dbinom{k}{x}\dbinom{N-k}{n-x}}{\dbinom{N}{n}}}{\dfrac{\dbinom{k}{x-j}\dbinom{N-k}{n-x+j}}{\dbinom{N}{n}}} = \frac{\dbinom{k}{x}\dbinom{N-k}{n-x}}{\dbinom{k}{x-j}\dbinom{N-k}{n-x+j}}$$

The theorem we want to prove holds if, and only if

$$A > 1 \quad \text{for all} \quad j = 1, 2, \ldots\ldots$$
$$B > 1 \quad \text{for all} \quad j = 1, 2, \ldots\ldots$$

and when $x = nk/N$.

I. We prove $A > 1$ by induction on j

(i) $j = 1$

$$A = \frac{\dbinom{k}{x}\dbinom{N-k}{n-x}}{\dbinom{k}{x-1}\dbinom{N-k}{n-x-1}} = \frac{(x+1)(N-k-n+x+1)}{(k-x)(n-x)}$$

when $x = \dfrac{nk}{N}$

$$A = \frac{nk - \dfrac{nk^2}{N} - \dfrac{n^2k}{N} + \dfrac{n^2k^2}{N^2} + \dfrac{nk}{N} + N - k + n + \dfrac{nk}{N} + 1}{nk - \dfrac{nk^2}{N} - \dfrac{n^2k}{N} + \dfrac{n^2k^2}{N^2}}$$

This ratio is > 1 if we can show

$$\frac{2nk}{N} + N - k - n + 1 > 0 \tag{1}$$

Now we show that for all values of n, k insofar as $n \leqslant N$, $k \leqslant N$, (1) holds.

Let k take any value, clearly when $n = 0$, $N - k + 1 > 0$
But even when $k = N$, $n = N$

$$\frac{2NN}{N} + N - N - N + 1 > 0.$$

Hence in any case, (1) holds.

(ii) Assume $A > 1$, (when $x = nk/N$), holds for $j = \theta$, we want to prove $A > 1$, (when $x = nk/N$), holds for $j = \theta + 1$.

By assumption,

$$\frac{\binom{k}{x}\binom{N-k}{n-x}}{\binom{k}{x+\theta}\binom{R-k}{n-x-\theta}} > 1.$$

Now

$$\frac{\binom{k}{x}\binom{N-k}{n-x}}{\binom{k}{x+\theta}\binom{N-k}{n-x-\theta}} \cdot \frac{(x+\theta+1)(N-k-n+x+\theta+1)}{(k-x-\theta)(n-x-\theta)} =$$

$$= \frac{\binom{k}{x}\binom{N-k}{n-x}}{\binom{k}{x+\theta+1}\binom{N-k}{n-x-\theta-1}}.$$

To show

$$\frac{\binom{k}{x}\binom{N-k}{n-x}}{\binom{k}{x+\theta+1}\binom{N-k}{n-x-\theta-1}} > 1.$$

We need to show

$$\frac{(x + \theta + 1)(N - k - n + x + \theta + 1)}{(k - x - \theta)(n - x - \theta)} \geqslant 1$$

$$\frac{(x + \theta + 1)(N - k - n + x + \theta + 1)}{(k - x - \theta)(n - x - \theta)} =$$

$$= (Nx - kx - nx + x^2 + x\theta + x + N\theta - k\theta - n\theta + x\theta + \theta^2 + \theta +$$
$$\frac{+ N - k - n + x + \theta + 1)}{kn - kx - k\theta - xn + x^2 + \theta x - n\theta + \theta x + \theta^2}$$

Substitute x for nk/N, we have

$$N - k - n + \frac{2kn}{N} + 2\theta + 1 + N\theta$$

But $N - k - n + \dfrac{2kn}{N} + 1 > 0$, $2\theta + N\theta$ is a positive integer.

Therefore

$$\frac{(x + \theta + 1)(N - k - n + x + \theta + 1)}{(k - x - \theta)(n - x - \theta)} > 1$$

Hence
$$\frac{\dbinom{k}{x}\dbinom{N-k}{n-x}}{\dbinom{k}{x + \theta + 1}\dbinom{N-k}{n - x - \theta - 1}} > 1$$

II. We prove $B > 1$ by induction on j.
(i) $j = 1$

$$B = \frac{\dbinom{k}{x}\dbinom{N-k}{n-x}}{\dbinom{k}{x - 1}\dbinom{N-k}{n - x - 1}}$$

$$= \frac{(x - 1)! \, (k - x + 1)! \, (n - x + 1)! \, (N - k - n + x - 1)!}{x! \, (k - x)! \, (n - x)! \, (N - k - n + x)!}$$

$$B = \frac{(k - x + 1)(n - x + 1)}{x(N - k - n + x)}$$

When $x = nk/N$

$$B = \dfrac{kn - \dfrac{nk^2}{N} + k - \dfrac{n^2k}{N} + \dfrac{k^2n^2}{N^2} - \dfrac{nk}{N} + n - \dfrac{kn}{N} + 1}{nk - \dfrac{nk^2}{N} - \dfrac{n^2k}{N} + \dfrac{n^2k^2}{N^2}}$$

To show this > 1, we need to show

$$k + n - \frac{2nk}{N} + 1 > 0$$

i.e.,

$$Nk + nN - 2nk + N > 0$$

This is obvious, for $Nk + nN > 2nk$.

(ii) Assume $B > 1$ (when $x = nk/N$) holds for $j = \theta$, i.e.,

$$\frac{\binom{k}{x}\binom{N-k}{n-x}}{\binom{k}{x-\theta}\binom{N-k}{n-x+\theta}} > 1$$

We want to show that $B > 1$ (when $x = nk/N$) holds for $j = \theta + 1$.

$$\frac{\binom{k}{x}\binom{N-k}{n-x}}{\binom{k}{x-\theta-1}\binom{N-k}{n-x+\theta+1}} > 1$$

But

$$\frac{(k-x+\theta+1)(n-x+\theta+1)}{(x-\theta)(N-k-n+x-\theta)} \cdot \frac{\binom{k}{x}\binom{N-k}{n-x}}{\binom{k}{x-\theta}\binom{N-k}{n-x+\theta}}$$

$$= \frac{\binom{k}{x}\binom{N-k}{n-k}}{\binom{k}{x-\theta-1}\binom{N-k}{n-x+\theta+1}}$$

Now, to prove

$$\frac{\binom{k}{x}\binom{N-k}{n-x}}{\binom{k}{x-\theta-1}\binom{N-k}{n-x+\theta+1}} > 1$$

We need to prove

$$\frac{(k - x + \theta + 1)(n - x + \theta + 1)}{(x - \theta)(N - k - n + x - \theta)} > 1$$

$$\frac{(k - x + \theta + 1)(n - x + \theta + 1)}{(x - \theta)(N - k - n + x - \theta)} =$$

$$= \frac{(kn - kx + k\theta + k - xn + x^2 - x\theta - x + \theta n - x\theta + \theta^2 + \theta + n - x + \theta + 1)}{(xN - kx - xn + x^2 - x\theta - N\theta + k\theta + n\theta - x\theta + \theta^2)}$$

To prove this > 1, we prove

$$k + n + 2\theta + 1 - \frac{2nk}{N} > - N\theta$$

$$k + n + 2\theta + n\theta + 1 - \frac{2nk}{N} > 0.$$

$$Nk + Nn + 2\theta N + N^2\theta + N - 2nk > 0.$$

This is obvious, for $Nk - Nn > 2nk$.

Q.E.D.

In the above, we have given a rigorous proof of 1. of the logical law of large numbers. To prove 2., we may also formulate it as a mathematical theorem in the probability theory. Given N, n, k, x as defined above, let d = the value by which the number of elements having the property t in a sample differs from the number of elements having the property t in a given sample. Then the cumulative probability that a sample has elements having the property t with a range of difference d is given by

$$P_d(N, k, n, x = nk/N) = \sum_{i=0}^{d} \frac{\binom{k}{x - i}\binom{N - k}{n - x + i}}{\binom{N}{n}} +$$

$$+ \sum_{j=1}^{d} \frac{\binom{k}{x + j}\binom{N - k}{n - x - j}}{\binom{N}{n}}$$

Then 2. in effect asserts the following
$P_d(N, k, n, x = nk/N) > P_d(N, k, n, x = m$, where $m >$ or $< nk/N)$
To prove this, we may utilize 1. and the following lemma

Lemma:

$$\frac{\dfrac{\dbinom{k}{x+a}\dbinom{N-k}{n-x-a}}{\dbinom{N}{n}}}{\dfrac{\dbinom{k}{x+a+1}\dbinom{N-k}{n-x-a-1}}{\dbinom{N}{n}}} = \frac{\dbinom{k}{x+a}\dbinom{N-k}{n-x-a}}{\dbinom{k}{x+a+1}\dbinom{N-k}{n-x-a-1}} > 1$$

$$\frac{\dfrac{\dbinom{k}{x-a}\dbinom{N-k}{n-x+a}}{\dbinom{N}{n}}}{\dfrac{\dbinom{k}{x-a-1}\dbinom{N-k}{n-x+a+1}}{\dbinom{N}{n}}} = \frac{\dbinom{k}{x-a}\dbinom{N-k}{n-x+a}}{\dbinom{k}{x-a-1}\dbinom{N-k}{n-x+a+1}} > 1$$

This lemma in other words says that the probability that a sample has
x + a or x − a elements having the property t is always smaller than
the probability that the sample has x + a + 1 or x − a − 1 elements
having the property t. We can prove this lemma by induction on a
in a way similar to our proof of 1.[1] Now by 1. we know that
$P_d(N, k, n, x = nk/N)$ is always greatest, and by the lemma we know
that all probabilities that a sample has less or more elements having
the property t (say, by a difference d) than a given sample has are
always smaller than the probability that the given sample has a
certain number of elements having the property t. Consequently, we
know that $P_d(N, k, n, x = nk/n)$ is always greater than

$$P_d(N, k, n, x > \text{ or } < nk/N) \quad \text{for any d.}$$

---

[1] 1. of the logical law of large numbers follows as a special case from this lemma
when a = 0.

PROBABILITIES OF ESTIMATES OF VALUES
OF POPULATION PARAMETERS

We begin by giving definitions of probability space, random variable, distribution function, probability function, and density function. A probability space consists of a set S (finite or infinite) of elementary events and a family F of events. Each event is a subset of elementary events in F. The family F of events satisfies the following axioms:

1. The set o containing no elementary event and the set S containing all elementary events are events.
2. The intersection of a countable set of events is an event.
3. The union of a countable set of events is an event.
4. The complement, Ā, of an event A is an event.

Associated with each event A is a probability P(A) with the following properties:

1. P(A) is defined for every event A.
2. $P(A) \geqslant o$ for every event A.
3. $P(S) = 1$.
4. The probability of the union of a countable set of mutually exclusive events is the sum of their probabilities.

A random variable X is a real-valued function on the elementary events of a probability space: to each elementary event corresponds a real number, the value of the random variable at that elementary event. Further, for every real number a, the set {X = a} of elementary events at which X assumes the value is an event, and for every pair of real numbers b and c the sets $\{b < X < c\}$, $\{b \leqslant X < c\}$, $\{b < X \leqslant C\}$, $\{b \leqslant X \leqslant c\}$, $\{X \leqslant c\}$, $\{X < c\}$, $\{X \geqslant b\}$, $\{X > b\}$ are events. The distribution function F(x) of a random variable X is the function of the real variable x defined by

$$F(x) = \Pr\{X < x]$$

The probability function f(x) of a discrete random variable X is the function of the real variable x whose value at each x is the probability that X will assume the value x:

$$f(x) = Pr(X = x)$$

then

$$F(x) = Pr(X < x) = \sum_{t<x} f(t)$$

The density function of a continuous random variable X is the function of the real variable x with the property that for every pair of real numbers a, b with a < b

$$Pr\{a < X < b\} = \int_a^b f(x)\ dx;$$

then

$$F(x) = Pr\{X < x\} - \int_{-\infty}^x f(t)\ dt$$

and

$$F(x) = F'(x)$$

at each point x where f is continuous.

Next we may introduce the definitions of expectation, variance and standard deviation of a random variable. The expectation, variance and standard deviation of the discrete random variable X are given by

$$E(X) = \sum_x xf(x)$$

$$V(X) = \sum_x [x - E(X)]^2\ f(x)$$

$$\sigma_x = \sqrt{V(X)}$$

The expectation, variance, and standard deviation of the continuous random variable X are given by

$$E(X) = \int_{-\infty}^{\infty} xf(x)\ dx,$$

$$V(X) = \int_{-\infty}^{\infty} [x - E(X)]^2\ dx,$$

$$\sigma_x = \sqrt{V(X)}$$

On the basis of the above definitions we may discuss random sampling from a population characterized by a hypergeometric distribution. The random variable of a hypergeometric distribution is the number of objects drawn with property A among the n drawn. Since this variable does not take into account the order in which the objects appear, it is immaterial whether the objects are actually drawn one at a time at random, without replacement, or drawn at random, without replacement, or drawn at random in a bunch. The probability function for a hypergeometric random variable X, the number of A's drawn in a bunch of objects taken from N objects of which M are A's, is as follows:

$$P(X = x) = p(x; N, M, n)$$

$$= P(xA\text{'s among the } n \text{ drawn})$$

$$= \frac{\binom{M}{x}\binom{N - M}{n - x}}{\binom{N}{n}} \quad \text{for } x = 0, 1, \ldots, n$$

$$= 0 \text{ otherwise}$$

This formula holds for all possible values running from the larger of 0 and n — (N — M) through the integers up to the smaller of n and N. The distribution function of the hypergeometric probability function is

$$F(x) = \sum_{t < x} \frac{\binom{M}{x}\binom{N - M}{n - x}}{\binom{N}{n}}.$$

Using the above definitions of expectation, variance and standard deviation, we reach the following expectation, variance and standard deviation of a hypergeometric distribution:

$$E(X) = \frac{nM}{N}$$

$$V(X) = npq \frac{N - n}{N - 1}$$

$$x = \sqrt{npq} \sqrt{\frac{N - n}{N - 1}}$$

where $p = M/N$, the probability of A for a single trial, and $p + q = 1$.

As an example of calculating hypergeometric probability we may suppose that a lot of 100 contains 20 defective and 80 good articles. Suppose that 20 articles are drawn from the lot at random, but without replacement, then the probability function for X, the number of defective articles among the drawn is

$$P(x; 100, 20, 20) = \frac{\binom{20}{x}\binom{80}{20-x}}{\binom{100}{20}}.$$

The variance of the distribution with this probability function of X is

$$V(X) = 20 \times \frac{20}{100} \times \frac{80}{100} \times \frac{100-20}{100-1} = 2.6$$

$$x = \sqrt{2.6} = 1.6$$

$$E(X) = 20\frac{20}{100} = 20\frac{1}{5} = 4$$

Now on consulting *Tables of the Hypergeometric Probability Distribution* (by Gerald J. Lieberman and Donald B. Owen, Stanford University Press, 1961), we find that the probability that the sample will have exactly 4 defective articles is 0.243688, and that the probability that the sample will have 4 defective articles, the expected value of X, within the range $-\sigma + 4 < X < +\sigma + 4$ is $0.215862 + 0.243688 + 0.191688 = 0.6515$. This shows that with known expected value of X, a random sample from a hypergeometric distribution will have a fairly high probability that it will have a proportion of good to defective articles with the expected value by a difference of σx.

Now the question occurs as to the following. If we do not know the proportion of good to defective articles in the population, if we take a sample of size 20 from the population and find that 4 of them are defective, how can we evaluate the proportion of defective to good articles in the population? At this point, we must introduce the conception of the sample mean and estimates of parameteric values in a distribution function.

If $X_1, X_2, \dots X_n$ are the sample random variables of a sample of size n from a population induced by a random variable X, we define the random variable, the sample mean, by $\bar{X} = 1/n \sum_{i=1}^{n} X_i$ the arithmetric average of the n sample random variables. A sample point $(x_1, x_2, \dots, x_n)$ represents the values of the sample mean of this particular sample is

$$X = \frac{1}{n} \sum_{i=1}^{n} x_i .$$

Since each x has the same distribution as does X, we have $E(X_i) = E(X)$ for each i. We calculate

$$E(\overline{X}) = E\left(\frac{1}{n} \sum_{i=1}^{n} x_i\right) = \frac{1}{n} \sum_{i=1}^{n} E(X) = \frac{1}{n} nE(X) = E(X)$$

Since the random variable X_i's are independent, we have

$$V(\overline{X}) = V\left(\frac{1}{n} \sum_{i=1}^{n} X_i\right) = \frac{1}{n^2} V\left(\sum_{i=1}^{n} X_i\right) = \frac{1}{n^2} \sum_{i=1}^{n} V(X_i)$$

Again, since each X_i has the same distribution as X, we have $V(X_i) = V(X)$ for each i, so that

$$V(\overline{X}) = \frac{1}{n^2} \sum_{i=1}^{n} V(X) = \frac{1}{n^2} nV(X) = \frac{1}{n} V(X)$$

As

$$V(X) = \sigma^2 \quad \text{or} \quad \sigma_x^2, \text{ then}$$

$$V(\overline{X}) = \frac{\sigma^2}{n}, \text{ or } \frac{\sigma}{x} = \frac{\sigma_x}{\sqrt{n}} .$$

We recall that the variance of a random variable in some sense measures the compactness or the dispersion of the probability distribution of the random variable about the mean or expectation. We observe that for large n the variance of $\overline{X}$ is very small, and accordingly suspect that if n is large the probability that $\overline{X}$ will assume a value near the mean will be high. Since $E(\overline{X}) = E(X)$, this means again that whatever the population distrubution (provided it has a finite variance), the distribution of the sample mean becomes more and more concentrated near the population mean as the sample size increases. This is essentially the law of large numbers. We may state this law of large numbers in a more exact form:

* *The Law of Large Numbers.* Suppose $X_1, X_2, \ldots$ is an arbitrary sequence of random variables, with exceptions $E(X_1), E(X_2)$ .... Suppose further that the random variable $\sum_{i=1}^{n} X_i$ has a variance for each positive integer n.
If

$$V\left(\frac{1}{n} \sum_{i=1}^{n} Y_i\right) \to 0 \text{ as } n \to \infty,$$

and if ε is a positive number, then

$$\Pr\left\{\left|\frac{1}{n}\sum_{i=1}^{n}[X_i - E(X_i)]\right| \geqslant \varepsilon\right\} \to 0 \text{ as } n \to \infty$$

or equivalently

$$\Pr\left\{\left|\frac{1}{n}\sum_{i=1}^{n}[X_i - E(X_i)]\right| < \varepsilon\right\} \to 1 \text{ as } n \to \infty$$

As the proof of this theorem can be found in any standard text book on probability theory, we omit it here. From this general law of large numbers, two important corollaries follow obviously:

* Corollary 1. If $\overline{X}$ is the sample mean of a random sample of size n from the population induced by a random variable X with mean μ and standard deviation σ and if ε > 0, then

$$\Pr\{|\overline{X} - \mu| \geqslant \varepsilon\} \to 0 \text{ as } n \to \infty$$

or

$$\Pr\{|X - \mu| < \varepsilon[\to 1 \text{ as } n \to \infty$$

In loose words, if the sample size is large, the probability is high that the sample mean $\overline{X}$ will be near the population mean μ. By choosing sufficiently large sample size, we can make the probability as near as we wish that the sample mean we shall obtain will be as near as we wish to the population mean.

* Corollary 2. (Bernoulli's Theorem) if S_n represents the number of successes in n independent trials of an event with probability P, and if ε > 0, then

$$\Pr\left\{\left|\frac{S_n}{n} - p\right| \geqslant t\right\} \to 0 \text{ as } n \to \infty$$

or

$$\Pr\left\{\left|\frac{S_n}{n} - p\right| < t\right\} \to 1 \text{ as } n \to \infty$$

With the help of the law of large numbers, we still cannot solve the question we raise concerning the evaluation or estimation of the proportion M/N in a population from a known value of sample mean $\overline{X}$ in a particular sample from the population. What we known from the Law of Large Numbers is merely that if our sample is sufficiently large, the probability will be high that the known value $\overline{X}$ will be very close to the expected value of X with the help of *Tables for Hyper-*

geometric Distributions. However, we may indeed decide how high a probability, with how large a variance that one $\bar{X}$ will be close to the expected value of X, if the size of the population is given. Without knowing how large the size of a population is, we may still evaluate the probability that the mean of population will be close to the sample mean and vice versa by utilizing a far more powerful theorem, the Central Limit Theorem.

    * *The Central Limit Theorem.* If a population has a finite variance σ^2 and mean μ, then the distribution of the sample mean approaches the normal distribution with variance σ^2/n and mean $\bar{X}_n$ as the sample size n increases. Now a random variable Z has normal distribution (standardized) if it has a probability density function $\varphi(Z)$ given by

$$\varphi(Z) = \frac{1}{\sqrt{2\pi}} e^{-z^2/2}.$$

The mean, variance, and standard deviation of such a random variable are:

$$E(Z) = \frac{1}{\sqrt{2\pi}} \int_{-\infty}^{\infty} z e^{-z^2/2} \, dz = 0$$

$$V(Z) = \frac{1}{\sqrt{2\pi}} \int_{-\infty}^{\infty} z^2 e^{-z^2/2} \, dz = 1$$

$$\sigma_z = \sqrt{V(Z)} = 1$$

    To state the Central Limit Theorem in a more rigorous form, we have: If $\bar{X}_n$ is the sample mean of a sample of size n from a population with mean μ and standard deviation σ, then for any real numbers a and b with a < b,

$$\Pr\left\{ a < \frac{\bar{X}_n - \mu}{\sigma/\sqrt{n}} < b \right\} \to \frac{1}{\sqrt{2\pi}} \int_{a}^{b} e^{-z^2/2} \, dz \quad \text{as} \quad n \to \infty$$

or

$$\Pr\left\{ \mu + \frac{a}{\sqrt{n}} < \bar{X}_n < \mu + \frac{b}{\sqrt{n}} \right\} \to \frac{1}{\sqrt{2\pi}} \int_{a}^{b} e^{-z^2/2} \, dz \quad \text{as} \quad n \to \infty$$

    The proof of Central Limit Theorem can be found in any standard text book on probability theory and hence it is to be omitted here.

The Central Limit Theorem is very important in the fact that given a sufficiently large sample of size n, we can always use the sample mean to estimate the population mean and use the variance of the sample mean to estimate the value of variance of the population mean divided by n, from which the value of variance of the population mean can be calculated. This is because when the sample has a sufficiently large size the distribution of the sample mean approaches normality, and therefore its mean approaches the mean of the population with a standard deviation $\sigma/\sqrt{n}$, where μ and σ^2 are variance and standard deviation of the finite population. In other words, we have the following:

$$\mu = \bar{X} = \frac{1}{n} \sum_{1}^{n} X_i$$

$$S^2 = \hat{\sigma}^2 = \frac{1}{n} \sum_{1}^{n} (X - \bar{X})^2$$

where $\hat{\mu}$ and $\hat{\sigma}^2$ are respectively called estimators of μ and σ^2 of the population when the sample n is large. It is also clear from the Central Limit Theorem that the larger the sample, the more certain we can be that the sample mean will be a good estimator of the population mean.

Now we may show that the Central Limit Theorem enables us to calculate probability of an estimate concerning a population parameter value by a known value of a sample parameter. There are following ways of doing this. (1) Let us consider an example. We have a large lot of items, and wish, by random sampling, to estimate the fraction which are defective. Let us use the Central Limit Theorem to find a number N with the property that if you take a sample of size N or larger, the probability will be at least 0.95 that the average number, $\bar{X}$, of defectives will differ from the true proportion by less than 0.1. We wish to have

$$\Pr\{|\bar{X} - p| < 0.1\} \geqslant 0.95$$

or

$$\Pr\{-0.1 < \bar{X} - p < 0.1\} \geqslant 0.95$$

Now $E(\bar{X}) = p$, $\sqrt{V(X)} = \sigma_x = \sqrt{pq/n}$. On dividing both sides of each inequality by σ_x we obtain

$$\Pr\left\{-0.1\sqrt{n/pq} < \frac{\bar{X} - p}{\bar{X}} < 0.1\sqrt{n/pq}\right\} \geqslant 0.95.$$

According to the Central Limit Theorem, the probability on the left is given approximately for large n by

$$\frac{1}{\sqrt{2\pi}} \int_{-0.1\sqrt{m/pq}}^{0.1\sqrt{n/pq}} e^{-z^2/2}\ dz$$

We find from the tables that this will be at least 0.95 if

$$0.1\sqrt{n/pq} \geqslant 1.96$$

or if

$$n \geqslant (19.6)^2\ pq.$$

Since $pq = p(1 - p) \leqslant 1/4$ for all p between 0 and 1, or will be at least $(19.6)^2\ pq$, no matter what p may be, if

$$n \geqslant (19.6)^2\ (1/4) \doteq 96.$$

Thus whatever the unknown proportion of defectives, the probability will be at least 0.95 that the average number found in a sample of size about 100 will differ from the true proportion by less than 0.1.

(2) Now suppose the density function of the sample mean is $g(\overline{X})$, where $\overline{X}$ is the mean of a sample of size n from a population with density function $f(x)$. We have found that the mean and variance of $g(\overline{X})$ are μ and σ^2/n, where μ and σ^2 are the mean and variance of $f(x)$. It follows from the definition of the variance that

$$\sigma_{\overline{X}}^2 = \sigma^2/n = \int_{-\infty}^{\infty} (\overline{X} - \mu)^2\ g(\overline{X})\ d\overline{X}$$

$$= \int_{-\infty}^{-(a\sigma/\sqrt{n})} (\overline{X} - \mu)^2\ g(\overline{X})\ d\overline{X} + \int_{-(a\sigma/\sqrt{n})}^{+(a\sigma/\sqrt{n})} (\overline{X} - \mu)^2\ g(\overline{X})\ d\overline{X} + \int_{+(a\sigma/\sqrt{n})}^{\infty} (\overline{X} - \mu)^2\ g(\overline{X})\ d\overline{X}$$

Where n is any arbitrarily chosen positive number.

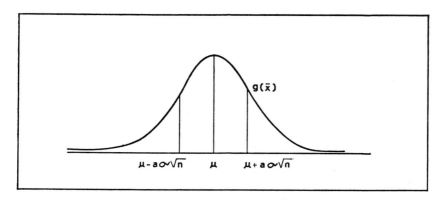

To reduce this equation to an inequality, we drop the second integral and replace $(\overline{X} - \mu)^2$ in the first integral by $a^2\sigma^2/n$ where $|\overline{X} - \mu| \geqslant a\sigma/\sqrt{n}$ we have then

$$\sigma^2/n > a^2\sigma^2/n \int_{-\infty}^{\mu-(a\sigma/\sqrt{n})} g(\overline{X})\ d\overline{X} + a^2\sigma^2/n \int_{\mu+(a\sigma/\sqrt{n})}^{\infty} g(\overline{X})\ d\overline{X}$$

Since the two integrals in this inequality give exactly the probability that X lies outside the interval $\mu - (a\sigma/\sqrt{n})$ to $\mu + (a\sigma/\sqrt{n})$, we have

$$1/a^2 > p(|\overline{X} - \mu| > a\sigma/\sqrt{n})$$

Then let $a\sigma/\sqrt{n} = b$, then $1/a^2 = \sigma^2/ab^2$, and we have

$$P(|\overline{X} - \mu| > b) < \sigma^2/ab^2$$

or

$$P(-b < \overline{X} - \mu < b) > 1 - \sigma^2/ab^2$$

This relation is known as Tchebysheff's inequality. Referring to this, we may choose any small number b and determine a small interval about the population mean; having done this, we may choose n large enough to give a value as near one as we please for the probability that the sample mean will be within the small interval containing the population man. An example of how to use this formula for calculating the probability that the sample mean will be within the small interval (determined by a chosen small value b) containing the population mean can be given as follows.

Suppose we have a sample of 30 items, in which we find 10 are defective. We set $b = 0.1$. Then the probability that the sample mean $\overline{X} = 1/3$ will be within the small interval $(\mu - 0.1, \mu + 0.1)$ is given by

$$P(-0.1 < 1/3 - \mu < 0.1) > 1 - \sigma^2/nb^2.$$

But we do not know σ^2 of the population. We may estimate on the basis of the Central Limit Theorem σ^2 by $S^2 = 2/9$. Thus $\sigma^2/nb^2 = 0.02/270 = 2/27000$. Thus

$$P(-0.1 < 1/3 - \mu < 0.1) > 1 - 2/2700 = 2698/2700.$$

(3) At this point, we may introduce the concepts of probable error and standard error for a normal distribution.

. The *probable error*, p.e., is defined as the particular deviation that divides the left (or right) half of the area under a probability distribution curve into two equal parts. Thus, the probability of observing a deviation within $\pm$ p.e. is $1/2$. This is indicated in the figure

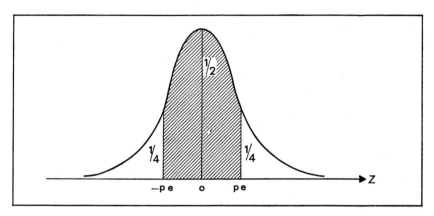

In other words, for a normal distribution,

$$\text{Total area} = \int_{-\infty}^{\infty} \frac{1}{\sqrt{2\pi}\,\sigma}\, e^{-x^2/2\sigma^2}\, dz = 1$$

p.e. is the particular value of z for which

$$1/2 = \frac{1}{\sqrt{2\pi}\,\sigma} \int_{0}^{x=pe} e^{-x^2/2\sigma^2}\, dx$$

p.e. $= 0.4769/(1/\sigma\sqrt{2}) = (0.4769/0.707)\,\sigma = 0.6745\sigma$

The probable error is the 50% *confidence limit* by definition; Any other confidence limit, e.g., the 90% confidence limit, may be deduced in the same manner as that for the probable error. Thus, for the 90% limit

$$0.90 = \frac{2}{\sqrt{2\pi}\,\sigma} \int_{0}^{x=(90\,\%\,cl)} e^{-x^2/2\sigma^2}\, dx$$

$90\% cl = (1.164/0.707)\,\sigma.$

Now for $x = \sigma$, the confidence limit is

$$\frac{2}{\sqrt{2\pi}\,\sigma} \int_{0}^{x=\sigma} e^{-x^2/2\sigma^2}\, dx = 0.6826.$$

That is, the probability of observing a deviation within $\pm\sigma$ is 0.683.

This σ is called the *standard error* of the normal distribution.

With the constant values of probability fixed for a normal distribution that the μ will be within small interval determined by the probable error and will be within a small interval determined by the standard error, it is easy to compute the probable error and standard error that a given sample mean $\overline{X}$ will estimate the population mean with a probability 1/2 and 0.6826, if the sample is fairly large.

One example can again be given. Suppose we draw a sample of 30 from a lot of items and find 10 are defectives. The standard error of the probability 0.6826 that 1/3 (a value of $\overline{X}$) estimates the population mean, i.e., the population will have a proportion 1/3 of defectives, is computed by the formula $\overline{X}/\sqrt{n} = \sqrt{(1/3\ (2/3)}/\sqrt{30} = 0.084$. That is to say, there is a probability 0.6826 that the population mean will be in the interval, containing the sample mean (1/3 − 0.084, 1/3 + + 0.084). The probable error is given by $0.6745 \times 0.084 = 0.0567$. Hence there is a probability 1/2 that the 1/3 will differ from the true proportion of defectives in the population by less than 0.0567.

The above Appendix is written on the basis of the following text books on probability theory and mathematical statistics:

Brunk, H. D. *An Introduction to Mathematical Statistics.* Ginn and Company, 1960.

Feller, William. *An Introduction to Probability Theory and Its Applications,* Vol. 1. Second edition. John Wiley and Sons, 1962.

Lieberman, Gerald J. and Donald B. Owen. *Tables of the Hypergeometric Probability Distribution.* Stanford University Press, 1961.

Lindgran, B. W. *Statistical Theory.* MacMillan Company, 1962.

McCarthy, Philip J. *Introduction to Statistical Reasoning.* McGraw-Hill Book Company, 1957.

Mood, Alexander M. *Introduction to the Theory of Statistics.* McGraw-Hill Book Company, 1950.

Parratt, Lyman G. *Probability and Experimental Errors in Science.* John Wiley and Sons, Inc. 1961.

Parzen, Emanuel. *Modern Probability Theory and Its Application.* John Wiley and Sons, 1960.

SELECTED BIBLIOGRAPHY

WORKS BY PEIRCE

Chance, Logic and Love, ed. with an Introduction by W. R. Cohen, New York: Harcourt, Brace & Co., 1923.
Collected Papers of Charles Sanders Peirce, Vols., I–VI, ed. by Charles Hartshorne and Paul Weiss; Vols. VII–VIII, ed. by Arthur W. Burks, Cambridge: Harvard University Press, 1931–1958.
C. S. Peirce: Essays in the Philosophy of Science, ed. with an Introduction by V. Tomas, New York: The Bobbs-Merrill Co., Inc., 1957.
The Philosophy of Peirce: Selected Writings, ed. with an Introduction by J. Buchler, London: Kegan Paul, Trench, Trubner & Co., 1940; Reprinted ed., *Philosophical Writings of Peirce*, New York: Dover Publications, 1955.

WORKS ABOUT PEIRCE

Berry, G. D. W. "Peirce's Contributions to the Logic of Statements and Quantifiers," Wiener and Young, 153–165.
Bernstein, Richard J., Ed. *Perspectives on Peirce, Critical Essays on C. S. Peirce*, New Haven: Yale University Press, 1965.
Bird, Otto. "Peirce's Theory of Methodology," *Philosophy of Science*, 26, 1959, 187–200.
—, "What Peirce Means by Leading Principles," *Notre Dame Journal of Formal Logic*, 3, 1962, 175–178.
Braithwaite, B. R. Review of *Collected Papers of C. S. Peirce*, Vols. I–IV, *Mind*, 43, 1934, 487–511.
Boler, J. F. *The Structure of Realism in the Philosophy of Charles Sanders Peirce*, Harvard University unpublished Ph.D. thesis, 1960.
—, *Charles Peirce and Scholastic Realism, A Study of Peirce's Relation to John Duns Scotus*, Seattle: University of Washington Press, 1963.
Buchler, J. *Charles Peirce's Empiricism*, London: Kegan Paul, Trench, Trubner & Co., 1939.
Burks, A. W. *The Logical Foundation of the Philosophy of Charles Sanders Peirce*, University of Michigan unpublished Ph.D. thesis, 1941.
—, "Peirce's Conception of Logic as a Normative Science," *Philosophical Review*, 52, 1943, 187–193.
—, "Peirce's Theory of Abduction," *Philosophy of Science*, 13, 1946, 301–306.
Feldstein, Leonard C. *The Norms of Science: An Evaluation of the Views of Meyerson, Duhem and Peirce*, Columbia University Ph.D. thesis, abstracted in: Dissertation Abstracts, 17, 1957, 1784–1785.

Goudge, T. A. *The Thought of C. S. Peirce*, Toronto: University of Toronto Press, 1950.

Holmes, Larry. *Charles Sanders Peirce and Scientific Metaphysics*, Harvard University Ph.D. thesis, 1962.

—, "Prolegomena to Peirce's Philosophy of Mind," Moore and Robin, 359–381.

Huggett, William J. *Charles Peirce's Search for a Method*, University of Toronto Ph.D. thesis, 1954.

Knight, Thomas Stanley. *Charles Peirce*, New York: Washington Square Press, 1965.

MacDonald, Audrey. *Peirce's Philosophy of Mind*, University of Texas Ph.D. thesis, 1963.

—, "Peirce's Logic: An Objective Study of Reasoning," *The Monist*, 48, 1964, 332–345.

MacDonald, Margaret. "Charles Sanders Peirce on Language," *Psyche*, 15, 1935, 108–128.

—, "Language and Reference," *Analysis*, 4, 1936, 33–41.

Madden, Edward H. "Chance and Counterfacts in Wright and Peirce," *Review of Metaphysics*, 9, 1956, 420–432.

—, "Charles Sanders Peirce's Search for a Method", in *Theories of Scientific Method*, Ralph M. Blake, Curt J. Ducasse, and Edward H. Madden, Seattle: University of Washington Press, 1960, 248–262.

—, *Chauncey Wright and the Foundations of Pragmatism*, Seattle: University of Washington Press, 1963.

—, "Peirce on Probability," Moore and Robin, 122–140.

McColl, Hugh. "A Note on Professor Charles Sanders Peirce's Probability Notation of 1867," *Proceedings of the London Mathematical Society*, 12, 1881, 102.

Milmed, Bella Kussy. *Kant and Current Philosophical Issues: Some Modern Developments of his Theory of Knowledge*, New York: New York University Press, 1961.

Moore, Edward Carter. *American Pragmatism: Peirce, James, and Dewey*, New York: Columbia University Press, 1961.

—, and Robin, Richard S., eds. *Studies in the Philosophy of C. S. Peirce*, Second Series, Amherst: The University of Massachusetts Press, 1964.

Moore, E. O. "The Scholastic Realism of C. S. Peirce," *Philosophy and Phenomelogical Research*, 1952, 12, 406–417.

Mullin, Albert Alkins. *Philosophical Comments on the Philosophies of C. S. Peirce and Ludwig Wittgenstein*, Urbana, Illinois: Electrical Engineering Research Laboratory, Engineering Experiment Station, University of Illinois, 1961.

Murphey, Murray G. *The Development of Peirce's Philosophy*, Cambridge, Massachusetts: Harvard University Press, 1961.

—, *The Synechism of Charles S. Peirce*, Yale University Ph.D. thesis, 1954.

Negal, E. "Charles S. Peirce, Pioneer of Modern Empiricism," *Philosophy of Science*, 7, 1940, 69–80.

—, "Charles Peirce's Guess at the Riddle," (Review of *The Collected Papers*, Vols. I–II), *Journal of Philosophy*, 30, 1933, 365–386.

O'Connell, J. "C. S. Peirce and the Problem of Knowledge," *Philosophical Studies*, 7, 1957, 3–42.

Quine, W. V. Review of *The Collected Papers*, Vol. II, *Issis*, 19, 1933, 220–229; Review of the *Collected Papers*, Vol. III, *Ibid.*, 22, 1934–1935, 285–297; Review of *The Collected Papers*, Vol. IV, *Ibid.*, 22, 1934–1935, 551–553.

Reese, William. "Philosophical Realism: A Study in the Modality of Being in Peirce and Whitehead," Wiener and Young, 225–237.

—, "Peirce on Abstraction," *Review of Metaphysics*, 14, 1961, 704–713.

Robin, Richard Shale. *Critical Common-sensism: A Critical Study in the Philosophy of Charles Peirce*, Harvard University Ph.D. thesis, 1958.
—, "Peirce's Doctrine of the Normative Sciences," Moore & Robin, 271–288.
Rorty, Richard. "Pragmatism, Categories, and Language," *Philosophical Review*, 70, 1961, 197–223.
Thompson, Manley. *The Pragmatic Philosophy of C. S. Peirce*, Chicago: The University of Chicago Press, 1953.
—, "The Logical Paradoxes and Peirce's Semiotic," *Journal of Philosophy*, 46, 1949, 513–516.
—, "The Paradox of Peirce's Realism," Wiener and Young, 133–142.
—, Review of Murphey, *Philosophical Review*, 72, 1963, 117–119.
Turquette, Atwell R. "Peirce's Icons for Deductive Logic," Moore & Robin, 95–108.
Wennerberg, Hjalmar. *The Pragmatism of Charles Peirce: An Analytical Study*, Lund: C. W. K. Gleerup, 1962.
Wiener, Philip P. *Evolution of the Founders of Pragmatism*, Cambridge, Massachusetts: Harvard University Press, 1949.
Wiener, Philip P. and Young, F. H., eds. *Studies in the Philosophy of C. S. Peirce*, Cambridge, Massachusetts: Harvard University Press, 1952.

WORKS BY LEWIS

An Analysis of Knowledge and Valuation, La Salle: The Open Court Publishing Co., 1946.
A Survey of Symbolic Logic, Berkeley: University of California Press, 1918.
Mind and the World-Order, New York: C. Scribner's Sons, 1929.
Our Social Inheritance, Bloomington, Indiana: Indiana University Press, 1957.
Symbolic Logic, with Harold Langford, New York and London: The Century Company, 1932.
The Ground and Nature of the Right, New York: Columbia University Press, 1955.
The Pragmatic Element in Knowledge, The University of California Publications in Philosophy, Berkeley: University of California Press, 1926.
"Logic and Pragmatism," *Contemporary American Philosophy*, G. P. Adams and W. P. Montague, London: G. Allen & Unwin, Ltd.; New York: The Macmillan Company, eds., 2, 1930, 31–51.
"The Modes of Meaning," in "A Symposium on Meaning and Truth-Part I," *Philosophy and Phenomelogical Research*, 2, 1943, 236–252.
"Some Suggestions Concerning Metaphysics of Logic," in *American Philosophers at Work*, ed. Sidney Hook, New York: Criterion Books, Inc., 1956, 93–105.

WORKS ABOUT LEWIS

Ambrose, Alice. "A Critical Discussion of Mind and the World-Order," *Journal of Philosophy*, 28, 1931, 365–380.
Baylis, Charles A. "C. I. Lewis's Theory of Ethics," *Proceedings of the Sixty-first Annual Meeting of the American Philosophical Association, Eastern Division, Journal of Philosophy*, 61, 1964, 559–566. (Comments by William K. Frankena, 567).
—, "Critical Comments on the Symposium on Meaning and Truth," *Philosophy and Phenomelogical Research*, 5, 1944, 80–93; The first section of the paper is on Lewis's "The Modes of Meaning,"
Firth, Roderick. "Coherence, Certainty, and Epistimic Priority," *Proceedings of the Sixty-first Annual Meeting of the American Philosophical Association,*

Eastern Division, Journal of Philosophy, 61, 1964, 545–556. (Comments by Richard B. Brandt, 557–558).

Frankena, William K. "C. I. Lewis on the Ground and the Nature of the Right," *Journal of Philosophy*, 61, 1964, 489.

Hempel, C. G. Review of *An Analysis of Knowledge and Valuation, Journal of Symbolic Logic*, 1948, 40–45.

Henle, Paul. Review of Lewis's *An Analysis of Knowledge and Valuation, Journal of Philosophy*, 45, 1948, 524–552.

Miller, Hugh. Review of *Mind and World-Order, Philosophical Review*, 40, 1931, 573–579.

Milmed, Bella Kussy. *Kant and Current Philosophical Issues: Some Modern Developments of his Theory of Knowledge*, New York: New York University Press, 1961.

Schiller, F. C. S. Review of *Mind and World-Order, Mind*, 39, 1930, 505–507.

Wells, R. S. Review of *An Analysis of Knowledge and Valuation, Review of Metaphysics*, 2, 1949, 99–115.

Williams, Donald C. "Clarence Irving Lewis 1883–1964," *Philosophy and Phenomenological Research*, 26, 1965, 159–172.

WORKS ABOUT INDUCTION AND PROBABILITY

Achinstein, Peter. "Circularity and Induction," *Analysis*,23, 1963, 123–127.

—, "The Circularity of Self-Supporting Inductive Arguments," *Analysis*, 22, 1962, 138–141.

Ayer, A. J. *Language, Truth and Logic*, New York: Dover, 1952.

—, *The Problem of Knowledge*, New York: St. Martin's Press, 1956.

Barker, S. F. *Induction and Hypothesis: A Study of the Logic of Confirmation*, Ithaca: Cornell University Press, 1957.

—, "On the New Riddle of Induction," with Peter Achinstein, *Philosophical Review*, 69, 1960; 511–522.

Bergmann, Gustav. "The Logic of Probability," *American Journal of Physics*, 9, 5, 1941, 263–272.

Black, Max. *Language and Philosophy*, Ithaca: Cornell University Press, 1949.

—, "Self-Supporting Inductive Arguments," *Journal of Philosophy*, 55, 1958, 718–725.

—, *Philosophy and Language*, Ithaca: Cornell University Press, 1941.

—, *Problems of Analysis*, Ithaca: Cornell University Press, 1954.

—, "Self-Support and Circularity: A Reply to Mr. Achinstein," *Analysis*, 23, 1962, 43–44.

Boole, George. *The Laws of Thought*. Chicago and London: The Open Court Publishing Company, 1940.

Braithwaite, R. B. *Scientific Explanation*, Cambridge: Cambridge University Press, 1953.

Broad, C. D. "On the Relation Between Induction and Probability," *Mind*, 27, 108, 1918, 26–45; 29, 113, 1920, 11–45.

—, "The Principles of Problematic Induction," *Proceedings of the Aristotelian Society*, 28, 1928, 1–46.

—, "Mr. von Wright on the Logic of Induction," *Mind*, 53, 1944, 1–24.

Brodbeck, May. "An Analytic Principle of Induction," *Journal of Philosophy*, 49, 1952, 747–750.

Buchdahl, G. "The Inductive Process and Inductive Inference," *The Australian Journal of Philosophy*, 24, 1956, 164–181.

Burks, A. W. "Reichenbach's Theory of Probability and Induction," *Review of Metaphysics*, 4, 1951, 377–393.
—, "The Presupposition Theory of Induction," *Philosophy of Science*, 20, 1953, 177–197.
Carlsson, Gösta. "Sampling, Probability, and Casual Inference," *Theoria*, 18, 1952.
Carnap, Rudolf. *Logical Foundations of Probability*, Chicago: University of Chicago Press, 1950.
—, "On Inductive Logic," *Philosophy of Science*, 12, 1945, 72–97.
—, "On the Application of Inductive Logic," *Philosophy and Phenomenological Research*, 8, 1947, 133–147. (Reply to Goodman [1946]).
—, "Remarks on Induction and Truth," *Philosophy and Phenomenological Research*, 6, 4, 1946, 590–602.
—, *"The Continuum of Inductive Methods,"* Chicago: The University of Chicago Press, 1952.
—, "Remarks to Kemeny's Paper," *Philosophy and Phenomenological Research*, 13, 3, 1953, 375–376.
—, "Reply to Nelson Goodman," *Philosophy and Phenomenological Research*, 8, 1947, 461–462. (Reply to Goodman [1947])
—, "Replies and Systematic Expositions," *The Philosophy of Rudolf Carnap*, ed. by Paul Arthur Schilpp, La Salle: The Open Court Publishing Company, 1963.
—, "The Aim of Inductive Logic" *Logic, Methodology and Philosophy of Science*, ed. by Ernest Nagel, Patrick Suppes, and Alfred Garshi, Palo Alto: Stanford University Press, 1962.
Church, Alonzo. "On the Concept of a Random Sequence," *Bulletin of the American Mathematical Society*, 46, 1940, 130–135.
Churchman, C. West. "Carnap's On Inductive Logic," *Philosophy of Science*, 13, 1945, 339–342.
—, "Probability Theory," *Philosophy of Science*, 12, 13, 1945, 147–173.
Day, J. P. *Inductive Probability*, New York: The Humanities Press, 1961.
Dewey, John. *Logic, The Theory of Inquiry*, New York: H. Holt & Co., 1938.
Dubs, Homer H. "The Principle of Insufficient Reason," *Philosophy of Science*, 9, 21, 1942, 123–130.
Ducasse, C. J. "A Neglected Interpretation of Probability," *Proceedings of the Seventh International Congress on Philosophy*, Cambridge, Massachusetts: Harvard University Press, 1926; New York: Longmans, Green and Co., 1927.
—, "Some Observations Concerning the Nature of Probability," *Journal of Philosophy*, 38, 15, 1941, 393–403.
Edwards, Paul. "Russell's Doubts about Induction," *Mind*, 58, 1949, 141–163.
Feibleman, James. "Pragmatism and Inverse Probability," *Philosophy and Phenomenological Research*, 5, 1945, 309–319.
Feigl, Herbert. "Confirmability and Configuration," *Revue International de Philosophie*, 5, 1951.
—, "De Principiis non est Disputandum... on the Meaning and the Limits of Justification," *Philosophical Analysis*, Max Black, (ed.), Ithaca: Cornell University Press, 1950.
—, "Some Major Issues and Developments in the Philosophy of Science," *Minnesota Studies in the Philosophy of Science*, Minneapolis: University of Minnesota Press, 1, 1956.
—, "The Logical Character of the Principle of Induction," *Philosophy of Science*, 1, 1, 1934, 20–29. Reprinted in Feigl and Sellars, *Readings in Philosophical Analysis*. New York: Appleton Century Crofts, 1949.
Feyerliend, Paul K. "A Note on the Problem of Induction," *Journal of Philosophy*, 61, 12, 1964, 348–372.

Finch, Henry Albert. "An Explanation of Counterfactual by Probability Theory," *Philosophy and Phenomenological Research*, 18, 1958, 368–378.

Fisher, Ronald Aylmer. "Inverse Probability," *Proceedings of the Cambridge Philosophical Society*, 16, 1930.

—, "Inverse Probability and the Use of Likelihood," *Proceedings of the Cambridge Philosophical Society*, 18, 1932.

—, "The Logic of Inductive Inference," *Journal of the Royal Statistical Society*, 98, 1935.

Foster, Marguerite H. and Martin, Michael L., eds., *Probability, Confirmation, and Simplicity: Readings in the Philosophy of Inductive Logic*, New York: The Odyssey Press, Inc., 1966.

Goodman, Nelson. "A Query on Confirmation," *Journal of Philosophy*, 43, 1946, 383–385.

—, "On Infirmities of Confirmation-Theory," *Philosophy and Phenomenological Research*, 8, 1947, 149–151. (Reply to Carnap [1947, 133–147]).

—, *Fact, Fiction and Forecast*, Cambridge, Massachusetts: Harvard University Press, 1955.

Hailperin, Theodore. "Foundations of Probability in Mathematical Logic," *Philosophy in Science*, 4, 2, 1936–1937, 125–150.

Harrod, Roy. *Foundation of Inductive Logic*, New York: Harcourt, Brace and Company, 1956.

Hawkins, David. "Existential and Epistemic Probability," *Philosophy of Science*, 10, 4, 1943, 255–261.

Helmer, Olaf, and Oppenheimer, P. "A Syntactical Definition of Probability and the Degree of Confirmation," *Journal of Symbolic Logic*, 10, 1945, 26–60.

Hempel, Carl G. "Inductive Inconsistencies," *Synthese*, 12, 1960, 439–469; Reprinted in his book *Aspects of Scientific Explanation*, New York: The Free Press, 1965.

—, "A Purely Syntactical Definition of Confirmation," *Journal of Symbolic Logic*, 8, 1943, 122–143.

Hesse, Mary. "Induction and Theory-Structure," *The Review of Metaphysics*, 18, 1, September 1964, 109–122.

Hume, D. A. *A Treatise of Human Nature*, Oxford: L. A. Selby-Bigge, ed., 1896.

—, *An Inquiry Concerning Human Understanding*, La Salle, Illinois: The Open Court Publishing Company, 1955.

Katz, Jerrold. *The Problem of Induction and Its Solution*, Chicago: University of Chicago Press, 1962.

Kaufman, Felix. "The Logical Rules of Scientific Procedure," *Philosophy and Phenomenological Research*, 2, 4, 1942, 457–471.

Kemble, Edwin C. "Is the Frequency Theory of Probability Adequate for All Scientific Purposes?," *American Journal of Physics*, 10, 1, 1942, 6–16.

Kemeny, J. G. "A Contribution to Inductive Method," *Philosophy and Phenomenological Research*, 13, 3, 1953, 371–374.

—, "Fair Bets and Inductive Probabilities," *Journal of Symbolic Logic*, 20, 3, 1955, 263–273.

—, "The Use of Simplicity in Induction," *Philosophical Review*, 7, 1953, 391–408.

—, "Carnap on Confirmation," *The Review of Metaphysics*, 5, 1, 1951, 145–156.

—, "Carnap on Probability," *The Review of Metaphysics*, 5, 1, 1951, 145–156.

—, Review of Carnap, *Logical Foundations of Probability*, *Journal of Symbolic Logic*, 16, 3, 1951, 205–207.

—, and Oppenheimer, Paul. "Degree of Factual Support," *Philosophy of Science*, 19, 4, 1952, 307–324.

Keynes, J. M. *A Treatise on Probability*, London: Macmillan and Company, 1921, 1929, 1952.

Kiekkopf, Charles F. "Deduction and Intuitive Induction," *Philosophy and Phenomenological Research*, 26, 3, March 1966, 379–390.

Kneale, William Calvert. *Probability and Induction*, Oxford: Clarendon Press, 1963.

Korner, W., ed. *Observation and Interpretation*, London, Colston Research Society, ed. by S. Körner with M. H. L. Pryce, New York: Academic Press, 1957.

Kyburg, Henry. "The Justification of Induction," *Journal of Philosophy*, 53, 12, 1956, 394–400.

—, *Probability and the Logic of Rational Belief*, Connecticut: Wesleyan University Press, 1961.

—, *Studies in Subjective Probability*, with Howard E. Smokler, eds. New York: John Wiley and Sons, Inc., 1964.

—, "The Justification of Deduction," *Review of Metaphysics*, 12, 1, 1958, 19–25.

—, "Demonstrative Induction," *Philosophy and Phenomenological Research*, 21, 1, 1960, 80–92.

—, "Braithwaite on Probability and Induction," *British Journal for the Philosophy of Science*, 11, 1958.

Laplace, Pierre Simon de. *A Philosophical Essay on Probabilities*, translated by F. W. Truscott and F. L. Emory, New York: Dover Publishing Company, 1951.

Leblanc, Hughes. *Statistical and Inductive Probabilities*, New Jersey: Prentice-Hall, 1962.

—, "The Positive Instances are No Help," *The Journal of Philosophy*, 60, 16, 1963, 453–462.

—, "Two Probability Concepts," *Journal of Philosophy*, 53, 22, 1956, 679–688.

Lehman, R. Sherman. "On Confirmation and Rational Betting," *Journal of Symbolic Logic*, 20, 3, 1955, 251–262.

Lehrer, Keith. "Knowledge and Probability," *Journal of Philosophy*, 61, 1964, 368–372.

Lenez, John W. "Carnap on Defining Degree of Confirmation," *Philosophy of Science*, 23, 3, 1956, 230–236.

Levi, Isaac. "Deductive Cogency in Inductive Inference," *Journal of Philosophy*, 62, 1965, 68–77.

—, "Hacking Salmon on Induction," *Journal of Philosophy*, 62, 1965, 481–487.

Lloyd, A. C. "The Logical Form of Law Statements," *Mind*, 64, 255, 1955, 312–318.

Lucas, J. R. "The One Concept of Probability," *Philosophy and Phenomenological Research*, 26, 2, December 1965, 180–201.

Madden, Edward H. "The Riddle of Induction," *Journal of Philosophy*, 55, 1958, 705–718.

Mill, C. S. *Philosophy of Scientific Method*, ed., with an Introduction by E. Nagel, New York: Hafner Publishing Co., Inc., 1950.

Mises, R. von, *Probability, Statistis and Truth*, New York: The Macmillan Company, 1939.

—, with G. L. Doob, "Discussion of Papers in Probability Theory," *Annals of Mathematical Statistics*, 12, 2, 1941, 215–217.

Moore, Asher. "The Principle of Induction," *Journal of Philosophy*, 49, 24, 1952, 741–758.

—, "Induction (II), a Rejoinder to Miss Brodbeck," *Journal of Philosophy*, 49, 24, 1952, 750–758.

Nagel, Ernest. "A Frequency Theory of Probability," *Journal of Philosophy*, 30, 20, 1933, 533–554.

—, *Principles of the Theory of Probability*, Chicago: University of Chicago Press, 1939.

—, "Probability and the Theory of Knowledge," *Philosophy of Science*, 6, 2, 1939, 212–253.

—, "Probability and Non-Demonstrative Inference," *Philosophy and Phenomenological Research*, 5, 4, 1945, 485–507.

—, "Is the Laplacian Theory of Probability Tenable?," *Philosophy and Phenomenological Research*, 6, 4, 1945–1946, 614–618.

—, "Reichenbach's Theory of Probability," Review, *Journal of Philosophy*, 47, 1950, 551–555.

—, *The Structure of Science*, New York: Harcourt, Brace & World, 1961.

Nelson, E. J. "Professor Reichenbach on Induction," *Journal of Philosophy*, 33, 21, 1936, 577–580.

Nicod, F. *Foundations of Geometry and Induction*, London: Routledge and Kegan Paul, 1930.

Oliver, W. Donald. "A Re-examination of the Problem of Induction," *Journal of Philosophy*, 49, 25, 1952, 769–780.

Oliver, James Willard. "Deduction and the Statistical Syllogism," *Journal of Philosophy*, 50, 26, 1953, 805–807.

Pap, Arthur. *Elements of Analytic Philosophy*, New York: The Macmillan Company, 1949.

—, *An Introduction to the Philosophy of Science*, New York: The Free Press of Glencoe, 1962.

Plantinga, Alvin. "Induction and Other Minds," *The Review of Metaphysics*, 19, 3, 1966, 441–461.

Popper, Karl R. "A Set of Independent Axioms for Probability," *Mind*, 47, 86, 1938, 275–277.

—, "Probabilistic Independence and Corroboration by Empirical Tests," *British Journal for the Philosophy of Science*, 10, 1960, 315–318.

—, *The Logic of Scientific Discovery*, New York: Basic Books, Inc., 1961.

Ramsey, Frank P. *The Foundations of Mathematics*, London: Routledge and Kegan Paul, 1931.

Reichenbach, Hans. *Experience and Prediction*, Chicago: The University of Chicago Press, 1938.

—, "On the Justification of Induction," *Journal of Philosophy*, 37, 4, 1940, 97–103.

—, "Reply to Donald C. Williams' Criticism of the Frequency View of Probability," *Philosophy and Phenomenological Research*, 5, 4, 1945, 508–512.

—, "The Theory of Probability," Berkeley and Los Angeles: University of California Press, 1949. Translation of his *Wahrscheinlichkeitslehre*, Leiden, 1935.

Royce, Josiah. "The Principles of Logic," in *Encyclopedia of the Philosophical Sciences*, ed. by W. Windelband and A. Ruge, 1, 1913, 67–135.

Russell, B. *Human Knowledge, Its Scope and Limits*, New York: Simon and Schuster, Inc., 1948.

Ryle, G. "Induction and Hypothesis," *Proceedings of the Aristotelian Society Supplement*, 16, 1937, 36–62.

Salmon, Wesley C. "Inductive Inference," *Philosophy of Science: The Delaware Seminar*, ed. by Bernard H. Baumrin, New York: New York Interscience Publisher, 2, 1963.

—, "Regular Rules of Induction," *Philosophical Review*, 6, 1956, 385–388.

—, "Should We Attempt to Justify Induction?," *Philosophical Studies*, 8, 1957, 33–48.

—, "The Uniformity of Nature," *Philosophy and Phenomenological Research*, 14, 1, 1953–1954, 39–48.

—, "Verification of Induction," (with comments by S. Barker and R. Rudner), in H. Feigl and G. Maxwell (eds.) *Current Issues in Philosophy of Science*, New York: Holt, Rinehart and Winston, Inc., 1961.

Shimony, Abner. "Coherence and the Axioms of Confirmation," *Journal of Symbolic Logic*, 20, 1, 1955, 1–28.

Stove, D. "Hume, Probability and Induction," *Philosophical Review*, 74, 2, 160–177.

Strawson, P. F. *Introduction to Logical Theory*, London: Methuen and Company, Ltd. 1952.

Symposium on Probability – Part I, *Philosophy and Phenomenological Research*, 5, 4, 1945, 449–532. Papers presented: Donald C. Williams, "On the Derivation of Probabilities from Frequencies," 449–484; Ernest Nagel, "Probability and Non-Demonstrative Inference," 485–507; Hans Reichenbach, "Reply to Donald C. Williams' Criticism of the Frequency Theory of Probability," 508–512; Rudolf Carnap, "The Two Concepts of Probability," 513–532.

Symposium on Probability – Part II, *Philosophy and Phenomenological Research*, 6, 1, 1945, 11–86. Papers presented: Henry Margenau, "On the Frequency Theory of Probability," 11–25; Gustav Bergmann, "Frequencies, Probabilities and Positivism," 26–44; R. von Mises, "Comments on Donald Williams' Paper," 45–46; Donald Williams, "The Challenging Situation in the Philosophy of Probability," 67–86.

Wald, Abraham. "Contributions to the Theory of Statistical Estimation and Testing Hypotheses," *Annals of Mathematical Statistics*, 10, 1939, 299–326.

—, *On the Principles of Statistical Inference*, Notre Dame, 1942.

Whiteley, C. H. "On the Justification of Induction," *Analysis* 7, 1939–1940.

Will, F. L. "Is There a Problem of Induction?," *Journal of Philosophy*, 39, 19, 1942, 505–513.

—, "Generalization and Evidence," in *Philosophical Analysis*, Max Black (ed.), Ithaca: Cornell University Press, 1950.

—, "Justification of Induction," *Philosophical Review*, 68, 1939, 359–372. (Review of G. H. von Wright, *The Logical Problem of Induction*, 2nd rev. ed.; New York: Macmillan Company, 1957).

Williams, Donald C. *The Ground of Induction*, Cambridge, Massachusetts: Harvard University Press, 1947.

Wittgenstein, L. *Philosophical Investigations*, New York: Macmillan Company, 1953.

Wright, George Henrick von. *A Treatise on Induction and Probability*, London: Routledge and Kegan Paul, 1961.

—, "On Probability", *Mind*, 49, 195, 1940, 265–283.

—, *The Logical Problem of Induction*, New York: Macmillan Company, 1957.

INDEX